W9-BBH-292

Confrontations with the Reaper

Confrontations with the Reaper

A Philosophical Study of the Nature and Value of Death

FRED FELDMAN

New York   Oxford
OXFORD UNIVERSITY PRESS

Oxford University Press

Oxford   New York   Toronto
Delhi   Bombay   Calcutta   Madras   Karachi
Kuala Lumpur   Singapore   Hong Kong   Tokyo
Nairobi   Dar es Salaam   Cape Town
Melbourne   Auckland   Madrid

and associated companies in
Berlin   Ibadan

Copyright © 1992 by Fred Feldman

Published by Oxford University Press, Inc.
198 Madison Avenue, New York, New York 10016-4314

First issued as an Oxford University Press paperback, 1994

Oxford is a registered trademark of Oxford University Press

All rights reserved. No part of this publication may be reproduced,
stored in a retrieval system, or transmitted, in any form or by any means,
electronic, mechanical, photocopying, recording or otherwise,
without the prior permission of Oxford University Press.

Library of Congress Cataloging-in-Publication Data
Feldman, Fred, 1941–
Confrontations with the reaper :
a philosophical study of the nature
and value of death / Fred Feldman.
p.   cm.   Includes bibliographical references and index.
ISBN 0-19-507102-6   ISBN 0-19-508928-6 (pbk)
1. Death.   2. Life.   3. Abortion.   4. Suicide.
I. Title. BD444.F44 1992 128′.5—dc20 91-3640

4 6 8 9 7 5 3

Printed in the United States of America
on acid-free paper

For Lindsay

forts, the present book is clearer and more coherent than it otherwise would have been. (This is not to suggest that they now agree with everything I say in it.)

I am grateful to the editors of *The Philosophical Review* for permission to publish (in Chapter 9) quite a lot of material that overlaps with my "Some Puzzles about the Evil of Death"; to the editor of *Philosophy and Phenomenological Research* for permission to publish (in Chapter 5) material that overlaps with my "On Dying as a Process"; and to the editor of *Philosophia* for permission to publish (in Chapter 4) material that overlaps with my "The Enigma of Death." I am also grateful to the University of Massachusetts at Amherst for granting me a sabbatical during the fall of 1990 during which much of the final rewriting of this book took place.

The production of this book has been, in some ways, a cooperative project. Many friends, students, and colleagues have offered all sorts of beneficial suggestions. Although I have not acted on all of these suggestions, I am grateful to all for offering them. I fear that I may not have mentioned all who deserve to be mentioned here. I hope they will understand.

Amherst, Mass.   F. F.
May, 1991

Contents

Confrontations with the Reaper

Introduction:
Confronting the Reaper

The Reaper—Mysterious and Evil

In art and mythology, death is sometimes represented as a ferry-man, eager to take his passengers to the other side. It is also sometimes represented as a moth, fluttering mindlessly into the flame of a candle. But the most compelling image of death is provided by the Reaper—the hooded skeleton bearing the huge curved scythe.

The Reaper is ugly and menacing. He stares directly at us, and with an outstretched bony finger, he beckons us to come to him. He is patient. If we escape today, surely he will have us tomorrow. He is democratic. He takes all; high and low alike will be "harvested" when the time comes. He is unforgiving. Once we are in his grasp, there is no return.

Two aspects of the Reaper are especially noteworthy. He is *mysterious*. This is illustrated by the fact that the Reaper's face is often hidden in the shadows of his hood. Death is taken to be weird or uncanny—something about which we have no real understanding.

Death is also taken to be *evil*. This is illustrated by the Reaper's malevolent glare. A visit from the Reaper is to be feared almost beyond comparison. What he does to us is the standard by which misfortunes can be measured.

While most of us find nothing remarkable in the claims that death is mysterious and evil, each of these claims has been vigorously rejected by certain philosophers. Some insist that there is nothing mysterious about death. In a remarkably level-headed and

3

sensible paper, Paul Edwards argues for the conclusion that death is no more mysterious than any other biological phenomenon.[1] As he sees it, a person's death is simply the event that takes place when he or she ceases to be alive. We understand (well enough) what life is; we know what cessation is. Thus, since death is just the cessation of life, we understand what death is. The Reaper is thus unmasked.

Edwards suggests that if you seek more knowledge about the nature of death, you may seek something that does not exist. Some apparently want to know what it feels like to be dead. Since no one returns from death, the living apparently have no informants who can tell us what death is like. Thus, according to these people, a certain important aspect of death remains mysterious. We cannot know what it feels like. Edwards points out the absurdity of any such quest. Death surely does not "feel like" anything; once dead, we cease to feel. We have no experience. If you are troubled because you cannot know what it feels like to have no feelings, you are simply confused.

Other philosophers argue that the Reaper is not really evil. Epicurus—perhaps the most eloquent spokesman for this position—says in effect that we have an utterly failsafe way of protecting ourselves from the evil of death.[2] At the very moment when the Reaper clutches us in his bony embrace, we go out of existence. Since the nonexistent cannot be harmed, death cannot harm us.

Epicurus summarizes this point by saying that "death . . . is nothing to us, since so long as we exist death is not with us; but when death comes, then we do not exist. It does not concern either the living or the dead, since for the former it is not, and the latter are no more."[3]

Many modern philosophers, biologists, and theologians have defended similar positions. They have claimed that death is neither so mysterious nor so evil as the naive would suppose. The Reaper, according to these thinkers, is really no more mysterious or evil than the stork who symbolizes birth or the flowing stream that symbolizes life. In each case, all we have is a biological phenomenon that has by now been thoroughly studied in the full light of day.

In this book, I defend the naive view on both counts. I try, in Part I, to show that death really is a mystery. Perhaps it is not mysterious in quite the way some have said, but it is mysterious nonetheless. In Part II I try to show how death can be a great evil, especially for its victim.

If I merely *claimed* that death is mysterious and evil, there would be no reason to read any further. You probably already accept these points and think that anyone who says otherwise is engaging in self-deception. But the issue is more complex. Wise and thoughtful philosophers have presented subtle arguments designed to show that death cannot be evil. Equally sensible thinkers have claimed to take the mystery out of death by telling us, in straightforward biological terminology, what death is. In order to deal responsibly with these views, we must first understand the arguments and proposed definitions. If, after appropriate scrutiny, the arguments and definitions can be seen to be defective, than we can reinstate the naive views. Of course, under those circumstances, the views will no longer be so naive.

The Structure of the Book

This book, as a whole, is about the nature and value (or, perhaps more properly, *disvalue*) of death. Part I is about the nature of death. According to a popular view, there is nothing mysterious about death—it is just the cessation of life. In Chapter 1, "The Search for Death Itself," I present a somewhat more detailed account of the sort of question I mean to ask about death. In other words, I try to explain what is meant by the question "What is the nature of death?" I also try to locate the target concept ("the biological concept of death"), and I indicate some criteria that must be satisfied by any adequate answer.

Since the concept of life apparently plays a role in the definition of death, we must first understand what is meant by 'life'. In Chapters 2 and 3, I present several of the most plausible accounts of the nature of life. I attempt to show that each of them fails. Life itself turns out to be a bit of a mystery.

Suppose we understand life well enough. Can we then use the

concept of life in our definition of death? Would it be correct to say that death is just the cessation of life? In Chapter 4, "The Enigma of Death," I explain why death cannot be defined in this way. One problem concerns suspended animation. Things that go into suspended animation cease to live, but don't die. So death is not the cessation of life. Furthermore, there seem to be certain other ways of getting out of life without dying. I claim, in light of all this, that even if we understood the nature of life, it is not clear how we could use it in the effort to define the nature of death. Death is thus a double enigma.

Chapter 5 concerns "Dying as a Process." Suppose we understand life and death well enough. Can we then explain what we mean when we say that something is "dying"? Roughly, the idea seems to be that something is dying if it is still alive, but on an irreversible downhill path that will soon terminate in death. Further reflection on a variety of cases makes it clear that any such rough characterization of dying is wrong. I propose a novel analysis.

When Hamlet says, "To be or not to be, that is the question," he really means "To die or not to die, that is the question." Hamlet apparently supposes that when a living thing dies, it stops existing—it ceases to be. Very many philosophers agree. But this "termination thesis" blatantly conflicts with some obvious facts. There actually exist very many dead bodies. Each of these formerly was alive. Hence, these seem to be things that died but did not cease to exist. In Chapter 6, "The Survival of Death," I try to unravel this conceptual tangle.

Chapter 7, "A Materialist Conception of Death," contains my proposed conceptual scheme for death and related concepts. I try to explain the central concepts ("death," "dying," "a death," "dead," "person," etc.) and I defend some answers to fundamental metaphysical questions involving these concepts. Can a person survive death? Can a person die more than once? Can a person get out of life without dying? Can something die if it never lived? This chapter provides a summary of a proposed materialistic conceptual scheme for death.

In Part II, I turn to questions about the value of death. The central ethical problem, as I see it, is whether death is bad for the one who dies. Will my death be a misfortune for me? Epicurus and

Lucretius presented a famous argument designed to show that since I will not exist after death, and will not then suffer any pain, my death cannot be bad for me. In Chapter 8, I explain and criticize the Epicurean argument. I defend a version of the "deprivation approach"—death is bad for those who die because it deprives them of the goods they would have enjoyed if they had continued to live.

Chapter 9, "More Puzzles about the Evil of Death," contains a discussion of four philosophical puzzles that confront the defender of the deprivation approach. One of the most interesting of these is a puzzle presented by Lucretius. If early death is bad for us because it deprives us of the goods we would have enjoyed if we had died later, then "late birth" must be equally bad for us, since it deprives us of the goods we would have enjoyed if we had been born earlier. Yet we do not lament the fact that we were born so late. Why is this?

One of the most notorious scandals of moral philosophy is this: no moral philosopher has presented a clear and plausible answer to the question "Why is it wrong to kill people?" In Chapter 10 I discuss two of the standard answers and explain why they fail. In Chapter 11, I propose a better answer of my own. I try to show that my view gives plausible results in a variety of very puzzling cases. One feature that makes my proposal especially unusual is that it is a form of utilitarianism—a view often thought to be incapable of dealing with the morality of killing.

In Chapter 12, I discuss applications of my view to a thorny and pressing practical difficulty. I defend a view about the morality of abortion. In connection with the discussion of abortion, I try to show how one's view about murder and abortion may come into conflict with one's view about the morality of failure to conceive. My own view, I argue, does not run into this difficulty.

Finally, in Chapter 13, I discuss a special sort of murder—the murder of a person by him- or herself. Some, perhaps influenced by St. Thomas Aquinas, have claimed that suicide is inevitably immoral. I try to show that Aquinas's arguments are inconclusive. For all he has shown, suicide might sometimes be morally permissible.

Other philosophers have insisted that suicide cannot be a rational choice. I attempt to draw out the main arguments for this counterintuitive conclusion, and to show that they fail. This involves drawing distinctions among several sorts of rationality. I then try to show that there are circumstances in which the Reaper is to be welcomed. In these circumstances it is rational (in several senses) to choose to die.

Let us then turn to our first topic—the alleged mystery of death.

I

THE NATURE OF DEATH

1

The Search for Death Itself

The Problems of Death

Although some writers speak of "the problem of death," I think it would be better to speak instead of "the problems of death," for death is problematic in very many different ways.

There are *psychological* problems concerning death: How do we feel about our own impending death? How do we react to the death of loved ones? Are there typical psychological stages in the adjustment to the recognition of impending death? At what age do we come to have a satisfactory understanding of mortality? etc.

There are *legal* questions about death: Do dead persons have any legal rights? Should the law permit people to kill themselves?

There are *biological* problems of death: Why do organisms die? Are there any organisms that never die? Would it be possible to treat people in such a way that they would never die? Is it possible to treat people or other organisms in such a way as to make them live again after they have died?

There are also theological, literary, sociological, economic, medical, and other questions about death. All of these are interesting and deserve to be considered. But the central question of Part I is distinct from all of these questions. It is the most fundamental question that can be asked about death. It is a philosophical question. It is this: What is death?

Although the question is surely sufficiently short, it may nevertheless be a bit obscure. Its meaning will become clearer as we proceed, but it will be useful to say a few words by way of preliminary clarification. The fundamental question ("What is death?") can be formulated in a variety of different ways. We could ask for an explanation of what we mean when we say that something has died. Another possibility would be to ask for an account of the nature of death itself. We could also state the question as a sort of challenge: can we formulate a satisfactory philosophical analysis of the concept of death itself?

Conceptual Analysis

Before we go any further, I should say a few words about conceptual analysis.

If you want to understand the engine in your motorcycle, you may study an "exploded view." This is a diagram showing all the main parts of the engine, but showing them apart from each other. Generally there are lines indicating how the parts would be connected in the functioning engine. When you come to know about the sizes and shapes of the various parts, and you come to know how they are supposed to be related to one another when the engine is properly assembled, you come to understand the engine—you begin to know how the engine works. This is a humble example of a pervasive fact about one sort of understanding. We understand complicated things by understanding their simpler parts and their relations. This is "analytical understanding."

What's true of motorcycle engines is widely thought to be true of properties. Some properties seem to be complex entities, composed of parts. Of course, the parts are not physical objects such as pushrods and valves. The parts of a property are other properties. These are related by logical relations, such as conjunction and conditionalization. For example, suppose someone is interested in the property of motherhood. We can explain this by saying that it is the conjunction of parenthood and femaleness. A person who already understands parenthood and femaleness, and who knows what 'and' means, should be able to understand motherhood. There is an ancient philosophical tradition according to which one of the best ways to come to understand a complex property is to come to understand its parts and their relations. Philosophers in this tradition focus on interesting and important complex properties and attempt to describe their parts and the way in which the parts are organized in the whole. (Since properties are sometimes called concepts, this activity is often called 'conceptual analysis'.) There are several different ways in which an analysis may be stated. We can consider motherhood again. We may present our analysis in any of the following forms:

M1: Motherhood is the conjunction of femaleness and parent-hood.
M2: To be a mother is to be a female parent.
M3: Being a mother is being a female parent.
M4: 'Mother' means the same as 'female parent'.

For certain personal reasons, I happen to prefer to formulate analyses as definitions. Thus, if I were attempting to analyze motherhood, I might present my results in this form:

M5: x is a mother at t = df. x is a female parent at t.

One necessary condition of success for an analysis is lack of counterexamples. Thus, if M5 is correct, we will be unable to conceive of a case in which something would clearly be a mother but not a female parent (or vice versa). When searching for counterexamples, we must beware of unclear or controversial border-line cases. These do not make satisfactory counterexamples. A satisfactory counterexample must be an uncontroversial case. It must be a case with respect to which there is nearly unanimous and relatively firm agreement.

A proposed analysis of a concept must get the uncontroversial cases right. If it gets them all right, we can consider what it legislates concerning the controversial cases. We should be open-minded. Perhaps a proposed analysis will yield surprising results with respect to the controversial cases. That would be no mark against it. It would merely show that we can learn things from good philosophy.

A second necessary condition of success for an analysis is this: the proposed definition must not make use of any terms that are as obscure in meaning as the term being analyzed itself. Suppose, for example, we find the concept of death puzzling and attempt to clear things up by offering an analysis. We say that to die is "to drift across the great divide into the other realm." Such remarks obviously shed very little light on the nature of death. Our analysis would be much more useful if it employed only clear, simple, and literal terminology. A closely related point is that the proposed definition must not be circular. If we are trying to explain what death is, the word 'dies' must not appear on the right-hand side of the definition. The problem with any such definition is obvious: we'd have to understand the meaning of 'dies' before we could use the definition to learn what 'dies' means. How could the definition be of any value?

A somewhat more subtle point concerns covertly circular definitions such as this one:

D2: x dies at t =df. x reaches thanatological termination at t.

We note a strange term in D2—'thanatological'. We look it up in the dictionary. We discover that 'thanatological' means 'having to do with death'. We thereby discover that D2 is covertly circular. We have to understand the meaning of death in order to understand the meaning of one of the terms in the proposed analysis of death. Our rule against circularity must be understood to prohibit covertly circular definitions, too.

Analysis of Death or Criterion for Death?

It is important to distinguish clearly between what I am here calling the analysis of the concept of death, and a quite different project that is sometimes called "defining death." For legal purposes, it is sometimes extremely important to determine whether someone is alive or dead. For example, before we remove the organs from someone's body for transplantation, we want to be sure that the person is dead. Similarly, before we expend huge amounts of energy and money trying to heal someone's wounds, we want to be sure that the person is not already dead. Thus, philosophers and others have set about trying to isolate some clear marks or criteria of death. Confusion arises because these criteria are sometimes called 'definitions'.

A criterion of death would be a fairly easily recognized property that serves as an indicator of death. Someone is dead if and only if he or she displays the criterion. Since it is important to be able to specify a precise moment of death, some would insist that a really good criterion of death would be an "all-or-nothing" property, rather than a property that comes in degrees. Suppose, for example, that in absolutely every case, a certain sort of brain activity ("z-waves") could be detected in living human beings. Suppose also that this sort of brain activity abruptly stops when a person dies. Suppose it is relatively easy to determine whether a brain is emitting z-waves. We might then "define" death as the cessation of that brain activity. Thus, we could say:

D3: x dies at t iff x's brain ceases to emit z-waves at t.

No matter how good a criterion of death D3 might be, it is not an analysis of the concept of death. One obvious point is that it has no relevance to plants and other mortal things that have no brains. It applies only to human beings (and perhaps other animals whose brains emit z-waves). Another point is that if something like D3 is true, it is only contingently so. Thus, even if earthly humans always cease to emit z-waves at the moment of death, things surely could have been otherwise. If evolution had progressed in some other possible way, it might have turned out that no living human being's brain ever emitted a z-wave. We can also conceive of other possible ways in which evolution might have progressed. In some of these, it might have turned out that corpses would continue to emit z-waves long after death. Finally, and perhaps most important, D3 sheds no light on the nature of death—it doesn't help us to understand what death is. It merely purports to help us determine the moment when death arrives.

There are other important differences between an analysis of the concept of death and a criterion for human death. One of them concerns what counts as *success.* When a criterion of human death is proposed, the aim is to offer something that can be acted upon; something that might be useful; something that might be adopted. It is suggested that people in the legal, mortuary, and medical professions should adopt the criterion and use it in their activities. The proposed criterion is successful if it gains widespread acceptance. An analysis is not like this. It does not purport to be useful.

It is not intended as a solution to any practical problem. Success for an analysis is measured by the extent to which it serves to enlighten us about the nature of death itself.

A closely related and important point concerns the adoption of a criterion. People in the medical, mortuary, and legal professions are often called upon to determine whether or not someone is dead. Such determinations have profound and immediate practical implications. Thus, for example, a mortician may be asked to bury a certain body. For a variety of reasons, he doesn't want to do this if the body is not yet dead. One reason might be this: if it should later come to light that he buried a still-living body, he might be found guilty of a crime—or at least of professional incompetence. He might lose his license. Thus, the mortician wants to be sure that the body is really dead.

Furthermore, he wants to be able to demonstrate that he took proper precautions before proceeding with interment. If the z-wave criterion were universally accepted, he could proceed as follows: he could attach the z-meter to the body and check for z-waves; he could ask two reliable observers to sign the printout, certifying that there were no z-waves; he could attach a notarized copy of the printout with the death certificate. Later, if a question should arise, the mortician would be protected. He could claim that he took all the legally mandated steps. He checked for z-waves, found none, and filed the necessary papers—all *before* burying the body.

It is consistent with all this to suppose that medical technology could advance in the area of z-waves. New procedures might be introduced that make it possible to revive a person even though he has emitted no z-waves for several minutes. If an advance of this sort were to occur, the z-wave criterion would have to be abandoned. Perhaps there would be a period of transition, during which new criteria would be proposed and debated; perhaps symposia would be held during which the merits and defects of these proposals would be argued; perhaps eventually a new criterion would be adopted. Thereafter (until yet another criterion is adopted) morticians would ignore the z-waves and check instead to determine whether or not the new criterion was satisfied.

Nothing quite like this could happen with respect to the *analysis* of the concept of death. Suppose there is such a thing as the concept of death. In other words, suppose the word 'dies' has a certain literal meaning in the English language. Experts may gather to debate about this meaning. At the end of their conference, they may reach a conclusion about the meaning of 'x dies at t'. They might hope that others would agree with them. However, their conclusion might simply be wrong. It is possible that the word just does not mean what they say. They were mistaken about the concept of death. Perhaps there is an obvious counterexample to their agreed analysis. No amount of consensus can overrule a fact of this sort. On the other hand, if their analysis is correct, it will express a metaphysical necessity. Nothing could later happen that would call for a revision of their decision. No change in medical technology could make it necessary to alter the analysis of the concept of death.

(Of course, the word 'dies' has a history; it is possible that it might come to express some new concept. In that case, a new analysis might be in order. However, it would not be a new analysis of the original concept—if the old analysis was correct, it would still be correct. What might be sought would be an analysis of the concept that the word now expresses.)

So there are many differences between the analytic project and the criterial project:

1. A criterion of death purports to help us locate the moment when death comes. An analysis of death purports to tell us what death is.

2. A criterion of death may be formulated in such a way as to apply only to human beings. An analysis of death must apply equally to anything that can die.

3. A criterion of death may be quite useful even if only contingently true. Indeed, it might be quite useful even if there are a few rare counterexamples. An analysis of death is, if true at all, then necessarily true. There cannot be even so much as a *possible* falsifying instance.

4. A criterion of death may be "in force" during a certain period of time, and then, with advances in technology, abandoned. An analysis of death, on the other hand, is eternally true if true at all.

5. A criterion of death is a success if enough people, thinking it would be useful, decide to adopt it. An analysis of death is a success if it is true—even if no one adopts it.

I am inclined to think that the analytical project has a sort of conceptual priority over the criterial project. Perhaps this may be brought out by reflecting on what might happen when experts assemble to formulate a new criterion. Suppose some experts propose a criterion according to which people are to be counted as dead when their hearts stop beating. Others object to this criterion, pointing out that hearts can easily be restarted by the careful administration of electric shocks. They claim that this shows that the proposed criterion is unacceptable—it conflicts with the "fact" that once a person dies, he cannot come back to life. Suppose advocates of the proposal grant that it has the indicated feature. But they insist that this is no defect. As they see it, people *can* come back to life after dying. Thus, the fact that their criterion permits this is a *virtue* of the proposal, not a defect.

I think this sort of disagreement would show that there is a certain amount of confusion about the nature of death itself. In the example, some of the conventioneers take death to have a certain "logic." As they understand it, someone can die and then live again. Other conventioneers think that the concept of death rules this out. Death, for them, must be *permanent.* Thus, it appears that the conventioneers do not have their eyes on the same target. Some are trying to formulate a criterion for one concept of death, and others are tying to formulate a criterion for some other concept of death. Perhaps some are trying to formulate a criterion even though they don't yet have any clear concept of death in mind.

This sort of confusion reveals one way in which the analytical project might have priority over the criterial project. It might be good for the conventioneers to agree at the outset about the nature of death. If they all agreed about what death is, they could more fruitfully go about their business of trying to agree on a clear mark of its arrival.

When I speak here of the search for death itself, I mean to indicate the effort to discover a satisfactory philosophical *analysis* of the concept of death. It is the attempt to answer the question 'What is death?', not the question 'What is the conventionally accepted indicator that death has arrived?'

The Biological Concept of Death

Some of the literature on death seems to be based on the assumption that the target concept is some special concept of death that is applicable only to *people*. Thus, for example, one writer says that to die is to cease permanently to be conscious of one's own psychological experiences.[1] He obviously does not assume that when a tree or a bacterium dies, it too ceases to be conscious in this way.

This assumption about death seems rather odd to me. I am more inclined to suppose that there is a single concept of death that has application throughout the biological realm. Perhaps I can clarify my view by appeal to some examples. Consider the following sentences:

1. JFK died in November 1963.
2. The last dodo died in April 1681.
3. My oldest Baldwin apple tree died during the winter of 1986.

I cannot think of any reason to suppose that the word 'died' has one meaning in sentence (1) and different meanings in the other two sentences. It seems to me that what we say about JFK in (1) is precisely the same as what we say about an apple tree in (3). Some slight evidence for my view can be derived from the fact that there would be nothing amusing, paradoxical, or otherwise out of the ordinary about the claim that if (1), (2), and (3) are all true, then at least three different things have died. If 'died' were used in different senses in these sentences, then the inference would be an eyebrow-raiser. It would be a play on words; it would be like the case in which a man tells us he owns two planes—one a single-engine Cessna that he uses on business trips and the other a single-bladed Stanley that he uses in his woodworking shop.

So I think there is a single concept of death that has application throughout the biological realm. This is not to say, of course, that all deaths are equally important; or that all deaths are manifested in the same way; or that one *criterion* of death must apply to every sort of entity. It is just to say, among other things, that the word 'died' has a certain intension, or meaning, and that it is possible that sentences (1), (2), and (3) may be used in such a way that the word 'died' in each of them expresses precisely this intension. In other words, it is to say that 'died' as used in (1) might mean exactly what it means as used in (2) and (3).

Someone might agree that there is a universally applicable concept of death but insist that there is also another concept of death applicable only to people. I think this is a mistake. I do not believe that there is a special concept of death applicable only to people. I do not believe that the word 'died' has a sense for which it would be a necessary truth that if a thing died, then it must have been a person. However, quite a few philosophers seem to believe that there is such a sense, and I see no way to prove them wrong. Thus, I should be cautious in describing my project: I am here interested in the analysis of the biological concept of death—I want to know what we mean when we say that something (whether human being, apple tree, or bird) dies; if there is a specifically "personal" concept of death, then I am also interested in it. But at least at the outset, I seek to understand the biological concept of death.

Life as a Part of Death

Our question is this: What is death? What do we mean when we say, using the biological concept of death, that something dies? According to the most popular answer, death is the cessation of life. In other words, to die is to cease to live. I call this "the standard analysis":

D1: x dies at t =df. x ceases to be alive at t.

D1 may seem to satisfy some of our requirements for success in conceptual analysis. It apparently does not violate the circularity condition. It seems to satisfy the necessity condition (we will reconsider this point later in Chapter 4). However, some philosophers would say that D1 trades one mystery for another; they would point out that D1 purports to clarify the concept of death by appeal to the concept of life; and they would say that the concept of life is hopelessly obscure—too obscure to be useful in the explication of the concept of death. Perhaps this objection would be an overstatement. In any case, this much is surely true: if we don't know what life is (what 'alive' means) then D1 is less than fully satisfactory. It is a definition per obscurius; it purports to tell us what a mysterious term means, but it makes use of yet another term at least as mysterious as the one originally in question.

We want to understand the biological concept of death. According to the standard analysis, death is the cessation of life. Thus, it may appear that we must first understand life. Let us then consider the nature of life. What does 'alive' mean? What do we mean when we say that something is alive? What is the nature of life? If we can answer this question, we can make use of the concept of life in our analysis of the concept of death. We can rebut the charge of obscurity in D1.

In Chapter 2, I consider some of the most popular analyses of the concept of life.

2

Life-Functional Theories of Life

Life itself

At least in part because it seems to play a crucial role in the analysis of death, I am interested in life—that is, I am interested in the property expressed by the phrase 'is alive'. The very same property (I think) is expressed by a variety of other phrases. For example, when we say that something 'has life' or 'is a living thing' then, if we use these terms in their central literal sense, we attribute life to it. These expressions also express the property of being alive. The challenge is to formulate a satisfactory philosophical analysis of that property.

There are other standard ways of referring to this property. Sometimes, especially when we are attending to the fact that people can be aware of properties, we call them "concepts" or "ideas." Thus, we may speak of the concept of life, or the idea of life. I take this to be the property of life, but thought of as an object of thought. In other words, it seems to me that when some property becomes the object of someone's thought, we can call that property a concept, or an idea. Properties also play a central role in the explanation of meaning. The property of being alive is the *intension* of the phrase '. . . is alive'. Since intensions are often taken to be "meanings," we may refer to the same entity when we speak of 'the meaning of "alive" '. Finally, some philosophers and biologists must surely be thinking of life itself when they speak of "the nature of living things."

It might seem that there's no difficulty in identifying our target. We all have some rough idea of what life is supposed to be. We all understand typical sentences in which the word 'alive' appears. But even at this early stage there are serious complications.

One complication concerns the fact that 'life' is also used in English to indicate something like the "history" of a living thing. For example, consider the statements "Her life lasted only sixteen and one half years," "A cat has nine lives," "His life was filled with joy," "His life was more interesting than mine." It would be implausible to interpret 'life' (or 'lives') in these sentences as referring to a certain property. In each case, it seems to refer to something with duration—something that lasts through a period of time. Life itself seems not to be like that. Furthermore, in these examples 'life' is used in such a way that it makes sense to say that different people have different lives. Yet one of the most striking facts about the property of life is that (apparently) every living thing exemplifies that very same property. It is a "universal"; it is common to all living things. Thus, these "lives" are distinct from life itself. For present purposes, we must put aside these "lives."[1] We are interested in a property that each living thing has throughout its life— the property of being alive, or "life."

A closely related complication concerns the fact that 'life' is sometimes used as a mass term indicating the aggregate of "living stuff." For example, when a man says that a certain region is "filled with life," or is "teeming" or "bursting" with life, he probably is not using 'life' as the name of a property. He's probably using it as a mass term for a kind of stuff—living stuff. For present purposes, we must also put aside this stuff. We are interested in the property, life itself, that characterizes this stuff.

Another complication is that 'life' and 'alive' are used in a variety of semantically distinct ways. Some of these are uncontroversially literal, and others are uncontroversially metaphorical. For example, suppose there has been a train wreck, and casualties are being removed from the wreckage. We might want to know if a certain passenger survived the accident. We ask, 'Is she still alive?' 'Alive' here is almost certainly used literally. On the other hand, when someone sings 'The hills are alive with the sound of music,' she almost certainly uses 'alive' metaphorically. Similarly, when we say that an automobile 'springs to life' when you turn the key, we use 'life' metaphorically (except perhaps in the Stephen King novel *Christine*). The complication arises because there are many intermediate cases—cases in which it is not clear whether 'alive' is being used literally or metaphorically. These can lead to confusion.

An interesting example concerns ponds. Environmentalists sometimes tell us that ponds are living things. They describe the geological conditions that "give birth to" a pond; they describe the way in which the pond "grows" and "flourishes"; they may describe the way in which the pond "becomes sick" when it fills up with silt or rubbish; finally, they may describe the way it "dies" when it ultimately turns into a swampy bog or a meadow. There are several possibilities here. (1) The environmentalists may think that ponds are literally alive—that they exemplify true life just as their fish and frogs do. (2) They may think that ponds are not literally alive, but that the history of a pond is like the history of a genuinely living thing, such as a fish or a frog. This recognition of similarity may provoke the use of 'living' in a strictly metaphorical way. (3) Finally, the environmentalists may be engaging in loose talk. If pressed, they might admit that they do not know whether they meant their expression literally or figuratively.

Another troublesome case is the so-called Gaia Hypothesis, introduced by J. E. Lovelock in his book *Gaia: A New Look at Life on Earth*. The biosphere is the part of the Earth that contains living stuff—roughly the part starting at the bottom of the topsoil and rising to the lower part of the atmosphere. The biosphere also contains the seas, lakes, rivers, and other bodies of water. Gaians claim to believe that the biosphere is alive. Perhaps they are using 'alive' metaphorically. Perhaps all they mean is that the biosphere is in interesting ways *like* a living thing. In this case, their claim seems uncontroversial. It's obvious that the earth is like a living thing in some ways. Perhaps Gaians find these similarities interesting.

On the other hand, it is possible that Gaians are using 'alive' in what they take to be its literal sense. Consider an ordinary fish happily swimming in an ordinary pond. We can use the word 'alive' in its literal sense to characterize the fish. It is possible that some Gaians use the word 'alive' in just this sense to characterize the biosphere. If so, their view seems to me to be silly. However, in the absence of a widely accepted understanding of the concept of life, it may be hard to adjudicate such disagreements.

I intend to proceed on the assumption that 'alive' has a central, literal sense. We generally use the word with that sense when we use it to describe an ordinary fish swimming in an ordinary pond. I will also assume that when used in this literal sense, 'alive' expresses a certain property. This is "life itself." I take it that the attempt to "define life" is the attempt to formulate an adequate definition of 'alive' when used in this way. This project is equivalent to the project of formulating an analysis of the concept of life, or an analysis of the property of being alive.

Some Preliminary Objections

In *The Growth of Biological Thought,* Ernst Mayr makes the following statement:

> Attempts have been made again and again to define "life." These endeavors are rather futile since it is now quite clear that there is no special substance, object, or force that can be identified with life.[2]

A few pages later, Mayr says:

> Life . . . is simply the reification of the processes of living. Criteria for living can be stated and adopted, but there is no such thing as an independent "life" in a living organism. . . . The avoidance of nouns that are nothing but reifications of processes greatly facilitates the analysis of the phenomena that are characteristic for biology.[3]

It is not entirely clear that Mayr means to say that 'alive' cannot be defined, but his words strongly suggest this. He says that there is something that has been tried "again and again" and that is "rather futile." He characterizes this as the attempt to "define life." If he is not talking about our topic, it is hard to understand what he is talking about. In any case, let us consider the objection.

I think that Mayr is probably correct in saying that there is no special substance, [physical] object, or force that can be identified with life. But it surely does not follow from this that life cannot be defined. There is no substance, physical object, or force that can be identified with motherhood, but motherhood can be defined. Equally, there is no substance, physical object, or force that can be identified with primeness (as in "three is a prime number"), but that fact does not rule out analyses of the concept of primeness.

Mayr's words suggest that he thinks that there is no such thing as life. One who thinks that life is a property, as I do, does not think that life is a physical object or substance, and he or she very well may reject the notion that it is a force. No property is a physical object, and quite a few fail to be forces. Thus, Mayr's remarks give us no reason for agreeing that there is no such thing as life. So long as we are careful to keep life in its proper ontological category, I see no danger in supposing it to exist.

Others have given other reasons for thinking that life cannot be defined. One reason is that living things are a very varied and heterogeneous group. Some have suggested that living things are so varied that they have nothing in common—hence there is no such property as life. This objection to our project strikes me as being premature. In the first place, it is obvious that living things in fact do have a lot in common—they share all necessary properties, and they are all alive. In the second place, huge variations in other respects are compatible with important similarities in some respects. For example, consider the class of mothers. It displays enormous heterogeneity—some are people and others are bugs; some weigh only a fraction of an ounce, and others weigh over a ton. Nevertheless, its members have something in common. They are all female parents.

So it seems to me that we may continue. No good reason has been given for supposing that our quest is wrongheaded from the start. Let us then turn to some of the most important traditional attempts to define life itself.

Aristotle's Life-Functional Analysis of Life

No approach to the analysis of life itself has a more distinguished history than the one we may call the "life-functional" approach. Aristotle himself is the founder and chief advocate of this approach. Since his time, hundreds of philosophers and biologists have defended variants of his view. Let's begin by considering Aristotle's version of the theory.

Although different texts suggest different lists, Aristotle seems to have recognized the following main life functions:

Nutrition: the capacity to get food, absorb it into oneself, and thereby to grow. Surprisingly, Aristotle maintains that nutrition is inseparable from reproduction; that these are both functions of the same "soul"—the nutritive soul. "Nutrition and reproduction are due to one and the same psychic power."[4] Reproduction is the capacity to produce offspring. Aristotle maintains that the capacity to engage in nutrition is the most basic and widely distributed life function. His view seems to be that every living thing, plant or animal, has this capacity; no nonliving thing has it. Thus, apparently according to Aristotle, a thing is alive if and only if it can engage in nutrition and reproduction.

Sensation: An organism has sense if it is capable of "receiving into itself the sensible forms of things without. . . ."[5] This capacity operates in two different modes. Certain senses (touch and taste) operate on objects that are in contact with the organism. Aristotle seems to have believed that all animals have the capacity to engage in this "immediate sensation."[6] Plants, however, do not have it.

The second mode of sensation involves the perception of objects that are not in direct contact with the organism. Sight, smell, and hearing are the instances of this mediate form of sensation. Aristotle claims[7] that these senses are not found in every sort of animal, but only in animals that can move. He apparently felt that there would be no point in giving sight, for example, to a fixed animal such as a barnacle. After all, even if the barnacle could see a tasty bit of food a few inches away, it would not be able to do anything about it. Having sight would not improve the well-being of a barnacle. Hence, nature did not give barnacles eyes.

Motion: An organism has "the locomotive soul" if it is capable of moving itself from place to place. Aristotle apparently held that the locomotive soul is always found in conjunction with the far sensitive soul. Stripped of its soulful terminology, the claim amounts to this: a creature can move itself about if and only if it can see, hear, or smell.

Thought: some organisms are able to think. This includes people and perhaps some other rational beings. Aristotle says[8] that this sort of "rational soul" is "capable of existence in isolation from all other psychic powers." Perhaps he is thinking of gods. There seems to be a slight tension between this remark and his later remark that "the nutritive soul then must be possessed by every-thing that is alive. . . ."[9] Perhaps he means to say this: among mortal beings, the nutritive soul is universal. If we include immortal beings, we find instances of things with rational souls but without nutritive souls.

Aristotle maintains that "Of the psychic powers above enumerated, some kinds of living things, as we said, possess all, some less than all, others one only."[10] If we simplify slightly, and emphasize certain texts rather than others, we can present the outlines of Aristotle's view in a chart.[11]

	Plants	Fixed Animals	Beasts	People	[Gods]
Nutrition	Yes	Yes	Yes	Yes	No
Reproduction	Yes*	Yes*	Yes*	Yes*	No
Near Sensation	No	Yes	Yes	Yes	No
Far Sensation	No	No	Yes	Yes	No
Motion	No	No	Yes	Yes	No
Thought	No	No	No	Yes	Yes

A few comments may be in order. First, it is important to recognize that Aristotle views nutrition and reproduction as functions of the same "soul"—the nutritive. Furthermore, he explicitly acknowledges[12] that there are many cases in which individual plants and animals are incapable of engaging in reproduction. Thus, I have asterisked the "yes" in each occurrence concerning reproduction. Second, the column marked "[Gods]" is just a guess on my part. Aristotle merely indicates that in his view, people are the only *mortal* beings with rational souls. This leaves open the question of whether there might also be some *immortal* beings with souls.

While the chart is surely suggestive, it does not yet constitute an answer to our fundamental question, What is Life? One natural answer, based on these Aristotelian ideas, would be this:

LF1: x is alive at t =df. x is able to perform at least one of the life functions at t.

It seems to me, however, that there are very serious problems for LF1. One of these problems concerns motion. If we understand motion in a straightforward manner, we will have to say that any mechanical device that is capable of setting itself into motion displays this sort of life function. As a result, LF1 seems to imply that alarm clocks, robots of various sorts, automatic lawn sprinkling devices, and the like, are all alive.

Aristotle himself seems to have been particularly impressed by the apparent universality of the nutritive soul. In a widely quoted passage, he says:

> This [the power of self-nutrition] is the originative power the possession of which leads us to speak of things as *living* at all. . . .[13]

And in another just a few paragraphs later we find:

> First of all we must treat of nutrition and reproduction, for the nutritive soul is found along with all the others and is the most primitive and widely distributed power of soul, being indeed that one in virtue of which all are said to have life. The acts in which it manifests itself are reproduction and the use of food.[14]

On one interpretation, Aristotle might be taken to be maintaining this view about life itself:

LF2: x is alive at t =df. x is able to engage in nutrition and reproduction at t.

Obviously, however, this won't do. As Aristotle himself pointed out, very many living things cannot engage in reproduction.[15] He cites three sorts of cases in which living things lack the capacity to reproduce. Some cannot reproduce because they are too young. (I suppose we could add that some cannot reproduce because they are too old.) He goes on to mention organisms that are "mutilated." Finally, he mentions organisms whose mode of reproduction is spontaneous. Aristotle seems to have thought that some creatures were produced by spontaneous generation. Be this as it may, the first two points are surely conclusive. Many things cannot engage in reproduction even though they are alive. Thus, LF2 is clearly wrong.

We could modify LF2 merely by deleting the second conjunct. This would yield:

LF3: x is alive at t =df. x is able to engage in nutrition at t.

Aristotle devotes several pages to his discussion of nutrition. He presents a fascinating discussion of the analysis of the concept of food, and he talks about the nature of growth. In the end, however, stripped of complexities, his view seems to be this: a creature can engage in nutrition at a time if and only if it is able at that time to acquire some food, absorb that food and make it part of itself, and as a result, grow and have the energy needed to do what needs to be done.

By way of criticism of LF3, I here quote at length a moving passage from *The Nature of Living Things* by C. Brooke Worth and Robert K. Enders. Worth and Enders have been describing an experiment with a cecropia moth. Shortly after the moth emerged from its pupal shell, Worth and Enders tied a string around its waist and placed it outdoors where a male could find it. According to their account, a male did find the moth:

Copulation lasts through the day. In the evening we untether the female and put her in a shoe box for an hour or so. By this time she has laid fifty eggs, so we let her go. For the next few nights she will dot the rest of her eggs, some two or three hundred, on various trees. What then? Already her gorgeous wings are a bit tattered. Her abdomen has shrunk and she is beginning to tremble. But naturally! She has been so busy that food has been forgotten. Now she is faced with tragedy greater than one would suspect, for her entire race has forgotten about food. The caterpillar's digestive tract, taken to bed in the pupa's interior, was completely demolished during moth-formation, but no substitute was provided. So here flits the *cecropia,* completely absolved of her responsibilities to posterity, but unable to taste the rewards of accomplishment. No mouth, no stomach—only a small additional reserve of stored energy. The moth flies about bright lights for a few evenings more but then falls ragged and quivering to the ground, where ants slowly extinguish the rest of its waning life.[16]

The case of the cecropia moth demonstrates, I think, that a creature can be alive at a time even though it is not then able to engage in nutrition. Other examples come to mind. While undergoing abdominal surgery, a person's digestive system might be temporarily detached and shut down. Furthermore, the patient might be unconscious and paralyzed. Such a patient is clearly alive, yet unable to take in any food (because of being paralyzed and unconscious) and unable to absorb any food (because the intestines are detached). As it stands, LF3 is unsatisfactory.

It should be obvious that we cannot modify LF3 in anything like this way:

> LF3′: x is alive at t =df. either (i) x is able to engage in nutrition at t, or else (ii) x was able to engage in nutrition at some time earlier than t.

The problem with LF3' is that nearly every dead organism satisfies the second disjunct of the definiens. Corpses are nonliving things that *formerly* were able to engage in nutrition.

It seems clear, then, that Aristotle's version of the life-functional approach suffers from some serious problems. Perhaps two thousand years of biological research has provided the basis for a more plausible formulation. Let us therefore consider some typical modern examples of the life-functional approach to the analysis of the concept of life.

Some Modern Life-Functional Analyses of Life

In *Philosophy: an introduction to the art of wondering,* James Christian says:

> At present, it appears that "life" can be defined with two qualities: self-replication and mutability. Any organism possessing these two qualities can be considered alive. In these two characteristics is contained the essential processes of evolution: continuity and adaptation. . . . But mutability—the ability to effect changes from one generation to another and adapt to a fluid environment—is essential. Without the ability to change and adapt no species could long

survive. Environmental conditions are forever changing; species must be able to change along with their environments. So far as we know, only living organisms have these two qualities, and an organism must possess both qualities to be considered alive.[17]

It is interesting to compare Christian's view with a view presented in Richard Goldsby's *Biology*. Goldsby reports that exobiologists at NASA have been interested in the nature of life. One of their missions, apparently, is to send spaceships to other planets on a search for living things. Since conditions on other planets are undoubtedly quite different from conditions here on earth, the NASA exobiologists recognized that it would be a big mistake to design their equipment to recognize "life as we know it." The equipment would have to recognize life even if it appeared in forms quite different from the forms we know. According to Goldsby:

> These scientists have tried to reduce the functional definition of life to the most simple, general, and abstract criteria. Their conclusion is that only two characteristics distinguish living entities from inanimate nature: the ability to *reproduce* themselves, and the means of producing and perpetuating *genetic variations* among the offspring.[18]

Goldsby goes on to claim that this very abstract definition of life has certain corollaries. In order to reproduce, an organism has to stay alive at least for a little while. This requires *metabolism* (the ability to "absorb, transform, and use material from the environment") and *adaptation* (the ability to make useful, genuinely "homeostatic" responses to changes in the environment). Christian also mentions these other life functions[19] along with a few others, but it isn't clear that he views them as "corollaries" of the core definition.

Thus it appears that NASA (at least according to Goldsby) and Christian would agree that life itself can be defined as follows:

LF4: x is alive at t =df. x is able to reproduce at t, and x is able to produce and perpetuate genetic variation among offspring at t.

The influence of Charles Darwin is obvious in this account of life. As both Christian and Goldsby point out, this analysis of the concept of life very naturally leads to the conclusion that living things will be able to evolve as their environment changes (so long as the environment changes at a suitable rate, and the mutations occur at a suitable rate). Because of this emphasis, this sort of analysis is sometimes called "the genetic analysis of life." It is nowadays quite popular with philosophers and biologists.

Nevertheless it is clear that, as it stands, LF4 won't work. As we have already noted, lots of living things are unable to reproduce. In some cases, infertility is only temporary, but in other cases it is permanent and lifelong. Among ants and bees, for example, many living individuals are permanently sterile. The same holds true for certain hybrids, such as mules. Obviously, if a thing can't produce offspring at all, then it surely cannot produce offspring manifesting genetic variations from itself. Thus, each conjunct of the the proposed analysis of life is clearly too narrow, and the analysis itself fails.

One natural modification of LF4 suggests itself. We must distinguish between the concrete, individual organism (this particular mosquito—the one that just bit my ear) and the species (in this case, I suspect, *Culex pipiens*). Living individuals may be unable to reproduce. But as a number of authors going back to Aristotle have remarked, a viable species must have some standard method (or methods) of reproduction. Typical adult, unmutilated instances of the species generally reproduce in the method standard for the species.

In the case of mutation, or variation, the focus on the species rather than the individual is even more obvious. It makes virtually no sense to say that an individual mosquito undergoes genetic variation from generation to generation. The individual has the same genetic makeup throughout its existence and is a member of exactly one generation, no matter how long it lives. However, it does make sense to say that a *species* undergoes genetic variation from generation to generation. Roughly, what this means is that individuals of one generation are genetically different from individuals of other generations.

In order to simplify our discussion, let us introduce some simplifying terminology. We can say that a species is *reproductive* when there is a method of reproduction such that typical members of that species reproduce by that method. Thus, the amoeba is reproductive because typical members undergo fission; the tomato is reproductive because typical members produce viable seeds; the lion is reproductive because males inseminate females who then carry their cubs to term; and so on. Going beyond this, we can say that a species is *variably reproductive* when it is reproductive and when individuals of one generation are capable of producing offspring that manifest small genetic differences from their parents. We need not attempt to define what is meant by "small" genetic differences.

Making use of these abbreviations, and taking note of the distinction between species and individuals, we could replace LF4 with:

> LF5: x is alive at t =df. x is a member of some variably reproductive species at t.

The advantage of LF5 over LF4 is clear. Immature, "mutilated," and postreproductive individuals are not counterexamples to LF5. Such individuals are counted as living not because they can reproduce, but because they are members of reproductive species. Furthermore, sterile ants and bees also count as alive, since they are members of variably reproductive species. Their own sterility is here irrelevant. Unfortunately, a moment's reflection will reveal that LF5 casts the net of life much too widely. It correctly counts the senile as alive; it incorrectly counts the deceased as alive. A dead chicken is still a chicken; it's still a member of a variably reproductive species. LF5 therefore tells us that each such chicken is still alive.

Someone might insist that a dead chicken is really not a chicken. Such a person might claim that the corpse of a member of a species is not itself a member of that species. This seems to me to be wrong. If we reflect for a moment on the activities of taxonomists, its wrongheadedness will become even clearer. Entomological taxonomists, for example, do virtually all of their work with dead specimens. They sort individuals into species—but the individuals are rarely living. They point to their cases of dead butterflies and say, "This is the Monarch; that is the Viceroy. Notice the difference in the pattern." If the current proposal were correct, the taxonomists would be wrong. Strictly speaking, there would be no Monarchs or Viceroys in their case. Only a dedicated philosopher could say such a thing with a straight face.

This sort of approach gives rise to further profound difficulties. Perhaps the most intractable of these is this: LF5 makes use of the notoriously obscure concept of "species." In order to make LF5 fully satisfactory as a philosophical analysis of the concept of life, we would have to give some account of the concept of species, and that would be a most difficult task. However, if we insist on altering our conception of species in such a way that, as a matter of conceptual necessity, each species contains only *living* members, then the task becomes vastly more difficult. Furthermore, as should be obvious, the task presupposes a solution to our present problem. In order to define 'species', we would have first to define 'alive'.

The Matthews Approach

A modern, sophisticated version of Aristotle's approach has been developed by my colleague, Gary Matthews.[20] Matthew's idea involves several refinements of Aristotle's approach. One of these is the idea that capacities that are life functions for the members of one species might not be life functions for the members of another species—it varies from species to species. Thus, a fundamental concept is expressed by 'F is a life function for the members of species S' (which Matthews expresses by 'x is a psychic power for species s').

It would be natural to suppose that a *life-functional* property is one that an individual needs in order to be alive, but it is clear that the properties on Aristotle's list don't have this feature. Individuals can live without them. Obviously, an individual can continue to live even if it cannot engage in reproduction or locomotion. Matthew's idea is that life functions are capacities without which a *species* cannot be preserved.

More exactly, the idea is that a certain capacity is a life function for a species if and only if *most* members of that species must have that capacity in order for the *species* to be preserved.

Consider the capacity to reproduce. An individual mosquito might be able to survive quite well even if it were unable to reproduce. However, if most mosquitoes were unable to reproduce, the species would soon begin to die out. Eventually, there would be no more mosquitoes. Thus, the capacity to reproduce in the mosquitoish way is a life function for mosquitoes. It is a capacity that members of that species must have if the species is to be preserved. In a comment, Matthews mentions the following as plausible candidates for vital functions: reason, sense perception, locomotion, appetite, metabolism, and reproduction.[21] Presumably, he means that certain forms of these are vital functions for certain species.

Making use of his novel concept of vital function, Matthews proceeds to offer an Aristotelian analysis of life itself. He says that for a thing to be alive is for it to be able to exercise at least one vital function for its species.[22] In other words:

LF6: x is alive at t =df. at t, x is able to exercise at least one capacity that is a vital function for x's species.

Matthew's proposal is subtle and insightful. However, there are a few difficulties.

I think that most of the properties Matthews mentions are not vital functions according to his definition. Consider reproduction, for example, among ants or bees. In certain species of social bees, one female out of ten thousand engages in reproduction.[23] Most of the members of the hive are sterile workers or drones. Now consider the property of *reproducing in the manner peculiar to bees*. It is clear that it is *not* the case that individual organisms belonging to *Apis mellifera* must exercise that property in order for the species to be preserved. In fact, most individuals do not exercise that property, and the species has been preserved for thousands of years. It is not on the endangered species list.

Consider any species that is profligate, that is, far more offspring are produced than are needed to keep the species going. Just a few individuals produce enough offspring to populate the whole next generation. Making allowances for the need for genetic variation, we can suppose that it is important that 10 percent reproduce. So it is not necessarily for the survival of the species that most of them reproduce, or that members of the species *in general* reproduce.

Indeed, human beings could get by indefinitely if only 5 percent of us engaged in reproduction (provided that each reproductive female worked at it full time).

Similarly for distant perception. Suppose 51 percent of humans became deaf, blind, and unable to smell. This would be very bad for those individuals, but surely they could reproduce. Even if they were somehow unable to reproduce, their difficulties might not interfere with the reproductive efforts of the other 49 percent, who could have somewhat larger families if need be. The species might continue to exist for thousands of years. Thus, far sensation is not a psychic power on Matthew's definition.

It goes almost without saying that our species could continue to exist even if all of us lost the distinctively human power to reason. Suppose we all behaved as irrationally as ponies. We would probably be somewhat better off, and we surely would be able to have lots of children.

Other properties may be vital functions according to Matthews's analysis. For example, some evergreens have this feature: the seeds are in cones. The cones burst open only if exposed to very considerable heat. The heat is produced by forest fires. The forest fires occur only if the old trees burn. Consider this property: being able to burn. If most evergreens of the relevant sort lacked this property, the species would die out. So it is a psychic property of the species. So any still-combustible tree is alive. But some dead trees are still combustible.

A deeper problem with Matthews's proposal is that it may be circular. As we saw above, Matthews defines a vital function as one without which a species will not long be *preserved*. What do we mean when we say that a species is "preserved"? Surely not this:

D9: S is preserved up to t =df. at t, S still exists.

The problem is that if species are such things as the property of being a tiger, then they exist necessarily (I think). Instances need do nothing in order to keep the species in existence. Surely Matthews didn't mean that. What then? Presumably this:

D10: S is preserved up to t =df. at t, there are still some living members of S.

But if this is what 'preserved' means, then Matthews's approach as a whole is clearly circular. We propose to analyze the concept of life by appeal to the concept of vital property; we analyze the concept of vital property by appeal to the concept of preservation; we analyze the concept of preservation by appeal to the concept of life. On the other hand, he might try:

> D11: S is preserved up to t =df. at t, there are still some existing members of S.

But then you don't have to be alive to preserve your species. And then a species could be preserved even if none of its members were alive—all we would need would be suitable formaldehyde baths for at least some members of the species.

Conclusion

In spite of its magnificent pedigree and its popularity, the life-functional approach to the analysis of life is unsuccessful. I see no satisfactory way to define life by appeal to some set of life functions. Let us then turn to some other approaches to the analysis of life itself.

3

Vitalist Theories of Life

I want to understand the nature of death itself. In other words, I want to discover a suitable philosophical analysis of the concept of death. According to the most popular view, death is the cessation of life. It appears then that in order to understand death properly, we must first understand life. So I have been considering some proposed analyses of the concept of life. In Chapter 2, I presented and discussed several versions of the Aristotelian idea that life can be explained by appeal to the life functions. None of these seemed successful. I know of no more plausible variant of the life-functional approach. In this chapter, I turn to a consideration of some other approaches to the analysis of life. These are vitalism, DNA-ism, and the genetic informational theory of life.

Vitalism

Aristotle is the first and perhaps greatest advocate of the life-functional approach to the analysis of life. Strangely enough, he is also the first and perhaps greatest advocate of a wholly distinct approach to the analysis of life. This second approach is generally known as "vitalism."

In order to explain the distinguishing characteristic of vitalism, we have to appeal to the distinction between "substances" and "attributes." Unfortunately, the substance/attribute distinction is notoriously difficult to draw. I will not be able to draw it very precisely here. Perhaps I can hint at the distinction in this way: such things as my body, the blood in my body, the air in my lungs, the earth, and the like, are *substances*. The shape of my body, the color of my blood, the temperature of the air, the weight of the earth, and the like, are *attributes,* or properties.

Substances are also known as objects, individuals, things, particulars. Attributes are also known as properties, characteristics, features, or universals. A given substance, such as my body, for example, is said to *exemplify* various attributes, such as being six feet tall, weighing over one hundred and fifty pounds, being at a temperature of approximately 98.6°F. These attributes are said to *characterize* this substance.

It is natural to think that living things differ from nonliving things fundamentally because living things have some special organization or capacity—that being alive is primarily a matter of having "vital properties." Thus, in this view, life itself is an attribute that living things have because they also have certain other attributes. Vitalists, however, disagree. They think living things differ from nonliving things in virtue of the fact that living things contain a special substance, which can be called their "life." Thus, for the vitalists, life itself is a substance rather than an attribute. They think that living things are alive because they contain some of this substance. Aristotle used the term 'psyche' (or 'soul') apparently to refer to this substance. In a famous passage in *De Anima* ("On the Soul"), Aristotle says: "[W]hat has soul in it differs from what has not in that the former displays life."[1]

If this is meant to be a suggestion of a definition of 'alive', and 'soul' is meant to refer to a substance rather than an attribute, then this passage contains an ancient formulation of the vitalist conception of life. According to this view, to say that a thing is alive is to say that it contains a certain object, a "soul."

Later vitalists characterized life in other ways. One of the most popular forms of vitalism is based on the idea that life is a fluid— "vital fluid." Hans Driesch, one of the best known of modern vitalists, insisted that life is some sort of substance, but he wrote in such an impenetrable style that it is nearly impossible to figure out what sort of substance he took it to be.[2] Perhaps in part because it was generally presented in such obscure terminology, vitalism has passed from the scene.

Vitalism is dead. Since there is no point in beating a dead horse, it may seem that there is no point in trying to refute vitalism. However, my main purpose here is not to refute vitalism but to engage in a sort of postmortem examination. I want to consider why vitalism died. Having done this, I will turn to some living alternatives, to consider the state of health of vitalism's descendants. During its life, vitalism took many forms. It will be necessary at the outset, therefore, to sketch one relatively clear version of the view.

At the heart of our form of vitalism is the commitment to "vital fluid." Vital fluid is an "imponderable substance." When we say, in this context, that vital fluid is a "substance," we imply that it is a kind of "stuff" rather than, for example, a force, a property, or a set of dispositions. Perhaps it would also be correct to say that each unit of vital fluid is supposed to be a concrete, individual thing rather than a property or attribute. Thus, a drop of vital fluid belongs in the same ontological category as a drop of blood, a drop of cerebrospinal fluid, or a drop of transmission fluid.

But vital fluid is different from transmission fluid in several important respects. One of the most important of these is that vital fluid is supposed to be "imponderable." To say that it is imponderable is to say that it has no weight. In this respect, vital fluid is like ether and phlogiston. Furthermore, vital fluid is colorless, tasteless, odorless, and in general unobservable. We can recognize that it is present (if at all) only by the consequences of its presence.

Let us also agree that from the perspective of chemistry and physics, vital fluid is not an ordinary liquid or gas. It does not have any chemical structure. It is not made of atoms and molecules. In light of this, we have to recognize that it would not be possible to synthesize vital fluid in a laboratory. At best, it might be possible to *collect* some. No one will ever be able to *make* any—at least, no one will be able to make any *by ordinary chemical processes*.

According to our version of vitalism, every living thing contains at least some vital fluid. In the case of human beings, vital fluid is contained in the sperm. When the sperm and egg unite, the vital fluid "vitalizes" the resulting embryo, and it is therefore alive. The living embryo has the capacity to enlarge its original portion of vital fluid. As the embryo grows, a portion of vital fluid is incorporated into every new cell. Eventually, the mature, living individual is permeated with vital fluid—every living cell in the body contains a tiny drop. As death approaches, the vital fluid begins to leave the body. In some cases, it may gradually ooze away as the various formerly living parts of the body become moribund and start to die. At some point, the body contains so little vital fluid that it can no longer function. We say that it is dead. After a few days, perhaps no vital fluid is left. The body is thoroughly dead—no part of it remains alive.

The version of vitalism that I mean to discuss here is not an empirical hypothesis about living things. That is, it is not just the contingent claim that, as a matter of fact, every living thing happens to contain some vital fluid. Rather, it is a theory about "life itself." That is, it is a theory about the nature of life, or the property of being alive. In its simplest form, the theory can be stated as a definition:

V1: x is alive at t =df. there is some vital fluid in x at t.

If V1 is correct, then it is impossible for something to be alive without vital fluid, and it is impossible for something to contain vital fluid without being alive. To say that something is alive is, in this view, simply to say that it contains vital fluid. This is not merely a contingent, empirical hypothesis.

The Empirical Problem

One of the most serious problems for V1 arises from the fact that there probably is not any vital fluid. If there is not any vital fluid, then, according to V1, nothing is alive.

Of course, in light of the fact that vital fluid is supposed to be unobservable, it is not easy to determine whether any exists. Driesch apparently performed a number of experiments on sea urchin eggs in an effort to establish the existence of vital fluid.[3] In one experiment, he allowed a fertilized sea urchin egg to undergo one cell division. Then he separated the two cells. Each cell continued to grow and eventually developed into a full-fledged (but pint-sized) sea urchin. Driesch declared that the experiment had succeeded—it showed, he said, that the original fertilized sea urchin egg contained vital fluid. Driesch's reasoning here eludes me. I can not see any connection between the facts about the sea urchins and the existence of vital fluid. The experiment seems to me to be utterly pointless.

The Jonah Problem

There is an another obvious and unanswerable objection to V1. This objection conclusively refutes V1 even if every living thing contains the appropriate amount of vital fluid. A trivial variant of the story of Jonah and the whale will make the objection clear. Suppose Jonah is swallowed by the whale, just as the Bible says. Suppose, however, contrary to what the Bible says, that as a result of eating Jonah, the whale suffers a huge bout of indigestion and dies. Suppose several days pass. Jonah remains very lonely and frightened but fully alive inside the whale. The whale becomes utterly dead. Suppose, in order to give the story a not-too-grisly ending, that the whale washes up on a beach, some fishermen hear Jonah's cries and cut open the whale, thereby freeing Jonah at last. Perhaps Jonah's ordeal teaches him that he cannot escape God's commands, and so he goes off to Nineveh to preach to the Ninevites as God originally told him to do.

For present purposes, the crucial period of time is the period during which the whale is dead and Jonah is alive inside the whale's carcass. According to V1, every living thing contains vital fluid. If V1 were true, it would follow that Jonah contained vital fluid during his captivity. Since Jonah was entirely inside the whale during this period, it follows that there was some vital fluid (Jonah's) inside the whale during the period of Jonah's captivity. If V1 were true, therefore, it would follow that the whale was alive during that period. But it wasn't. So V1 is false.

Perhaps someone will say that Jonah's vital fluid was not really "inside" the whale during his captivity. It might be insisted that for something to be truly "inside" the whale, it has to be inside the cells in the whale's body—merely being in the whale's belly would be insufficient. This suggests:

V2: x is alive at t =df. there is some vital fluid inside the cells of x at t.

Since Jonah's vital fluid was not inside the cells of the whale's body, V2 generates more plausible results in the Jonah case. However, V2 is hardly an improvement over V1. Suppose the whale died because of an infection. Suppose the still-living infectious agents are located inside some of the whale's cells. Then the vital fluid in the infectious agents is really "inside" the whale—it is inside his cells. But the whale is still dead.

These examples show quite conclusively that V1 and V2 are false. To state a more plausible version of vitalism, we might try to distinguish between cases (such as the one involving the whale and Jonah's vital fluid), in which some vital fluid is in an object in the "wrong way," and other more typical cases (such as the one involving Jonah and Jonah's vital fluid) in which the vital fluid is in the object in the "right way"—the way that serves to make the thing alive.

We can say that vital fluid "animates" an organism when it is in the organism in the "right way." Thus, during his captivity, Jonah's vital fluid animated Jonah, but it did not animate the whale. Now, instead of V1, we can consider:

V3: x is alive at t =df. some vital fluid animates x at t.

Since we have not even tried to explain what is meant by 'animates', V3 suffers from a certain amount of obscurity, but the cases I have described do not refute it.

The real problem with V3, as I see it, is that the appeal to vital fluid now begins to seem irrelevant. Perhaps the difficulty can be brought to the surface by comparing V3 with a nonvitalistic competitor:

V4: x is alive at t =df. something animates x at t.

Suppose some sea urchin were animated by ether, or by phlogiston, or by some other imponderable fluid, instead of by vital fluid. So long as it were truly *animated,* it would behave in every way like a living thing. We could never tell that it was animated by the wrong substance. But what is most important in the present circumstances is that there seems to be no plausibility to the claim that such a sea urchin really would not be alive. We would all say that it is alive, and I think we would be right. In light of this, it is hard to see what difference the vital fluid makes. Animation (whatever that may be) seems to be the crucial factor. So the nonvitalistic V4 is just as plausible as the vitalistic V3. Each, of course, is hopelessly obscure.

The Failure of Analyticity

Suppose a flying saucer lands on the Mall in Washington. A door opens, and a little green man walks out. Suppose he breathes air, eats hamburgers and french fries, and talks to us about his hopes and fears. Suppose also he shows us photos of his wife and children back home on Mars. We would all say that he is alive, and we would be literally right.

However, it is consistent with all this to suppose that life on Mars developed in a genuinely "unearthly" way. Suppose the Martian allows some scientists to take a tiny sliver of his skin for laboratory study. Suppose the scientists discover that there is no vital fluid in the Martian skin sample. Perhaps the Martian's cells contain "zoetic fluid" instead of vital fluid. (How this could be determined is another matter.) The scientists say:

1. The Martian is alive, but he contains no vital fluid.

It is important to notice that the scientists' statement, (1), is not self-contradictory. Such a statement *could* be true. That is, there is no conceptual problem in the supposition that something is alive but has no vital fluid. This shows that 'alive' does not entail 'has vital fluid'. Hence, "life itself" does not involve vital fluid. Even if every living thing on earth contains vital fluid, the property we ascribe to such things when we say that they are alive is not properly defined by V1, V2, or any other vitalistic definition. The case of the zoetic Martian shows that the property of being alive cannot be identified with the property of containing, or being animated by, vital fluid. We can easily imagine a case in which something is alive even though it contains no vital fluid.

So there are several reasons for rejecting vitalism. In the first place, there is no reason to suppose that there is any vital fluid.

This is the empirical problem. In the second place, even if there is vital fluid, it is hard to state in any useful way how the vital fluid is supposed to bear on the life of living organisms. Consideration of the story of Jonah demonstrated the difficulty. Finally, there is the failure of analyticity. The case of the zoetic Martian shows that there is no conceptual link between being alive and having vital fluid. With these reflections in mind, let us now turn to a consideration of a much more respectable view. According to this view, which we can call "DNA-ism," the essence of life is the containment of DNA or RNA.

DNA-ism

In *The Growth of Biological Thought,* Ernst Mayr seems to maintain a somewhat confusing combination of positions on the question concerning the definability of life itself. On the one hand, in a passage I quoted earlier, he asserts that attempts to define 'life' "are rather futile, since it is now quite clear that there is no special substance, object, or force that can be identified with life."[4] On the other hand, he says that "The process of living, however, can be defined. There is no doubt that living organisms possess certain attributes that are not or not in the same manner found in inanimate objects."[5] Mayr lists eight attributes that are allegedly characteristic of living things. One of these attributes is the possession of a genetic program. Mayr says:

> All organisms possess a historically evolved genetic program, coded in the DNA of the nucleus of the zygote (or in RNA in some viruses). Nothing comparable to it exists in the inanimate world, except for manmade computers. . . . Except for the twilight zone of the origin of life, the possession of a genetic program provides for an absolute difference between organisms and inanimate matter.[6]

Mayr does not say that the "process of living" can be defined simply by appeal to DNA. Seven other characteristics of living things are also mentioned. Yet his remarks clearly entail some sort of strong conceptual link between life and the possession of DNA or RNA. Let us consider a non-Mayrian form of DNA-ism—the view that life can be defined strictly by appeal to the containment of DNA.

This view may be stated as a new definition of life itself:

DNA1: x is alive at t =df. x contains some DNA or RNA at t.

One of the serious objections to vitalism is that there is no evidence to support the claim that there is vital fluid. Earlier, I called this "the empirical problem." DNA1 faces no comparable difficulty. There is overwhelming empirical evidence that DNA and RNA actually exist. My older daughter once worked in a biology laboratory. Together with others, one of her jobs was to extract DNA from ground-up mouse spleens. One day she brought home a little test tube containing a few drops of purified DNA. So DNA exists. I've seen it with my own eyes. Obviously, then, DNA-ism has certain advantages over vitalism.

However, this little story about my daughter and the test tube provides the basis for a thoroughly devastating objection to DNA1. My daughter's test tube contained DNA. According to DNA1, it would follow that the test tube was alive. But it was not. Therefore, DNA1 is false. The reader is invited to consider the analogy between this objection to DNA1 and the Jonah Problem discussed above in connection with V1. I think the similarity is quite striking.

The natural way to modify the theory is to say that living things differ from nonliving things, not simply by virtue of the fact that they *contain* some DNA or RNA, but that the DNA or RNA is contained *within their cells*. Thus we can modify DNA1 as follows:

DNA2: x is alive at t =df. DNA or RNA is contained in the cells of
       x at t.

Since my daughter's test tube was not made of cells, it would not be correct to say that its cells contained DNA. Thus, DNA2 yields more satisfactory results in that case. Nevertheless, DNA2 is obviously wrong. It is vastly too generous with life. Consider any reasonably fresh corpse. Its cells contain just as much DNA as they contained when the organism was alive, yet it is now dead. According to DNA2, the corpse is alive. But it isn't. Thus, DNA2 is false.

Cases such as this last one concerning the fresh corpse show that vitalism has certain advantages over DNA-ism. It is open to the vitalist to insist that all the vital fluid has gone out the fresh corpse. Since vital fluid is unobservable, no one can prove the vitalist wrong. But the defender of DNA-ism has no such "out." DNA is observable. Unfortunately for DNA-ism, it can readily be observed in dead organisms.

There are a number of ways in which we might try to modify DNA2. One follows the pattern of V3. Instead of saying (as we do in DNA2) that DNA or RNA is merely "contained in" the cells of x, we can require that the DNA or RNA be more productive—we can require that x be *animated* by the DNA or RNA in its cells. This would yield:

> DNA3: x is alive at t =df. x is animated at t by some DNA or RNA
> in x's cells.

One could reasonably maintain that DNA3 does not run afoul of the corpses in the morgue. Although their cells contain plenty of DNA, we can always insist that their DNA fails to animate them. Thus, DNA3 yields the correct results in such cases.

Nevertheless, DNA3 faces a very serious difficulty. The difficulty is quite like the difficulty that faced V3. 'Animate' is a pretty fancy word. What does it mean? Let us consider three main possibilities.

1. My dictionary (*The Oxford Paperback Dictionary,* 1983) says that 'animate' means 'to give life to'.[7] In other words:

> A1: x animates y at t =df. x gives life to y at t.

For certain purposes, this might be a fine dictionary definition of 'animate'. However, we cannot make use of it in the present context. We are trying to give an account of the concept of life. The proposal currently under consideration is DNA3. It makes use of 'animate'. If, in this context, we define 'animate' as we do in A1, the project as a whole becomes hopelessly circular. We define life by appeal to animation, and animation by appeal to life. Obviously, the combination of DNA3 and A1 sheds no light on the nature of life.

2. A second proposal concerning animation would involve an appeal to the "life functions." These are such activities as nutri-

tion, reproduction, motion, and thought. The precise details of the list of life functions should not detain us here, since they were discussed in Chapter 2. The important point is that we give some independent account of the life functions, and then we say:

A2: x animates y at t =df. x causes y to be able to perform the life functions at t.

It should be obvious that the combination of DNA3 and A2 is a failure. In the first place, as I attempted to establish in Chapter 2, no one has been able to give a satisfactory account of the life functions. However, if someone were to give such an account, it would make DNA3 and A2 pointless. We could define life directly by appeal to the life functions, and skip the business about DNA as well as the business about animation. What I have in mind, of course, is just this:

L1: x is alive at t =df. x is able to perform the life functions at t.

3. A third proposal concerning animation would involve taking this concept as a conceptual primitive—that is, we propose that animation is both indefinable and familiar. In virtue of its indefinability, we are absolved of the responsibility of providing a definition. In virtue of its familiarity, we are permitted to make use of it in the effort to define other, less familiar concepts.

Clearly, however, we cannot take animation as a primitive here. That would be tantamount to taking life itself as a primitive. In other words, it would be tantamount to admitting that we cannot discover an analysis of the concept we set out to analyze.

Earlier, in connection with V3, I presented what I called "the analyticity problem." I pointed out that the sentence "The Martian is alive, but contains no vital fluid" is not self-contradictory. Even if all and only actual living things contain vital fluid, this shows that V3 is unacceptable. Let us now consider whether a similar objection can be raised against DNA3.

Consider this scenario: A flying saucer lands on the Mall in Washington, D.C. A door opens and out steps a little green man. He breathes air; he eats hamburgers and french fries; he speaks to us about his hopes and fears. He shows us photos of his wife and children back home on Mars. As an expression of interplanetary scientific generosity, he allows some scientists to remove a sliver of skin for analysis in the laboratory. To their surprise, they find that the Martian's skin cells contain no DNA or RNA. Perhaps they find that his cells contain a substance never before seen on earth—"ZNA". They say:

2. The Martian is alive, but he contains no DNA or RNA.

It seems to me that (2) is not self-contradictory. It *could* be true. Therefore, it is metaphysically possible for a thing to be alive even though it does not contain DNA or RNA. This shows that the concept of life does not involve the concept of containment of DNA or RNA. Any definition along the lines of DNA1 or DNA2 has got to be wrong.

It may be interesting to note that Francis Crick, one of the co-discoverers of the structure of DNA, commented on this very point. In his book *Life Itself,* in the chapter "The General Nature of Life," he discusses the idea that there may be forms of life utterly different from everything we know here on earth. He describes what he takes to be some of the necessary conditions for life (these involve storage and replication of genetic information). He points out that the earthly system, based on chemical features of the carbon atom, is well suited to these tasks. But he goes on to say:

Of course, elsewhere in the universe life may exist based on other materials. At lower temperatures liquid ammonia might serve as the solvent, though it is not as versatile a solvent as water, which is an exceptionally good one. Instead of carbon, silicon has been suggested. . . . Thus, a form of life based on other materials is not impossible.[8]

It appears, then, that Crick recognized that there is no conceptual connection between life and DNA containment. He saw that statements similar to (2) might be true. Thus, he would not endorse any definition of life that entails that life essentially involves DNA.

As we saw above, Mayr mentioned eight attributes in his attempt to "define the process of living." It appears that Mayr intended his "definition" to be conjunctive in form. Thus, he might endorse some definition according to which 'x is alive at t' means the same as some eightfold conjunction whose final conjunct mentions the containment of DNA or RNA.

Any such definition yields the result that there is a necessary connection between life and DNA- or RNA-containment. If such a definition were correct, it would be *necessary* that every living thing (or its zygote) contain DNA or RNA. On conceptual grounds alone, DNA or RNA containment would be a necessary condition of life. Crick's reflections concerning life on other planets show that this is wrong. While life as we know it seems to involve DNA or RNA, life itself does not. There is no conceptual connection between being alive and having DNA or RNA.

We saw above that vitalism faces three main objections. In the first place, it runs into difficulty because it is doubtful that there is any vital fluid. We called this "the empirical problem." DNA-ism has no similar difficulty. The second problem for vitalism was the Jonah problem. If there were vital fluid, merely *containing* it would not be sufficient for life. We found that DNA-ism suffers from a variant of the Jonah problem. The mere *containment* of DNA is also not sufficient for life—a nonliving test tube might *contain* DNA. A fresh corpse contains plenty of it. It is very hard to describe in any clear or helpful way how life is related to DNA. The third objection to vitalism was the analyticity problem. There seems to be no conceptual link between life itself and the containment of vital fluid. This objection applies equally to DNA-ism. There is no conceptual link between life itself and the containment of DNA. We can easily understand what would be meant by saying that something is alive but contains no DNA.

Genetic Informationism

In another passage in *Life Itself,* Crick presents a more positive suggestion concerning the nature of life. He says that life itself may be identified with the conjunction of five features involving "genetic information." The five features are these: (1) each living thing contains some genetic information that it is able to reproduce, together with "machinery needed for execution"; (2) when it produces replications, it will do so with a high degree of accuracy, but not perfectly; (3) the genetic information and the objects (on earth, it is cells) thereby created are held in close contact; (4) the system is open, and able to receive some raw material for its chemical operations; and (5) it is also able to receive energy from the environment.

It seems to me that Crick's view is a combination of a pure genetic information theory (like the one suggested by Mayr in the passage cited above) and some version of the metabolism theory (similar to Aristotle's). If we emphasize conditions (1) and (2), we get something quite reminiscent of what Mayr said.

All this is quite interesting and surely contains more than just a grain of truth, but what precisely is the view? One serious problem concerns the notions of "instructions," "information," and the like. What do we mean when we say that the genetic material in a living cell contains "information" about the cell? I think it is clear that one thing we do not mean is "semantic information." A book might contain semantic information about a cell. It would do so if it contained sentences that expressed facts about that cell. The genetic material in a cell does not in this way express facts about the cell.

Some information seems to be "non-semantic." Consider a footprint in the mud. It might contain lots of information about the person who left it. From its depth, we might infer the weight of the person; from the shape of the print, we might infer the sort of shoe the person was wearing and that it was a man's shoe; from the location of the print, we might infer that he was here; from the amount of stuff that has fallen into the footprint, we may infer how long ago he was here; and so on. In general, then, one thing contains information about another when properties of the first are related to properties of the second in such a way that observations of properties of the first enable sufficiently well-informed persons to infer corresponding properties of the second.

What about "instructions"? Strictly speaking, instructions are semantic entities. Instructions for creating a cell would be statements such as: "first take some carbon atoms; then add some oxygen; then mix that with a bit of nitrogen; and so on." The genetic material in a cell does not contain any literal instructions.

Once again, however, we can give sense to the concept of "nonsemantic instructions." Suppose we want the lights to go on when it gets dark, and to go off again when it gets light. We might hire a lightkeeper, and give him or her suitable semantic instructions. On the other hand, we might rig up a photosensitive switch. When sufficient sunlight shines on the switch, a current is induced, a relay is tripped, the circuit is broken, and the lights go off. When the sun goes down, insufficient current goes across the circuit, a spring trips the relay, and the lights go back on. This is a purely causal process—there is nothing semantic about it—but we might want to say that the photosensitive switch acts in accord with the "instructions" to turn the lights on when there is insufficient sunlight; to turn them back off when there is sufficient sunlight.

A more complicated sort of switch might be made in such a way as to act in accord with more complex "instructions" such as these: when there is insufficient sunlight, then turn the lights on, except if they have been off for less than a minute. Maybe it would be possible to characterize a program as a sufficiently complex sequence of nonsemantic instructions such as these.

What about the genetic material in living cells? It contains nonsemantic information about many of the important features of the cell itself and cells that could be produced by replication from that cell. It also contains nonsemantic information about the organism as a whole from which it has been taken. It also contains nonsemantic instructions about the productions of replicated cells, and whole reproduced organisms. All of this information and instruction is contained, among earthly organisms, in the DNA or RNA.

Obviously, however, it would be a mistake to try to define life by appeal to DNA-containment. As we saw in above, most organisms contain just as much DNA when they are dead as when they were alive. Furthermore, as Crick points out, "a form of life based on other materials is not impossible."[9] Thus, for all we know, living Martians may contain ZNA rather than DNA or RNA. It is more plausible to suppose that the idea is this: living things contain tiny parts that contain nonsemantic information and instructions concerning the construction of near replicas of themselves; furthermore, living things are able to make use of this information in the production of such near replicas of themselves.

Let us say that an object contains a "genetic representation" of itself just in case it contains some tiny parts that encode some nonsemantic information and instructions concerning the construction of near replicas. Thus, since we contain DNA, and DNA encodes such information and instructions, we contain genetic representations of ourselves. If there are Martians, and they contain ZNA, then they also contain genetic representations of themselves. In this way, we focus on the *function* of DNA rather than on the particular chemical features of the stuff that serves that function in us.

Now we can formulate a theory about life itself based on these ideas:

GI: x is alive at t =df. x contains a genetic representation of x at t.

I think that GI generates correct results in a wide variety of cases, and that it is close in spirit to a central component of the proposals suggested by Mayr and Crick in the passages cited.

Problems for Genetic Informationism

Any living thing that is capable of reproducing is alive according to D3. However, I believe that many dead things are counted as alive by this definition. Consider a dead female frog. Suppose this frog contains a lot of still-viable eggs. If the eggs are removed from the frog, they can be fertilized, and they can then grow into "near replicas" of the original frog. In this case, though the frog is clearly dead, it still contains genetic representations of itself. Thus, GI implies, incorrectly, that it is alive.

Similarly, consider what happens in the gardens of careless gardeners. They may neglect to remove their tomato plants at the end of the season. Frost will kill the plants. During the winter, the plants stand dead and blackened against their stakes. Miserable-looking, shriveled tomatoes may hang from the branches. In those tomatoes are many still-viable seeds. Though the plants are clearly dead, they therefore still contain genetic representations of themselves. In the spring, seeds from the dead tomatoes may sprout into near replicas of the now-dead parents. Thus, GI is clearly false.

While there are still other proposed analyses of the concept of life itself, I think I have discussed most of the interesting variants. Each of them has proved unsatisfactory. Other theories, it seems to me, are no more successful. Thus, my view is that life is a mystery. Though professional biologists may have huge amounts of very detailed information about typical features of living things here on earth, it appears that no one has succeeded in formulating a satisfactory philosophical analysis of the concept of life itself.

4

The Enigma of Death

The Gift of Life

The goal of this chapter is to consider whether it is possible to formulate a satisfactory philosophical analysis of the concept of death. If there is such an analysis, it seems likely that the concept of life plays a central role in it. Since any obscurity in the concept of life would apparently carry over into the analysis of the concept of death, I have devoted the previous two chapters to a discussion of the analysis of the concept of life. Unfortunately, it appears that life is enigmatic. I have been unable to say precisely what 'x is alive at t' means. Insofar as the concept of life is obscure, it will import obscurity into any analysis of death in which it appears.

Since I have not been able to analyze the concept of life, I propose to make use of the concept of life as an unanalyzed primitive. Thus, for present purposes, I simply give myself the gift of life. That is, I assume that our grasp of the concept of life is sufficiently firm to permit it to be used in the analysis of the concept of death. I recognize that any obscurity in the concept of life may make what follows somewhat less than crystal clear. So be it.

The Biological Concept of Death

Before turning to a consideration of some proposed analyses of the concept of death, it may be useful to try to be a bit more specific about the target concept. That is, I should try somehow to identify the concept whose analysis is here in question. As I remarked in

Chapter 1, some of the literature on death seems to be based on the assumption that the most interesting concept of death is one applicable only to people. Such analyses mention *brain function, consciousness,* or some other concept that has no application to lowly organisms. Thus, some writers seem to be trying to analyze a concept of death that could not possibly apply to any lower animal or plant.[1]

I also mentioned in Chapter 1 that this view seems quite odd to me. I see no reason to suppose that the word 'died' has different meanings in these sentences:

1. JFK died in November of 1963.
2. The last dodo died in April of 1681.
3. My Baldwin apple tree died during January of 1986.

I acknowledge that I cannot *prove* that 'died' is univocal in these sentences. Nor can I *prove* that there is no essentially "personal" sense of 'died'. However, I shall proceed here on the assumption that there is a concept of death that has application throughout the biological realm. As I see it, just as there is a single concept of life that applies to every living plant and animal, so there is a single concept of death that potentially applies to every organism from the lowliest plant all the way up to the most complex mammal. I call this "the biological concept of death." Our topic here is the analysis of this concept.

It may also be important to recall another point I made in Chapter 1. This concerns the distinction between two fundamentally different projects. One project is the attempt to discover a correct *analysis* of the concept of death. The other project is the attempt to formulate a useful *criterion* of human death.

As a sample criterion of death, we might consider:

4. A person, S, dies at a time, t, if and only if S's brain ceases to emit z-waves at t.

As a sample analysis of death, we have this:

D1: x dies at t =df. x ceases to be alive at t.

A *criterion* is something that is proposed for acceptance; that might be adopted if enough people think it would be useful; that might later be rejected if it proves inadequate or becomes obsolete as a result of technological advances. A criterion is better if it is more useful—easier to apply; more practical; more decisive. It would apply only to human beings. Thus, if enough morticians, prosecutors, judges, transplant teams, etc., agreed at a convention to adopt (4), it would be the criterion of death in human beings (until replaced).

A philosophical *analysis,* on the other hand, is supposed to report a necessary truth about the construction of a concept. If D1 is true, then the concept of death is constructed out of the concepts of life and cessation in the indicated way. No amount of voting or adopting could make D1 true if in fact it is false; nor could any human activity make it false if in fact it is true. (Of course, we could conventionally adopt some other meaning for the word 'dies'. But this would have no bearing on the analysis of the concept that word formerly expressed.)

Furthermore, the existence of possible counterexamples shows that a proposed analysis is simply false. It shows that the concept expressed by the term to the left of the '=df.' sign is not the same as the concept expressed by the term to the right. When this happens, the analysis fails. Counterexamples are not decisive against proposed criteria in this way. The excellence of a criterion is *usefulness,* not truth. It's not entirely clear what a counterexample would be. But the mere possibility of a few counterexamples to (4) has no bearing whatsoever on its suitability as a criterion of death for human beings. If actual counterexamples are sufficiently rare, (4) might remain perfectly acceptable as a criterion of death in human beings.

The topic under consideration here is the *analysis* of the biological concept of death. Let us now turn to an analysis that has recently been proposed.

Perrett's Analysis

In his book *Death and Immortality,* Roy Perrett seems to be discussing the nature of death itself. He distinguishes between *persons* and *biological organisms* and says that he is focusing on the question about what we mean when we speak of the death of a biological organism.[2] Thus, it appears that Perrett's target in his book is identical to my target in this chapter. He calls it "the concept of death that is neutral to all deaths."[3] He goes on to say: "My proposal is that death be identified with [the destruction of a functioning biological organism]."[4]

If Perrett said no more on this topic, the reader would surely assume that he meant to defend this analysis of the concept of death:

D2: x dies at t =df. x is a living biological organism up to t, but at t, x is destroyed.

However, Perrett has more to say.

In a passage just a sentence later than one already cited, Perrett says that "*death* is the annihilation of a functioning biological organism."[5] And only a page after that, he says that death is 'the disintegration of a living organism . . .'[6] These remarks seem to confuse matters, since it now appears that Perrett has committed himself to three different analyses of the biological concept of death. According to the first, death is the *destruction* of a living biological organism; according to the second, it is the *annihilation* of such an organism; according to the third, it is the *disintegration* of the organism.

The three proposals are distinct. We could investigate them independently. However, it seems to me that none is correct. One example suffices to show that each of Perrett's proposals is false. Suppose a butterfly collector captures a rare specimen. Suppose she carefully places it in the killing jar. Surely it is possible that she might kill it without breaking off any legs and without dislodging even so much as a single scale from the wings. The specimen might be "perfect." In such a case, I think, even though the butterfly had died it would be wrong to say that it has been "destroyed." It is even more obvious that it would be wrong to say that it has disintegrated or that it has been annihilated. Thus, Perrett's proposal, no matter how interpreted, is false.

In another passage, Perrett notes that death "marks the transition from being alive to being dead."[7] This hints at a much more popular conception of death—the conception according to which a thing dies at a time if and only if it then ceases to be alive. Since this conception is so popular, I refer to it as "the standard analysis." Let us turn to it.

The Standard Analysis

I think it is fair to say that something like the analysis formulated above in D1 is almost universally assumed to be correct. Some would accept D1 as it stands. Thus, in his recent book *Thinking Clearly about Death,* Jay Rosenberg says, "to die is to cease to live, to cease to be in the condition of life."[8] Others would modify this by adding that death occurs only if life *permanently* ceases. Rosenberg cites a dictionary definition that suggests this idea. According to this dictionary, death is "the total and *permanent* cessation of all the vital functions of an animal or plant."[9] Still others would modify it in a slightly different way by adding that death occurs when life *irreversibly* ceases. Rosenberg himself suggests this view when he says elsewhere in his book that ". . . an organism dies when it loses its power to preserve and sustain its self-organizing organization permanently *and irreversibly.*"[10] Since Rosenberg takes life to be the cited power, this is tantamount to saying that an organism dies when it irreversibly ceases to live. The variations may seem trivial. Let us say that each of the proposed analyses, and any others relevantly like them, are instances of "the standard analysis." According to this view, death is the (perhaps permanent, perhaps irreversible) cessation of life.

Puzzles About Suspended Animation

I think the three above-mentioned versions of the standard analysis are genuinely distinct and mutually incompatible. Furthermore, I think none of them is true. Although each of them is open to several sorts of objection, I want to discuss two main sorts of difficulty. The first difficulty is that the standard analysis is incompatible with some facts concerning suspended animation. Let us then consider this phenomenon.[11]

As a rough first approximation, we may say that an organism

undergoes suspended animation when it temporarily ceases to be alive. The most familiar type of suspended animation involves freezing. It takes place every day in biology laboratories all over the world. In a typical case, some sort of microorganism has been grown in a culture. The culture is then flooded with glycerol or some other suitable cryoprotectant, and the whole thing is gradually cooled until frozen solid. Subsequently, the frozen culture is placed for storage in liquid nitrogen at a temperature of −196°C. The glycerol prevents crystalization within the cells, which otherwise would rupture.

Later on, when there is need for the microorganisms, a lab technician can remove the culture from the freezer and allow it gradually to warm up. If the culture has been properly handled, the microorganisms will return to life merely as a result of being returned to room temperature.

This sort of procedure can be applied to all sorts of microorganisms, as well as to isolated cell cultures. It is also an important step in certain reproductive techniques. For example, consider in vitro fertilization as applied to cows. Sperm and eggs can be removed from adult animals and then mixed in a dish. Fertilized eggs can then be removed and allowed to undergo a relatively small number of cell divisions. The blastulas are then soaked in glycerol and frozen in liquid nitrogen. They cease to be alive.[12] Later, the frozen blastulas may be thawed and implanted in the reproductive tracts of suitable cows. They resume growth and eventually are born just like old-fashioned calves.

In vitro fertilization followed by fetal implantation is very common in cows and horses. It is much less common in human beings, but it has been used on hundreds of occasions during the past twenty-five years or so. All these cases illustrate suspended animation, since in every case a living organism (or cell culture, or blastula) temporarily ceases to be alive and then lives again.

I realize that it is currently impossible to freeze adult human beings (or any other large mammals) and subsequently revive them. Freezing destroys too many cells. However, it is reasonable to believe that the problems are all merely technical. Just as we can now freeze and later reanimate a day-old human blastula, so someday we will be able to freeze and then later reanimate an adult human being. Let us imagine that the technology has in fact been developed, and that an adult human being can be frozen and later reanimated. I prefer to proceed in this way primarily for dramatic effect, even though my argument could just as well be formulated by appeal to an example involving organisms that currently can be frozen and revived.[13]

To see how facts about suspended animation bear on the standard analysis of death, let us consider a case.

Case One. A man has a bad disease. There is currently no cure. Unless some way can be found to stop the disease, he will die in a few days. There is good reason to believe that a cure will be found in a dozen years or so. Cryogenics, Inc., offers to inject some specially formulated glycerol and to freeze the man solid. Then, when the cure has been perfected, they will thaw him out, reanimate him, and see to it that he is cured of the disease. The man accepts the offer and is injected and frozen. Ten years later, a cure for the disease is found. The body is thawed, reanimated, and subjected to the cure. The man goes on with his life.

In one of the passages cited above, Rosenberg said that to die is to cease to live.[14] This surely suggests the following version of the standard analysis of the concept of death:

D1: x dies at t =df. x ceases to be alive at t.

Case One refutes D1. For in Case One the man ceased to be alive when he was frozen. Without an accepted analysis of the concept of life, this point is hard to prove. But it seems reasonable to say that the man ceased to live when he was frozen. After all, he then ceased to engage in metabolism, growth, motion, and the other life functions. D1 therefore implies that the man died when he was frozen. But the implication is false—the man did not die when frozen. He went into suspended animation. Unless something went wrong with the procedures, and it became impossible to reanimate him, no one would want to say that Cryogenics, Inc., *killed* its client.

The mere possibility of suspended animation shows that death cannot be defined as the cessation of life. When an organism enters suspended animation it ceases to live, but it does not then die. We must alter the standard analysis to accommodate this fact. The analysis of death must be consistent with the fact that not all organisms that enter suspended animation die.

Perhaps we can think of suspended animation as the *temporary* cessation of life. Then perhaps we will want to say that death is the *permanent* cessation of life. This suggests another version of the standard analysis of death:

> D2: x dies at t =df. x ceases permanently to be alive at t.

Notice first that D2 yields a different result in Case One. Since the frozen man did not cease *permanently* to live when he was frozen, D2 (unlike D1) entails that he did not then die. This may seem to be an improvement, since it seems to be consistent with the facts about suspended animation. But another example shows that there is something implausible about D2.

Case Two. Each of two identical twins has the same currently incurable disease. Both are frozen and go into suspended animation. Unfortunately, about one year later, one frozen body is damaged. The damage is so severe that it would be impossible ever to reanimate the body. It is then thawed out and buried. That twin never lives again. The other twin remains frozen until a cure is found. He is then thawed, reanimated, and cured. The second twin goes on with his life.

D2 yields strange results in Case Two. Since the first twin in fact never lives again after being frozen, D2 entails that he died when he was frozen. His loss of life was *permanent*. On the other hand, even though there is no discernible difference between the twins during their first year on ice, D2 entails that the second twin did not die when he was frozen. This follows from the stipulated fact that the second twin comes back to life later. His loss of life was only *temporary*. But it seems to me that until the accident occurs, the twins are in relevantly similar conditions. We can imagine that, cell-for-cell, they are indiscernible. So either they are both dead, or they are both alive, or they are both neither dead nor alive. (My own view is that they are both neither dead nor alive. As I see it, suspended animation is a state that excludes both life and death. But the point of the example does not depend on my intuition.[15]) D2 entails that the twins are in different "vital states" during the first year on ice—one is dead, the other not. Since the twins are in fact not in different vital states during that period of time, D2 is wrong.

Consider yet a third analysis of death suggested by Rosenberg's remark[16] about *permanence* and *irreversibility:*

> D3: x dies at t =df. x ceases permanently and irreversibly to be alive at t.

D3 has truly bizarre implications in Case Two. Consider the twin whose body is damaged. According to D3, this twin *never* dies. He does not die when frozen, because at the time of freezing later reanimation is still possible. Though he then ceases permanently to be alive, he does not cease irreversibly to be alive. If he had been handled properly, his condition would have been reversed. He would have come back to life. Nor according to D3 does he die when the body is damaged in handling, for he does not cease in any way to be alive at that time. That is a time at which he is not alive to start with. So there is no time at which the twin "ceases permanently and irreversibly to be alive." Surely this is wrong; surely there is *some* time at which that twin dies.

Let us consider a variant of D3:

> D4: x dies at t =df. (i) x ceases permanently to be alive at or before t, and (ii) at t, it becomes physically impossible for x ever to live again.

The idea behind D4 is that the time of death is the time at which the loss of life becomes irreversible. The loss of life may have occurred years before. D4 implies that there is a time of death for the damaged twin. The time of his death, according to D4, is not the time when he was frozen but the time when the body is damaged beyond repair, for this is the time at which the loss of life becomes irreversible.

In more mundane cases, D4 implies that death occurs approximately when life ceases. For in more mundane cases, when life ceases, it is almost immediately impossible for it to return.

Some would reject D4 because it implies that it is impossible for an organism to live again after it dies. The comedian Jerry Lewis claims that he died several times while undergoing open-heart surgery. If D4 is correct, Lewis must be wrong. We can offer a somewhat less striking claim for Lewis. Perhaps he would be satisfied to say instead that he ceased to live several times while undergoing open-heart surgery. D4 permits that. Maybe that's all Lewis means.

A more serious problem with D4 can be brought about by consideration of a distinction. In some cases, later reanimation becomes impossible because of changes that take place *within* the body. Thus, for example, if the body is damaged beyond repair, internal changes make later reanimation impossible. In other cases, however, changes that take place *outside* the body may make later reanimation impossible. Perhaps the body is moved to a place where it cannot be reached; perhaps a crucial reanimation chemical is irretrievably lost; perhaps the atmosphere of the earth becomes so choked with pollution or radioactivity that it would be impossible to reanimate the frozen corpse (even if there were some technicans to try!).

Suppose a body is in suspended animation, and some such external change takes place, thereby making later reanimation impossible. Provided that the body is *internally* unchanged, I would be uneasy about saying that it had just died. I would rather say that the body remains undead until *internal* changes occur that would independently make subsequent reanimation impossible. Thus I propose:

D5: x dies at t =df. (i) x ceases to be alive at or before t, and (ii) at t, internal changes occur in x that make it physically impossible for x ever to live again.

While I think that D5 comes pretty close to solving the problem of suspended animation, I still have my doubts. I am troubled by the obscurity of the concepts of *internality, physical impossibility,* and *life*. But let us assume that we have come close enough. I want to turn to another problem for the standard analysis.

Problems Concerning Fission and Fusion

In spite of its plausibility and in spite of the fact that Rosenberg seems to endorse something quite like it, D5 is inconsistent with certain other plausible views Rosenberg maintains. In an interesting passage, Rosenberg asserts that death is not the only route out of life. To illustrate his point, he describes the case of an amoeba, Alvin.[17] He tells us that Alvin was a fat and healthy amoeba. According to the story, Alvin was so fat and healthy that at precisely midnight on Tuesday night/Wednesday morning, Alvin underwent fission and became two amoebas. According to Rosenberg, Alvin no longer existed on Wednesday. Apparently, Alvin was "replaced" by his two descendants, Amos and Ambrose. Rosenberg claims that Alvin's example shows that "there are other ways for a life to come to an end besides death."[18] So while Alvin is no longer among the living on Wednesday, it is ". . . clear that he did not die."[19] My own intuitive sense of the situation is identical to Rosenberg's. I would not say that Alvin died.

Fission is not the only biological process that may seem to provide a deathless exit from life. Rosenberg apparently thinks that metamorphosis does the same thing. As he sees it, when a caterpillar turns into a butterfly, the caterpillar ceases to exist but does not die.[20]

The point that Rosenberg seems to have missed is this: if Alvin ceased to be alive at midnight, but did not die at midnight, then death cannot be the cessation of life. When we say that a thing died, we cannot mean just that it ceased to live. For Alvin ceased to live without dying. If we think that the caterpillar gets out of life without dying, we will have to say that its case also refutes the idea that death is the cessation of life.

A natural "fix" would be based on a crucial feature that is common to division and metamorphosis. In each case, an organism seems to go out of existence, but the stuff of which it is made continues to exist—and this stuff continues to support life. We can make use of this common feature in a relatively economical new analysis of death:

D6: x dies at t =df. (i) x ceases to be alive at or before t, and (ii) at t, x undergoes internal changes that make it physically impossible for x ever to live again, and (iii) it's not the case that x turns into another living thing or a bunch of other living things at t.

It may be useful to say a few words about a phrase—'turns into'—that appears in D6. This phrase is intended to express what is traditionally called 'substantial change'. Some would say that the caterpillar undergoes substantial change when it turns into a butterfly. As I understand it, the crucial elements in a pure example of such a change are these: the first entity (the caterpillar) is a concrete individual substance—a "thing." It is made of some "stuff"—a certain parcel of protoplasm, perhaps. During the substantial change, the first entity goes out of existence, and a new concrete individual substance (in this case, the butterfly) comes into existence. The new entity is diverse from the old entity, but they are made of the same parcel of stuff (or "matter"). In such a case, we can say that the first entity "turned into" the second.[21]

D6 gets the fission example right. At the moment of division, Alvin turns into Amos and Ambrose. Each of these is a living thing. So, according to D6, Alvin does not die. Furthermore, in an ordinary case, in which some organism ceases to live and simply rots, D6 still yields the correct result. Since, in such cases, the organism does not turn into living things, D6 entails that it dies. D6 also preserves Rosenberg's intuitions concerning the caterpillar example.[22] At the moment of metamorphosis, the caterpillar allegedly turns into the butterfly, which is a living thing. So, although it ceases to be alive, it doesn't die.

Reflections such as these on cases of fission invite reflections on corresponding cases of fusion. Are there examples in which organisms go out of existence by fusing with others? Would we want to say that such organisms die when they fuse? Let us look into this.

Under certain environmental conditions, certain types of single-celled green algae engage in a sort of fusion. These creatures, called chlamydomonas, are flagellated, chlorophyll-bearing plants. In their normal state, each individual is haploid. Although they are all of approximately the same size, they come in two different mating types. When conditions are favorable, large clusters of individuals form.

Eventually the clustered cells move apart in pairs. The members of a pair are positioned end to end, with their flagella, which bear species-specific and mating-type-specific attractant sites at their tips, in close contact. The cells then shed their walls, and their cytoplasms slowly fuse. Finally, their nuclei unite in the process of fertilization, which produces a single diploid cell, the zygote.[23]

Suppose two chlamydomonas, $c1$ and $c2$, fuse to form a new zygote, $c3$. It seems reasonably clear that, in this process, $c1$ and $c2$ go out of their existence. Furthermore, it seems reasonably clear that neither one of them turns into any new living individual. No living part of the resultant individual, $c3$, can be identified as the part such that $c1$ turned into it. The stuff from which $c1$ and $c2$ were made is thoroughly blended in $c3$.

In this case, we must say that $c1$ ceases irreversibly to live and does not turn into another living thing or even into a bunch of living things. D6 then legislates that $c1$ dies at the moment of fusion. Yet I would hesitate to say that $c1$ dies at the moment of fusion. I would say that the example of the chlamydomonas shows that there are still more ways of getting out of life. In addition to death, suspended animation, and deathless fission, there is also a certain sort of deathless fusion that sometimes does the trick. So D6 is wrong.[24]

We can revise D6 in such a way as to take account of fusion, too. We merely add a clause specifying that if an organism engages in deathless fusion, then it does not die. In other words, if it is a member of a set of living things that fuses into a new living thing, then it does not die:

> D7: x dies at t =df. (i) x ceases to be alive at or before t, and (ii) at t, x undergoes internal changes that make it physically impossible for x ever to live again, and (iii) it is not the case that x turns into a living thing, or a bunch of living things, at t, and (iv) it is not the case that x is a member of a set of living things whose members fuse and turn into a living thing at t.

The fundamental idea behind D7 is reasonably simple: a thing dies if and only if it ceases irreversibly to live without making use of one of the deathless exits; the deathless exits are metamorphosis (turning into another living thing); a certain sort of fission (turning into a bunch of living things) and a certain sort of fusion (being a member of a set of living things that fuse into a living thing). I think D7 gets a wide variety of cases right. In simple cases, in which an organism ceases to live and simply rots, D7 says that the organism dies. In cases of fission like the one illustrated by Alvin, D7 says that the organism does not die, even though it ceases to live. Similarly for the chlamydomonas—they cease to live without dying because they make use of one of the deathless exits.

Nevertheless, it seems to me that D7 still fails. One problem is that there are forms of division that mimic deathless fission but that seem to involve the death of the divided organism. Consider an example. Imagine a device for use in biology laboratories—a "cell separator." This is a machine that grinds up mice and then emits a puree of mouse cells. The machine is constructed in such a way that all the mouse cells come out alive. Each cell can be placed in a suitable medium and kept alive indefinitely.

Suppose some mouse is placed in the cell separator and is ground up into a puree of living mouse cells. In this case, the mouse goes out of existence, and hence ceases to be alive. However, it turns into a bunch of living things. As a result, the mouse fails to satisfy the right-hand side of D7. D7 then legislates that the mouse does not die. It seems to me, however, that the cell separator kills the mouse.

Another example involves not cells, but bodily organs. Reasonably sane medical personnel sometimes want to harvest living organs from dying patients. Suppose a mad scientist wants to harvest *all* the organs from some perfectly healthy victim. Suppose he captures his victim, knocks him out, and then carefully dissects the victim's body in such a way as to waste nothing. Every organ is preserved alive. (If need be, we can imagine that each organ is transplanted into some needy body, where it remains alive for years to come.) In this case, it would appear that the poor victim goes out of existence and is replaced by a complete set of living bodily organs. If D7 were correct, we would have to say that the victim did not die. This seems wrong.[25]

If we allow ourselves to make use of another rather obscure concept, we may be able to revise D7 in such a way as to accommodate these examples. Let us assume that we have sufficient understanding of what we mean when we say that something is an *organism*. Now notice that when an amoeba deathlessly divides, it turns into living *organisms,* but that when a mouse is killed in the cell separator, it does not turn into living organisms. It turns into living cells. Similarly, in the case of the Mad Organ Harvester, the victim does not turn into living organisms. He turns into the members of a set of living *organs.* Perhaps this marks the distinction between deathless and deadly division.

We can revise D7 as follows:

> D8:   x dies at t =df. (i) x ceases to be alive at or before t, and (ii) at t, x undergoes internal changes that make it physically impossible for x ever to live again, and (iii) it is not the case that x turns into a living organism or a bunch of living organisms at t, and (iv) it is not the case that x is a member of a set of living organisms whose members fuse and turn into a living organism at t.

It seems to me that the introduction of talk about organisms in D8 is a fundamental mistake. It is a mistake, as I see it, because the concepts of life and death apply univocally to biological entities, whether organisms or not. The difficulty can be brought out by reflection on a variant of the example concerning Alvin the amoeba.

Suppose a researcher has removed a single cell from a frog and is keeping it alive in a suitable medium. Suppose the researcher is interested in cell division. She treats the cell in a special way. Subsequently, the cell divides, giving rise to two "daughter cells." Since neither daughter cell is an organism, the original frog cell does not turn into a bunch of living organisms. Thus, D8 entails that the frog cell dies at the moment of division. But it seems to me that the frog cell is relevantly like Alvin the amoeba. Since we don't want to say that Alvin dies when he divides, we should not say that the frog cell dies when it divides. Each of them gets out of life deathlessly. So D8 is wrong.

Fission and fusion are puzzling. I find that I cannot explain the difference between their deathless forms and their deadly forms.

The Mystery of Death

I think there is a single concept of death that applies across the biological board. When we say of some plant or animal, or of some cell or tissue, or of some organ, that it has died, we may be expressing this concept. I call this the biological concept of death. Roughly, what we seem to mean in such cases is that the biological entity has ceased to live but has not entered suspended animation and has not engaged in one of the deathless forms of fission or fusion. Explaining death in such rough (and circular) terms is not too difficult. The difficulty arises when we try to clarify the concepts of suspended animation and deathless fission and fusion. It is then that the enigma of death begins to reveal itself.

My main point is that when we say that some biological entity has died, we do not invariably mean that it has ceased to live. I am inclined to suspect that we never mean just this. If there is some single thing that we do mean, then it is hard to say precisely what it is. So, though death looms large in our emotional lives, though we hate it, and fear it, and are dismayed by the thought that it will someday overtake us and those we love, we really don't know precisely what death is. The Reaper remains mysterious.

5

On Dying as a Process

Two Senses of 'Dying'

'Winning' is ambiguous. In one sense, when we say that someone is winning a race, we mean roughly that he is just now being first to cross the finish line. If it is now correct to say that he is winning the race, then at all times in the future, it will be correct to say that he won. This is the "success" sense of 'winning'. The word has another sense. If a runner is leading the pack, and all the evidence suggests that he will win, we may say, even before he has won, that he is winning. This is the "process" sense of 'winning'. Ryle pointed out that a runner may be winning (in the process sense) even though it is going to turn out that he doesn't win (in the success sense).[1]

Lots of other verbs are like 'winning'. 'Finishing' is a good example. Suppose a man is interrupted just as he is nearing the end of a story. He could say, 'Just as I was finishing the story, I was interrupted. What with all the commotion, I never did finish that story.' The first 'finish' is in the process sense; the second is in the success sense. The man's statement could be true.

'Dying' is ambiguous in this way. It too has a process sense and a success sense. Let us use 'dying1' to indicate the success sense, and 'dying2' to indicate the process sense. The success sense is in one way utterly unproblematic—to say that a thing is dying1 at a time is just to say that it then dies. In another way, I think, the success sense is deeply problematic. As I tried to show in Chapter 4, it is hard to give a fully satisfactory philosophical analysis of what we mean when we say that a thing *dies* at a time. Thus, it is equally hard to give a fully satisfactory philosophical analysis of what we mean when we say that a thing is dying1 at a time.

I want to consider the concept of dying2—the concept expressed by 'dying' when used in the process sense. It is easy enough to give a rough account of what this word means. To say that a thing is dying2 is to say that it is "in a terminal decline," that it is "heading toward death," that it is "in grave condition." But these expressions are little more than metaphors. An organism can be dying2 even though it is not literally in a "decline"—it does not have to be losing altitude. Equally, a thing can be dying2 even though it is not literally "heading" toward its death—it does not have to be moving in space toward the spot at which it will die.

To help focus the discussion, let us introduce a clear example. Consider a former coal miner, Morton. Suppose Morton worked for many years in dusty coal mines and eventually developed black lung disease. Suppose his condition has deteriorated so that now he must make use of an oxygen mask all the time. Suppose Morton's doctors realize that there is no cure. Morton will get sicker and sicker and will eventually die of black lung disease—unless, of course, he dies of something else first. Under these circumstances, it would be correct to say:

1. Morton is dying2.

We can state our fundamental question quite simply: can we explain literally and precisely just what (1) means? Can we give an analysis of the concept expressed by 'dying2' as it is used in (1)?

Some Preliminary Proposals

It may seem that the most promising first step would involve recognition of the fact that Morton is in the midst of a process of deterioration that will end with his death. Perhaps this is all we mean when we say that a thing is dying2. Perhaps to say that a thing is dying2 is just to say that it is engaged in some process that will later end with its death. This may be stated as a definition of 'dying2':

D1 x is dying2 at t =df. at t, x is engaged in some process that will
    later end with the death of x.

While D1 may seem to capture a fairly attractive intuition, it is
wrong in several ways. I shall discuss just one central problem. It is
this: D1 entails that every living mortal thing is always dying2.
Consider a patient (call her Vivian) who has undergone a serious
operation. Suppose she is recovering nicely and getting stronger
every day. She is now eating solid foods and taking a few steps
around the hospital corridors. All the evidence correctly points to
the conclusion that the surgery was a success and that Vivian will
soon be released from the hospital to resume her normal activities.
Suppose the surgeon calls to inquire about Vivian's condition. The
nurse, trying to pull a joke on the surgeon, says,

2. Come quickly, Doctor! Vivian is dying2.

If D1 were an adequate definition of 'dying2', then the nurse's
statement would be true. For Vivian (like all of us mortals) is alive.
Thus she is engaged in a process (living) that will end with death.
However, it seems to me that the nurse's statement is in fact false.
In the example, Vivian is not dying2—she is getting better and
better each day and is on the road to recovery. Suppose the surgeon hurried to the hospital and found Vivian contentedly enter-
taining visitors in her hospital room. Surely the surgeon would
insist that the nurse had issued a false alarm. He would claim
(justifiedly) that Vivian was not dying2.
    A natural modification of D1 suggests itself. Perhaps the differ-
ence between Vivian and Morton is this: at the time of the utter-
ance of (1), Morton was engaged in a process that was going to end
with his dying in a relatively short period of time. At the time of
the nurse's statement (2), Vivian was engaged in no such process.
Though she was eventually going to die, she was not then going to
die in a relatively short period of time. Let us modify D1 by taking
note of the temporal length of the process leading to death:

D2: x is dying2 at t =df. at t x is engaged in a process that will end
     in a relatively short time with x's death.

It might seem that one serious problem for D2 is that it makes use of the very obscure notion of a "relatively short" period of time. However, it is not necessary to probe the meaning of 'relatively short' because, no matter how we interpret that phrase, D2 will still be false. The basic intuition behind D2 is fundamentally wrong. An example should make this clear. Consider another patient, Horton. He has a horrible disease. His condition is rapidly deteriorating. Horton's heart is beginning to function erratically; he is slipping into a coma. The nurse calls the doctor and says:

3. Horton is dying2.

The doctor rushes to Horton's room and quickly looks over his patient. He sees that the situation is really grave. As a last resort, the doctor orders that Horton be given some very dangerous experimental drugs. These are administered. Within a few hours, Horton's condition begins to stabilize. On the next morning, he is clearly "out of the woods." In a week, Horton is fully recovered.

My own sense of the situation is that the nurse's statement (3) was literally true when uttered. Even though Horton recovered, and didn't die from the disease he then had, at the moment of crisis he was dying2. It would be natural and correct to say, after the fact, that Horton was dying2 of that terrible disease, and that, if the doctor had not administered the experimental drugs, Horton would have died. If this is right, D2 is wrong. For in the example, Horton was not engaged in any short process that in fact was going to terminate with his death.

The necessary repair seems fairly obvious. Recall that in D2 we attempted to define 'dying2' in such a way that a thing can be dying2 only if engaged in a short process that *in fact* will take it to its death. In the most recent example, the process did not in fact lead to death, and so the example runs counter to the definition. However, Horton's condition was indeed grave. If the doctor had not interfered, Horton would have died. He was engaged in a process that would have resulted in death, were it not for the doctor's last-minute intervention. Let us attempt to make use of this as the basis for a revision of D2. We can do this as follows:

D3: x is dying2 at t =df. at t, x is engaged in a process that, if it were allowed to run its course without interference, would end in a relatively short period of time with x's death.[2]

It must be acknowledged, of course, that D3 suffers from some obscurities. We have not said what 'relatively short' means; we have not explicated the concept of interference; and we have not explained what death is. But the general idea behind D3 should be reasonably clear anyway.

D3 is defective in several ways. Perhaps the most obvious is that not all cases of dying2 involve "relatively short" periods of time. A sick elephant might be dying2 for a decade. A giant sequoia might be dying2 for half a century or more. This shows that it is possible for a thing to be dying2 even though it is not engaged in any process that would end, without interference, in its death *in a relatively short period of time.*

We might try to modify D3 by deleting the clause about "a short period of time" and replacing it with a clause to indicate that the deadly process must be one that would lead to death at a time that would be "premature" for the organism in question, considering the sort of organism it is. In other words, we could say:

D4: x is dying2 at t =df. at t, x is engaged in a process that, if it were allowed to run its course without interference, would lead to x's death at a time that would be "premature" for x, considering the kind of thing x is.

But D4 is really no improvement, since sometimes a thing is dying2 even though it is not heading toward a premature death. One obvious case involves things that are dying2 of old age. These things are dying2, but not prematurely. Other examples involve things that are dying2 of disease, but not prematurely. For example, suppose some old horse is dying2 of progressive heart failure. He may be dying2 slowly. Perhaps he is dying2 so slowly that, without medical interference, he will linger on for quite a few more years. Perhaps he will in this way live longer than most horses do— despite the fact that he will be dying2 all the time.

On the other hand, some things are engaged in processes that will take them to their premature deaths, but are not dying2 at all.[3]

Consider a man in perfect health who is walking across a street. Suppose that in a just a moment or two he will be hit by a fully loaded eighteen-wheeler going seventy miles per hour. This man is engaged in a process (walking across the street) that will end (unless somebody interferes) in a relatively short time (a moment or two) with his premature death. Yet he is not dying2. He is in perfect health. So D4 is wrong in the other direction, too.

Smart's Analysis of Dying2

In "Philosophical Concepts of Death," Ninian Smart proposes a somewhat more sophisticated analysis of the concept of dying2. The analysis has several components. Smart begins by mentioning an example. He imagines that some man has been shot. Smart goes on:

> From the perspective of what happened after the shooting, we can say that he was obviously dying. He was, that is, in a state where he was going to die, unless some remarkable interference in the process were to take place.[4]

But this statement is merely provisional. Smart recognizes that it would be wrong to say that everyone undergoing a process that would, failing interference, lead to death, is dying2. It is necessary to describe in greater detail the sort of process involved. One apparently important feature of the process is that it must be one that "normally issues in death."[5] Smart emphasizes[6] that it doesn't matter whether onlookers believe that the process will terminate with death; what matters is that it is a process of a sort that normally does so. Our evidence in particular cases can be misleading. Smart accepts the view (mentioned above in connection with Horton) that a person can be dying2 of something and yet not die of that thing. In support of this view, he cites the fact that there is nothing incoherent about the remark "Can't you see that this man is dying? For God's sake, do something about it!"[7] Thus, the process must be one that *normally* leads to death, but need not be one that *invariably* leads to death. Even though an organism is dying2, "remarkable interference" may still have some point. Perhaps it will prevent the expected death.

A second important feature of the process is that it must be "internal." "[D]ying is predicated of the person himself as though it is a process, as it were, originating in him."[8] "The source of dying is within the person rather than outside him."[9] The point can be illustrated by appeal to the example involving the shooting victim. At times when the bullet is still hurtling toward the victim, he is not yet dying2. At such times, the process is still "external." After the bullet has entered his body and internal organs have been damaged, he is dying2. At these times the process is "internal." The internality requirement is clearly also relevant to the case of the healthy pedestrian. Though he is engaged in a process (walking across the street) that will shortly terminate with his death, he is not dying2 until the process becomes internal.

Smart also mentions that it would be paradoxical to use the word 'dying' of a perfectly healthy five-year-old.[10] Such a person is eventually going to die—so he is engaged in an internal process that normally issues in death. However, "before we can say that someone is dying, we must have an idea of some rather specific condition or conditions *of* which he is dying."[11] Smart weakens this condition when he subsequently admits that in some cases, we do not have any idea of the nature of the malady that is killing someone. In such cases, however, we allegedly "certainly believe that there is some specific malaise which is responsible . . ." even if we do not know what it is.[12]

Thus, it appears that Smart's analysis of dying2 consists of four main elements. Smart seems to be claiming that when we say that something is dying2, what we mean is that it is engaged in some process (a) that will, in this particular instance, lead to death unless interrupted; (b) that normally leads to death; (c) that is "internal," and (d) that involves some specific malady, whether we know what it is or not. Let us call this "Smart's analysis."

Problems for Smart's Analysis

Smart's analysis seems to me to be insightful and plausible, and in some ways superior to the ones we considered earlier, but still not quite right. There are several difficulties. The internality condition is a source of trouble. Smart himself cites the case of a man with a bit of shrapnel embedded in his body.[13] Some process might be going on whereby the shrapnel is gradually becoming dislodged; at a later stage in the process, the shrapnel will break loose and become stuck in the man's heart and kill him.

Smart asserts[14] that we would not say, at earlier stages of a case such as this, that the shrapnel bearer is dying2. I think Smart is right about this. While the shrapnel is still lodged in some muscle far from the heart, I would not yet say that the man is dying2. However, I cannot see why this example fails to refute the analysis. The process certainly seems to be "internal"—every bit of it happens within the man's body; a wise enough person would be able to see that this particular form of embedded shrapnel does normally lead to death; the condition is surely sufficiently "specific." Thus, it appears to me that Smart's proposal is refuted by an example given by Smart himself.

The requirement that the process "normally" lead to death is also puzzling. On the one hand, there is nothing inconsistent about the statement that something is dying2 as a result of processes that do not normally issue in death. Perhaps, for unknown reasons, these processes lead to death in just 2 percent of cases.

On the other hand, there seems to be nothing inconsistent about the statement that something is undergoing processes that normally do issue in death, but that this organism is not dying2. Consider, for example, a normally frost-sensitive plant that has been injected with antifreeze. Suppose it is undergoing the process of having its internal temperature reduced below 32°F. Normally, this process leads to death in plants of this sort. However, in the present case, in virtue of the antifreeze, the plant is in no danger—it is not dying2. Thus, there is reason to be dubious about Smart's normality condition.

A final difficulty for Smart's analysis concerns the third component of the analysis—the "specific malady" requirement. Contrary to Smart, I see no reason to suppose that a "specific malady" must be involved. There are organisms that are genetically programmed to die after a fixed number of minutes of life. These things may not be "sick" at all—they just go into a terminal decline and die. While in decline they are dying2. Of course, these things cannot die "for no reason at all." There must be some cause of death. But it seems to me that the cause of death might be "general decrepitude" or "universal collapse" rather than some specific malady.

A New Proposal

With all this as background, I want to sketch the outlines of a new analysis of dying2. The basic idea behind my proposal can be stated simply. For each sort of organism, there are certain biologically crucial capacities. In the case of human beings, some examples might include the capacities to engage in respiration, blood circulation, acquisition of nutrients, regulation of internal temperature, etc. I call these "vital capacities" or "vital properties" of human beings. As I see it, when an organism is dying2, it is engaged in a causal process involving the sequential destruction of its vital properties—a process which, barring interference, will lead to the organism's death. So much for rough-and-ready suggestions. Let us consider the proposal in more detail.

The analysis makes essential use of the concept of "vital properties." I cannot provide a definition of 'vital property', but I can provide some examples. In order to stay alive in anything like the normal way, an organism has to be able to nourish itself. Some animals eat and digest grass; others eat mice; still others eat plankton. Plants send down roots that absorb nutrient-laden moisture from the soil. In light of this, I want to say that for each main kind of organism, the capacity to engage in a special style of nourishment is vital.

There are other vital properties. In the case of human beings, the relevant properties might include being able to take in and make appropriate use of oxygen; being able to fight off disease; being able to circulate oxygenated blood to various parts of the body; and being able to maintain body temperature somewhere around 98.6°F. A tree, on the other hand, would have different vital properties. Like a human being, it needs to be able to fight off disease. Unlike a human being, it needs to be able to engage in photosynthesis. It also needs to be able to draw moisture out of the soil and up into its leaves. It has no need to be able to circulate blood.

It would be wrong to define the vital properties of a kind as the properties things of that kind need for life.[15] In many cases, organisms remain alive even after they have lost some of their vital properties. For example, consider a human being undergoing open-heart surgery. For a while, he may lack the capacity to circulate his blood. Consider a human being who has undergone a bone-marrow transplant. For a short period of time, she may have no capacity to fight off disease. Although this is hardly a crystal-clear definition, perhaps it will help to say that the vital properties of a species are the biological capacities organisms of that species must have, at least to some degree, if they are to remain alive in anything like the normal way appropriate to their kind. If a thing loses a vital capacity, and the normal function of that capacity is not taken over by some substitute means, then the thing is in serious danger of death.

Vital properties are matters of degree. One organism may have the disease-fighting capacity to a greater extent than another. One organism may have the capacity to acquire nutrition to a greater extent than another. Similarly for the rest. Thus, it makes sense to say that an organism is suffering a "decrease" in a vital capacity.

Finally, I should mention that my list of vital properties is not intended to be just like Aristotle's.[16] As I mentioned in Chapter 2, Aristotle includes such things as reproduction, locomotion, and sensation. These are important properties for certain organisms, but they are not vital in my sense. A decrease in the capacity to engage in reproduction does not, by itself, make it harder for an organism to remain alive. Similarly for decreases in the capacity to move around or to see.

When a thing is dying2, it is engaged in a special sort of causal process. Let us next consider these processes. Imagine a row of dominoes standing upright. Suppose they are placed in such a way that if the first domino falls over, it will strike the second, causing it to fall. When the second domino falls, it will knock over the third, and so on. Though each fall of a domino "leads to" the next fall of a domino, no fall of a domino is by itself a sufficient causal condition of the fall of the next. It would be easy enough to interrupt the sequence. Any of various sorts of interference could abort the process. However, if nothing interferes with the process, each step will lead to its successor, and in the end, all the dominoes will fall.

A causal process is just a sequence of individual events. Suppose d1, d2, and d3 are certain dominoes. Suppose F1, F2, and F3 are three properties, each a variety of the property of falling. Suppose t1, t2, and t3 are certain times. Now consider these events:

Case One

    e1: d1's having F1 at t1.
    e2: d2's having F2 at t2.
    e3: d3's having F3 at t3.

Suppose that the dominoes are arranged in such a way that if e1 were to occur, that would lead to e2; and if e2 were to occur, that would lead to e3. Then the sequence <e1, e2, e3> is a causal process.[17]

For present purposes, a special sort of causal process is central: the "terminal" process. Morton (the coal miner mentioned at the outset) illustrates such a process. Morton had black-lung disease. His lungs were clogged with coal dust. As a result, he was losing his capacity to take in and make appropriate use of oxygen. Thus, he was suffering a decline in the capacity to engage in respiration—a property that is vital for human beings. The loss of this property would surely lead to the loss of the capacity to engage in proper brain function—brain cells work properly only if they get sufficient oxygen from the blood. The loss of proper brain function would in turn lead to the general loss of all other vital properties, and thence to Morton's death. Thus, Morton was engaged in what I will call a "terminal process."

In order for a process to be terminal for an organism of a kind, K, it must satisfy four conditions. First of all, it must be a causal process. Second, it must be possible to break down the process into a number of stages, each of which involves the decrease or elimination of a capacity that is vital for organisms of K. Third, the last stage of the process must be the death of the organism. To see how the first three conditions are intended to work, suppose F1, F2, and F3 are vital properties for human beings. Suppose a human being, m, is engaged in some process whereby the decrease of F1 leads to the decrease of F2; and the decrease of F2 leads to the decrease of F3; and the decrease of F3 leads to m's death. Then (provided the fourth condition is also satisfied) m is in a terminal process. We can represent the relevant process as a series of events <e1, e2, e3, e4> as follows:

Case Two

e1: m suffers a decrease in F1 at t1.
e2: m suffers a decrease in F2 at t2.
e3: m suffers a decrease in F3 at t3.
e4: m dies at t4.

To explain the fourth condition, it will be necessary to digress for a moment. Suppose a man owns some trees. Suppose he is a photosynthesis fanatic. Whenever one of his trees suffers a decrease in the capacity to engage in photosynthesis, this man promptly cuts down the tree for firewood. Suppose one of his trees, d, suffers a minor decrease in photosynthetic capacity—a decrease that surely would not have caused the tree any trouble if it had been owned by any sane owner. Consider the following sequence of events:

Case Three

e5: d suffers a decline in photosynthetic capacity at t1.
e6: d's owner notices at t2 that d has suffered a decline in photosynthetic capacity.
e7: d's owner cuts down d at t3.
e8: d suffers the loss of capacity to bring nutrients from the roots to the upper parts at t4.
e9: d dies at t5.

Since I do not want to say that d started dying2 at t1 when it suffered a trival decline in photosynthetic capacity, I do not want to say that the sequence of events <e5, e6, e7, e8, e9> is a terminal sequence. It seems to me that this sequence is not a terminal sequence, according to my account. After all, it has certain stages (e6 and e7) that are not themselves losses or declines in capacities that are vital for trees.

However, the problem is that it may seem that the sequence <e5, e8, e9> is a terminal sequence, since each stage in this sequence does represent the loss or decline in a vital capacity, and each stage does lead to the next in something like the approved way. I propose to deal with this difficulty by insisting that in genuine terminal processes, there are no "covert external linkages." A sequence has a covert external linkage when two of its adjacent events are causally linked in anything like the way in which e5 and e8 are linked. That is, they are linked by a complex causal process that involves events that are not themselves declines or losses of vital capacities, and are in some sense "external" to the dying2 organism. The most obvious examples of covert external linkages would be provided by cases in which events in a causal process are linked by beliefs and desires of other organisms. In any case, in order to qualify as a genuine terminal process, a sequence of suitably related events would have to satisfy this fourth condition—it must contain no covert external linkages.

In light of all this, we can now introduce the concept of the "terminal process."

D5: Process P is terminal for organism x =df. x is of some kind, K, such that (1) P is a causal process; (2) P can be broken down into a number of stages, each of which (other than the last) is the loss or decrease of a property that is vital for K; (3) P's last stage is the death of x; and (4) P contains no covert external linkages.

My general proposal concerning dying2 is this: an organism of whatever sort is dying2 if and only if it is engaged in a process that would be terminal for that organism if it were allowed to reach its conclusion without interference. In other words:

D6: x is dying2 at t =df. at t, x is engaged in a process that would be terminal for x, if it were allowed to reach its conclusion without interference.

Let us apply D6 to the case of the shrapnel bearer to see how it works, and to compare it with Smart's analysis. Consider some time at which the bit of shrapnel is still lodged in some muscle far from the heart. The shrapnel bearer can still engage properly in nutrition, respiration, circulation, disease fighting, etc. He has a full complement of undiminished vital properties for his kind. Since he has not yet begun to suffer a loss or decrease in vital properties, he is not yet in a terminal process. Thus, he is not dying2. This seems right to me. (Of course, we all know that he is engaged in an internal process that will lead to his death. That is why his case refutes Smart's analysis. The trick here is that the process, though internal and ending with death, does not yet involve the loss of any vital properties. Thus, it is not "terminal".)

Now consider a later time, when the bit of shrapnel has broken loose and has lodged in the man's heart. Now the man's capacity to engage in the normal sort of blood circulation has been disrupted. Being able to engage in circulation is a vital property for human beings. Since the loss of circulation will lead to the loss of brain function, and this will lead to death, we can see that the shrapnel bearer is now embarked on a causal process that, barring interference, will be terminal for him. Thus, once the shrapnel begins to interfere with his capacity to engage properly in blood circulation, the shrapnel bearer begins to be dying2.

Consideration of another example may shed some light on Smart's "normality" condition. Suppose there is a certain type of disease process that normally doesn't kill trees of a certain species. Suppose, however, that in 2 percent of cases, the disease process does result in the death of the tree. Suppose a certain tree is dying2 of this unusual disease. According to D6, there is no need that the abstract process be one that normally issues in death. The tree can be dying2 anyway, provided that the tree is in a terminal process. The tree can be in a terminal process—all that's necessary is that it be in a process in which the decrease of one vital capacity *in that particular tree* would lead, barring interference, to the decrease of others and eventually to the death of that tree. Whether other trees would die at the end of similar processes is irrelevant.

More Mysteries of Dying2

The analysis proposed in D6 contains a number of conceptual "soft spots." One important defect is that the concept of *vital properties* is not as clear as we might like it to be. I am unable to say precisely what I mean by 'vital property'. I gave some examples of properties I take to be vital for humans, and I gave some other examples of properties I take to be vital for certain trees. I suggested that a property is vital for things of a kind if it is relevantly like the capacities for respiration, nutrition, blood circulation, thermal regulation, and disease fighting are for human beings. Each of these is a biological capacity that human beings must have in order to live in the manner appropriate to them. If an organism loses one of these properties, and the loss is not compensated for, that organism will be in grave danger of dying.

But this is all obscure. I really have not given a fully satisfactory account of vital properties. Insofar as the concept of vital properties is obscure, so is the proposed analysis of dying2.

A second weakness concerns certain of the causal concepts that appear in the analysis. The concept of *interference* is especially troubling.

It must be acknowledged that more needs to be said about "covert external linkages." I suspect that, on examination, every terminal sequence will be found to have some covert linkages. That is, there will be some complex causal chain linking the loss of one vital capacity to the loss of the next. It would be good to be able to explain in detail the difference between cases in which the extra steps violate the fourth condition and the cases in which they do not. I have not yet provided that explanation.[18]

Finally, it should be clear that this proposed analysis of dying2 makes essential use both of the concept of death and of the concept of life. The concept of death appears in the explanation of terminal processes; the concept of life appears in the explanation of vital processes. Since life and death are enigmatic, so is dying2.

In light of all these difficulties, I think it must be admitted that the concept of dying2 is a bit of a mystery. Nevertheless, I think my proposed analysis is an advance over earlier suggestions. I think that it at least has the merit of revealing the outlines of the concept of dying2 and showing how it relates to some other concepts in the vicinity. It also has the merit of revealing and locating some of the more obscure conceptual components of the concept of dying2.

On Death and Dying2

Before leaving this topic, I would like to consider some general principles concerning the relations between death and dying2. We have already seen that it would be a mistake to suppose that whenever a thing is dying2, it is engaged in a process that will in fact take it to its death. Terminal processes may be interrupted. However, it might seem that if a thing is dying2, then it will surely reach its death *sometime* in the future. In other words:

P1: Necessarily, if a thing is dying2 at a time, then it will die at some later time.

I think P1 is false. As we saw in Chapter 4, some organisms manage to get out of life without dying. Let us consider a variant of Rosenberg's example involving Alvin the amoeba. Suppose Alvin is living in a drop of excessively acidic water. Suppose that as a result, he is dying2. His vital properties are dropping like dominoes. Suppose, further, that a kindly lab technician takes note of Alvin's plight. The technician then adds a drop of slightly alkaline water to Alvin's acidic drop, thereby getting the pH into the range suitable for amoebas. Suppose that Alvin recovers and sometime later gets out of life without dying by undergoing division. Thus, though he was dying2, Alvin never dies.

In the other direction, it seems to me that a thing may die even though it never previously was dying2.[19] This would happen, I think, in the case of an organism that suffers an instantaneous annihilation—as, for example, a butterfly that happens to be fluttering a few inches from ground zero at the time of a nuclear blast. Thus, we must not endorse:

P2: Necessarily, if a thing dies at a time, then it was dying2 at some earlier time.

In light of the failure of P1 and P2, it may seem that there is no connection between death and dying2. However, I think that to say this would be to overstate the case. For recall that 'dying2' was defined by appeal to the concept of *terminal process;* and 'terminal process' was defined by appeal to the concept of death. Thus, even if there is no guarantee that there is a causal connection, in particular cases, between death and dying2, there is some, however weak, conceptual connection between the concept of death and the concept of dying2.

6

The Survival of Death

One of the most profound and troubling questions about death is whether it can be survived. I take this to be the question whether people (and other living things) continue to exist after they die. I think I know how this question should be answered, and I think the answer contains some good news and some bad news.

Those who think that we do not survive death may be called "terminators." They accept the termination thesis, according to which people cease to exist when they die. It should be clear that the termination thesis is just the denial of the notion that we survive death. The termination thesis is my main focus in this chapter. In the first section, I attempt to formulate the doctrine clearly. In the second section, I indicate something of its popularity. Then, in the third section, I try to show how profoundly counterintuitive it really is. Various lines of argument in favor of the doctrine are then discussed. In each case, I try to show why the argument is unsuccessful. I conclude in the final section with a brief discussion of the implications of my view.

The Termination Thesis

To focus the discussion, let us introduce a general principle that expresses a version of the thesis that we cease to exist when we die. This version of the thesis is restricted to people. It says:

TTp: If a person dies at a time, then he or she ceases to exist at that time.

I should perhaps say a word or two about the intended meaning of TTp. Three concepts are especially interesting: the concept of a *person;* the concept of *death;* and the concept of *existence.*

I think we will have to begin our consideration of this issue without any explicit account of the concept of persons. Later, I will distinguish between two different meanings that the term may have. (Still later—in Chapter 7—I will consider two more concepts of personality.) For now, let us assume that we have sufficient grasp of the meaning of the term 'person' as it appears in TTp. I mean to use the word in such a way that it would be correct to say that I am a person, and you are a person.

'Dies' in TTp can be taken to express what I have been calling 'the biological concept of death'.[1] Although I cannot provide a satisfactory philosophical analysis of this concept, I think the concept is sufficiently familiar for present purposes. In typical cases, when a living organism ceases to live, it dies. In Chapter 4, I argued that there are some cases in which living organisms cease to live without dying. Organisms that go into suspended animation illustrate one important deathless exit from life; organisms such as amoebas that undergo certain forms of fission or fusion illustrate another. There may be more. Thus, we cannot define 'dies' as 'ceases to live'. At best, we might say that 'dies' means 'ceases to live but does not enter suspended animation and does not undergo deathless fission or deathless fusion.' Obviously, this is no definition of death. But it will have to do.

When I say that a thing "ceases to exist" at a time, what I mean is that for some period of time up to that time there was such a thing as it; subsequently there is no such thing. So, for example, imagine that I have a little wooden table. Suppose I break off the legs and then chop up the tabletop for kindling. Suppose I burn all the resulting wood and scatter the ashes. Then the table no longer exists. Of course, all the atoms from which it was made still exist. But the table no longer exists. Instead of the table, we now have scattered ashes and dispersed smoke.

We have to be clear on the distinction between two fundamentally different sorts of case. In some cases, such as the case of the little table, a certain object *simply ceases to exist.* In other cases, an object does not simply cease to exist, but merely ceases to exist *as something or other.* This may be illustrated by the case of a Jewish boy who reaches the age of thirteen. According to tradition, each such boy then ceases to exist *as a boy.* He then becomes a man. But unless something very unusual happens at his bar mitzvah, it would be entirely wrong to say that such a Jewish boy simply ceases to exist when he reaches age thirteen. He keeps on existing; he just stops being a boy.

The distinction can also be illustrated by a variant of the table example. Suppose I alter the table in some trivial ways, place it on top of my desk, and proceed to use it as a lectern. Perhaps the table has ceased to exist *as a table.* But it would be wrong to say that it has simply ceased to exist. The object that formerly was a table still exists. Now it is a lectern.

The case in which the table is smashed and burned illustrates a case in which a complex physical object is so profoundly altered that it simply ceases to exist. The case in which the table is converted into a lectern illustrates the sort of case in which a complex physical object is altered, but does not simply cease to exist. It only ceases to exist as a table. It would be good to be able to state, in fully general terms, the principles that explain the difference between the two sorts of case. We might want to know just why it is that in some cases things persist through change, whereas in others they do not. Unfortunately, I cannot provide such principles. We will have to proceed by appeal to our best metaphysical intuition.[2]

TTp is not the thesis that when a person dies, he or she ceases existing *as a person.* It is the thesis that when a person dies, he or she *simply* ceases to exist. The person goes out of existence; subsequently, there is no such thing as that person. No object that exists afterward is such that we could correctly say of it, 'this formerly was a living person.' Terminators believe this. Survivalists deny it. I am a survivalist.

Some Philosophers Who Have Accepted the Termination Thesis

In his letter to Menoeceus, Epicurus says that "death is nothing to us."[3] He supports this claim by appeal to some arguments. One premise of one of them is that if an individual does not exist at a time, then nothing bad can happen to him or her at that time. Another premise of that argument seems to be a version of the termination thesis. He says that "when death comes, then we do not exist."[4] So Epicurus apparently believed that when we die, we simply cease to exist. He was a terminator.

Epicurus's disciple Lucretius maintained the same view and defended it by appeal to similar arguments. He said that we have nothing to fear from death, since "he who exists not, cannot become miserable."[5] The remark would be pointless unless it were assumed that a person who is dead "exists not." Thus Lucretius also must have believed that death marks the end of our existence. So he too was a terminator.

Modern defenders of the Epicurean view about the evil of death sometimes assert TTp. For example, Peter Dalton says. "When a man is dead he no longer exists and will never again exist."[6] Similar remarks can be found in the writings of other modern-day Epicureans.[7]

In his book on *Death and Immortality,* Roy Perrett asserts: " 'A biological organism has died' does entail 'A biological organism has ceased to exist.' "[8] Further remarks in the context of the one cited make it clear that Perrett accepts the claim that death marks the end of existence not only for people, but for biological organisms of all other sorts as well. He would apparently endorse this more general version of the termination thesis:

TTo: If a biological organism dies at a time, then it simply ceases to exist at that time.

Reflection on TTo suggests an even broader version of the termination thesis. Instead of speaking just of persons, as TTp does, or just of organisms, as TTo does, we might formulate a version that applies to every living thing—whether person, organism, cell, tissue, or organ. This would be:

TTu: If a living thing dies at a time, then it simply ceases to exist at that time.

So far as I know, no modern philosopher has discussed the view more extensively than Jay Rosenberg. In *Thinking Clearly about*

Death, Rosenberg describes death as a "change in kind."[9] In a typical case, Rosenberg seems to maintain, when a person dies, she ceases to exist. Just as the person ceases to exist, a new entity, a corpse, begins to exist. According to Rosenberg, it is a matter of metaphysical necessity that a person's history comes to an end when she dies. "There is no possibility that a person's history might extend beyond that person's death."[10]

Rosenberg recognizes that ordinary speech is full of talk that seems to presuppose that people regularly continue to exist after death. Thus, for example, we say:

My Aunt Ethel died last week, and we're burying her tomorrow.

This statement clearly suggests that there is one thing ("Aunt Ethel") that both died last week and will be buried tomorrow. But Rosenberg maintains that this is mere "linguistic appearance." He goes on:

There is no one thing which both died last week and will be buried tomorrow. What died last week was Aunt Ethel. What will be buried tomorrow, however, is not Aunt Ethel but rather Aunt Ethel's remains. What will be buried tomorrow is a corpse, Aunt Ethel's corpse. But a corpse is not a person. Aunt Ethel's corpse is not Aunt Ethel.[11]

Lots of other philosophers apparently maintain similar views. So many, in fact, that it would be nearly impossible to cite them all, and, since the view is so common, it seems to me that there is little point in listing any more than the handful so far mentioned. So it is clear that lots of philosophers have maintained that people simply cease to exist when they die. Some have maintained that all biological organisms are relevantly similar—they all simply cease to exist at death.

Doubts About the Termination Thesis

A substantial portion of our common-sense thought about death conflicts blatantly with the termination thesis. Rosenberg mentioned one example. We often say such things as that Aunt Ethel died last week and we're burying her tomorrow. Anyone who finds this (from the metaphysical perspective) a fully satisfactory thing to say must therefore think that at least some entities continue to exist after they have died. Otherwise, they would say that Aunt Ethel died last week and we're burying something else tomorrow, for she is no longer here to be buried.

But Rosenberg's example is just one of a huge supply. Let us consider some others.

1. Consider what goes on in elementary biology courses. The aim is to teach children something about the anatomy of certain organisms—usually frogs. On the appointed day, the children cut open the dead frogs, carefully drawing diagrams of the mutilated guts. The poor frogs have been sacrificed on the altar of scientific education.

Imagine the reaction if someone informed the teachers and students that the items on their lab tables had in fact *never lived.* Suppose someone pointed to one of the dismembered frogs and said: "That very object was never alive. The thing you are dissecting never swam in a pond; never ate a fly; never dozed on a lily pad." Surely such remarks would be greeted with utter disbelief. They would be taken to be completely fanciful. Yet if TTo were true, these remarks would be entirely correct. The former frogs would have gone out of existence when they died. The items being dissected by the children must have come into existence approximately when the frogs departed. The biology students have spent a whole class period investigating the anatomy of objects that never lived. Why is this called "biology"?

2. Suppose a man has an old horse. The horse pulls the man's cart. One hot day, the horse dies. The man removes the harness, dumps it into the cart, and is about to walk off, leaving the horse where it collapsed in the road. Spectators draw near. One says, "Wait a minute there, fellow. What are you going to do with your horse? You can't just leave it there to rot." Suppose the man replied with these words, "You folks must be mistaken. That object is not my horse. My horse went out of existence a few minutes ago when it died. Thus I have no responsibility for this large object blocking the road. If you are worried about it, I suppose you will have to remove it."

Surely the man's remarks would be taken to be simply absurd. Yet if TTo were true, he would be quite right about his main point. If his horse went out of existence when it died, the large horse-shaped object on the road cannot be his horse. At best it might be something else "descended from" his horse.

3. I vaguely recall an occasion in my youth when I was taken to a seafood restaurant. On the napkins and bibs was printed a slogan attesting to the freshness of the food. As I recall, the slogan was: "The fish you eat today, last night slept in Chesapeake Bay." I do not know whether the claim was in fact true.[12] Perhaps the fish were not quite that fresh. Perhaps they hadn't slept in Chesapeake Bay for two or three days. But in any case it seemed to me that the fish being served in that restaurant surely had slept in some body of water at some time in the past. Yet if the termination thesis is true, the slogan was false. If living things cease to exist when they die, then any fish that slept in Chesapeake Bay ceased to exist before they made it to my platter. The "fish" I ate that day never slept or swam in any bay.

These examples, and many more of the same sort, decisively establish that the termination thesis (especially in the generalized forms) runs counter to common-sense views about death. We often think and speak about dead things in a way that reveals that we think that dead things formerly lived; that the dead bodies we encounter once walked or swam with full vitality.

Indeed, if you ask a person unperverted by philosophy to define "dead," he will probably say "formerly living, but no longer."[13] Clearly, however, if any version of the termination thesis is correct, this is an unacceptable way to define 'dead'. For if TTp is true, then no actually existing dead person formerly lived; if TTo is true, then no actually existing dead organism of any sort formerly lived; if TTu is true, then no actually existing dead entity of any sort formerly was alive. At best, dead objects are somehow descended from living things.

We have seen, then, that various versions of the termination thesis are very widely accepted by philosophers, even though it is blatantly inconsistent with common-sense views about death. This provokes a natural question. What do the terminators know that ordinary people do not know? Why do these philosophers accept such a paradoxical view about death?

The Argument from Definition

Some philosophers define death in such a way that the termination thesis appears to be an immediate consequence of the definition. Consider Perrett again. He suggests several definitions of death. In one passage, he discusses a concept of death that is intended to be applicable not only to human beings, but to organisms of all other sorts as well. This he calls "the concept of death that is neutral to all deaths."[14] He proposes to identify death, so understood, with ". . . the destruction of a functioning biological organism."[15] In the same context, presumably intending to express the same idea, Perrett says that death is "the annihilation of a functioning biological organism."[16] He also says that "death is the disintegration of the living organism as a whole."[17]

Although it seems to me that there are interesting differences between the concepts of annihilation and destruction, and further differences between these and the concept of disintegration, for present purposes it may be just as well to ignore them. Let us say, then, that Perrett defines the all-inclusive biological concept of death in this way:

D1: x dies at t =df. x is a functioning biological organism for some time up to t, and at t, x is annihilated, destroyed, or disintegrated.

Perrett goes on to say " 'A biological organism has died' does entail 'a biological organism has ceased to exist.' "[18] I take this to be a clear affirmation of the termination thesis in the form in which it applies to all biological organisms.

It appears, then, that Perrett defines death as the annihilation of a functioning biological organism, and then, noting that what is annihilated goes out of existence, infers that when organisms die, they go out of existence. If this is right, it would be appropriate to formulate his argument in this way:

The argument from definition

1. When an organism dies, it is annihilated, destroyed, or disintegrated.

2. When an organism is annihilated, destroyed, or disintegrated, it simply goes out of existence.

3. Therefore, when an organism dies, it simply goes out of existence.

Perrett could defend line (1) by pointing out that it is an immediate consequence of his definition of death. Line (2) is analytic—it is true in virtue of the meanings of 'annihilate', 'destroy,' and 'disintegrate.' The argument as a whole is logically valid.

It seems to me that if the definition were correct, the argument would be (near enough) sound.[19] However, it also seems to me that the definition is clearly incorrect. When a butterfly, for example, is captured and placed in the killing jar, the entomologist may do her job with exquisite care. She may treat the specimen so gently that not so much as a single microscopic scale is dislodged in the process. Though the butterfly dies, it is not destroyed or disintegrated. Surely it is not annihilated. It is a "perfect" specimen. Thus, it is a mistake to suppose that death should be identified with the "annihilation, destruction, or disintegration of a functioning biological organism."

The argument from definition depends on a most implausible and highly question-begging definition of death. If our central question is whether organisms cease to exist when they die, it is clearly pointless to argue as I have suggested Perrett does.

The Argument from Dualism

It appears that at least some philosophers have maintained the termination thesis at least in part because they also maintain a certain form of dualism. Lucretius seems to be a case in point. He apparently believed that a person is a compound entity, composed of a body and a soul. At the moment of death, the soul and body are separated, the union destroyed.[20]

This conception of persons and their death may seem to provide very strong support for the termination thesis. Let us consider it a bit more closely. According to Lucretius, every person is a compound entity, composed of two main parts. One part, the body, is a relatively ordinary physical object made of ordinary atoms. The other part, the soul or mind, is a wholly distinct entity. According to Lucretius, the soul is a physical object, but one made of "bodies exceedingly small, smooth, and round."[21] Bits of the soul are dispersed throughout the body of a living organism. The various parts of the soul are bound together with the various parts of the body to form a new entity, a person. In a particularly striking passage, Lucretius describes living persons as entities that ". . . by the binding tie of marriage between body and soul are formed each into one single being."[22] This doctrine we may call "Lucretian personal dualism."

Lucretian personal dualism is associated with a view about death. Lucretius affirms this view about death when he describes death as "a separation of body and soul, out of both of which we are each formed into a single being."[23] The Lucretian view is that when a person dies, his soul separates from his body. The two entities become "unstuck"—whatever mysterious force formerly bound them together somehow releases them.

From this view about the nature of death, Lucretius readily derives the conclusion that each person ceases to exist at the moment of death.[24] I think it would be fair to represent his argument for the termination thesis in this way:

The argument from personal dualism

    1. When a person dies, his soul separates from his body.
    2. When a person's soul separates from his body, he simply ceases to exist.
    3. Therefore, when a person dies, he simply ceases to exist.

In spite of its validity, the argument seems to me to be very weak indeed. One crucial problem is that I see no good reason to suppose that Lucretian personal dualism might be true. Thus, I am extremely dubious about line (1).

A more important problem with the argument is this: among terminators, there are very many who reject personal dualism and its associated view about death.[25] Hence, unless these philosophers are very confused indeed, their acceptance of the termination thesis cannot be based on the argument from personal dualism. They must have some other reason to think that people cease to exist when they die.

Furthermore, the argument would not have much bearing on the generalized forms of the termination thesis, unless the advocate of the argument wanted to insist that clams and pine trees and isolated cells also have souls, and that death for these entities also involves the separation of body from soul. This view is not very popular nowadays.

Before leaving this argument, I want to make a final comment. According to personal dualism, as I have described it, a person is a compound entity, composed of a body and a soul. At death, the components are separated, and the compound goes out of existence. But what about the body? What happens to it at the moment of death? Presumably, the personal dualist will say that in typical cases, *the body* of a person who dies does not go out of existence at the moment of death. It lingers on until it decomposes. This may seem unproblematic. However, it generates a problem for the generalized versions of the termination thesis.

Suppose we take as an example a certain corpse, which we will call "C." Suppose we ask a personal dualist whether in his view C was ever alive. Perhaps he will tell us that (i) C formerly was alive, back during those times when it was combined with a soul; back during the time when it helped to form a person. This may seem reasonable, but it straightforwardly entails that the generalized forms of the termination thesis are false. For in this view C is an object that formerly was a living organism, and then died—yet C continued to exist after death.

On the other hand, the personal dualist might maintain that (ii) C was never alive. Even when properly bound to a soul, C was always nonliving. What was then alive was only the person of which C was a part. Thus, the personal dualist may protect the generalized forms of the termination thesis. This alternative strikes me as being seriously implausible. The body was able to eat, drink, breathe, and grow; perhaps it was capable of reproduction. Its nervous system might have been in perfect working order. Yet the personal dualist is imagined as saying that in spite of all this, it was never alive. One wonders what it takes to count as a living thing.

Corpses and People

I earlier quoted a passage in which Jay Rosenberg discusses the sad case of Aunt Ethel. Rosenberg recognizes that we might say "Aunt Ethel died last week and we're burying her tomorrow." This suggests that the corpse that we are about to bury formerly was Aunt Ethel. But Rosenberg rejects this literal understanding of the sentence. He insists that we are not really burying Aunt Ethel; we are really burying Aunt Ethel's "remains." In this context, perhaps in support of his contention, Rosenberg says that "a corpse is not a person."[26] Rosenberg's remark suggests an argument for the termination thesis, but it is not clear just how the argument is intended to work.

My hunch is that Rosenberg's thought is roughly this: when something that has been a person dies, we have a corpse on our hands. But a corpse is not a person. Thus, when something that has been a person dies, it stops being a person. But if a thing that has been a person stops being a person, then it simply ceases to exist. Therefore, when a person dies, he or she simply ceases to exist.

If this is indeed the proper interpretation of Rosenberg's thought, then the argument can be reformulated as follows:

The argument from personality

    1. When a person dies, he or she ceases to be a person.
    2. When a person ceases to be a person, he or she simply ceases to exist.
    3. Therefore, when a person dies, he or she simply ceases to exist.

Each premise has some initial plausibility, and the argument as a whole seems to be valid. Thus, it appears that we have a fairly persuasive line of thought leading to the termination thesis in its personal form.

The argument makes essential use of the term 'person'. Earlier, I noted that there are ambiguities here, and I suggested that it would be useful to draw certain distinctions. I think there are at least four distinguishable concepts of personality. Fortunately, some of these probably have no relevance to the present discussion. They can be discussed later. In order to facilitate evaluation of this latest argument, let us then consider a distinction between just two of these concepts of personality. I have in mind the distinction between the *psychological* concept of personality and the *biological* concept of personality. These are often confused but can readily be distinguished. When we say that something is a biological person, we are merely saying that that thing is a human organism—a member of the biological species *Homo sapiens*. On the other hand, when we say that something is a psychological person, we are saying something about the psychological functions, abilities, and capacities of that thing. We are saying that the thing is capable of self-consciousness; that it can engage in purposeful action; that it instantiates a sufficiently rich psychological profile.

Here on earth, it appears that most of the living biological persons are also psychological persons, and most of the psychological persons are also biological persons. But once we recognize the conceptual distinction, we will want to insist that this large-scale coincidence is just a local accident. If there are sufficiently intelligent, self-conscious beings on Mars, then they are full-fledged psychological persons but almost certainly not biological persons. If dolphins are as smart as some marine biologists have suggested, they are psychological persons, too. But, of course, no matter how smart and sensitive they are, dolphins are not members of the species *Homo sapiens,* and so they are surely not biological persons. On the other hand, some unfortunate biological persons may fail to be psychological persons. Biological persons with severe brain damage, for example, may lack self-consciousness and the capacity to engage in purposeful action. Thus, they fail to be psychological persons.

Since there are at least two concepts of personality, we have at least two different ways of interpreting the argument from personality. We can take it either as an argument entirely about psychological personality, or as an argument entirely about biological personality.[27] Let us first consider the version of the argument that makes use of the psychological concept. In other words:

The argument from psychological personality

    1. When a psychological person dies, he or she ceases to be a psychological person.
    2. When a psychological person ceases to be a psychological person, he or she simply ceases to exist.
    3. Therefore, when a psychological person dies, he or she simply ceases to exist.

The argument is valid, and there is reason to accept the first premise. When a psychological person dies, his heart stops beating, and his brain is soon deprived of freshly oxygenated blood. It is reasonable to suppose that under these circumstances, the person quickly loses consciousness. Furthermore, in virtue of the fact that brain cells deteriorate relatively quickly, it is also reasonable to suppose that when a psychological person dies, he loses the abilities that are definitive of psychological personality. He no longer can engage in purposeful action; he no longer instantiates a psychological profile; he is no longer self-conscious. Thus, if we use the word 'person' to expresss psychological personality, it appears that we will have to say that at death, the object that formerly was a person stops being a person. Thus, line (1) seems correct. Perhaps when Rosenberg said that "a corpse is not a person," he meant to indicate that a corpse is not a *psychological* person. If so, I think he was right.

The puzzle here concerns the second premise. Why would anyone think that ceasing to be a psychological person entails simply ceasing to exist?

Perhaps someone will think that (2) instantiates a form that is universally true. Perhaps they will think that everything of this form is true: "When an F ceases to be an F, it simply ceases to exist." Thus, if a tree stops being a tree, it ceases to exist; when a fish stops being a fish, it ceases to exist. Line (2) might be based on this sort of consideration.

If it is not already obvious, a moment's reflection will make it obvious that not everything of the illustrated form is true. As I mentioned at the outset, when a boy ceases to be a boy, he generally does not cease to exist. He becomes a man. When a student ceases to be a student, he or she generally does not cease to exist.

He or she continues to exist either as a graduate or else as a dropout. So we cannot defend (2) by appeal to the claim that everything of its form is true.

Premise (2) might be defended by appeal to the notion that every psychological person is *essentially* a psychological person. Let us look into this.

When we say that every psychological person is essentially a psychological person, our statement has implications for each and every thing that is a psychological person. If our statement is true, then no such thing could have existed without being a psychological person; no such thing can exist at any time without being a psychological person at that time; psychological personality is a sine qua non for anything that in fact is a psychological person. If we accept this view about psychological personality, we will also want to accept premise (2) of the argument. For whenever a thing loses an essential property, it simply ceases to exist.

But I see no reason to suppose that psychological personality is essential to the things that have it. Consider some biological person who is also a psychological person. Suppose she comes down with some terrible disease that leads to gradual psychological degeneration. As time goes by, she loses more and more of her psychological capacities. Eventually, she goes into a vegetative state and gradually ceases to be a psychological person. Clearly, however, the very organism that formerly was a psychological person still exists—it has merely ceased having the properties definitive of psychological personality. The same horrible misfortune might befall any of us. Thus, however important psychological personality may be to us, it is not a property we have essentially. We could exist without it. So we are fortunate to be psychological persons. It could have been otherwise.

I think the plausibility of (2) derives in part from the fact that it is easy to confuse psychological personality with biological personality, and it is far more reasonable to suppose that everything that is a biological person is essentially a biological person. In that case, it would be correct to say that when a thing ceases to be a biological person, it simply ceases to exist. Thus, we would have a plausible version of the second premise. Let us consider a revised version of the argument that makes use of this line of thought:

The argument from biological personality

1. When a biological person dies, he or she ceases to be a biological person.
2. When a biological person ceases to be a biological person, he or she simply ceases to exist.
3. Therefore, when a biological person dies, he or she simply ceases to exist.

This version of the argument is also valid. Premise (2) can be defended by appeal to the doctrine that each organism has its species essentially. Since this is a reasonable doctrine, (2) seems plausible.

The problem with this version of the argument is line (1). What (1) really says is that when a thing that has been a member of the human species dies, it ceases to be a member of the species. But this seems implausible. I see no reason to suppose that biological organisms lose their species membership merely by dying. A dead horse is still a horse; a collection of dead butterflies still serves to instantiate a collection of butterfly species. Why should human beings be different? Recall that the concept *biological person* is not an "ability concept"; when we say that something is a biological person, we are not saying that it is able to think, to act purposefully, or to be self-conscious. We are merely allocating that object to a certain biological species. It seems to me that dead members of the species *Homo sapiens* are still members of the species *Homo sapiens*. Suppose there has been a terrible disaster, and dead bodies are strewn about. Someone might suggest that the dead dogs and cats be dumped into a common grave, whereas the dead humans ought to be brought to the stadium for identification. Although they are dead, they are still humans. Thus, in this version of the argument, the faulty premise is (1), not (2). My conclusion is that no version of the argument from personality serves to establish the termination thesis.

Death and *Nonexistence As*

The termination thesis, in its various guises, is the view that when they die, things simply cease to exist. In other words, it is the view that when a living entity dies, that very entity goes out of existence. In my discussion above, I tried to show how counterintuitive this view really is. In subsequent sections, I have been trying to show that the main arguments for it are inconclusive. On balance then, it seems reasonable to reject the termination thesis. It is more reasonable to suppose that many things continue to exist after they die.

I should acknowledge that I agree that when a living thing dies, it ceases to exist *as a living thing;* when a psychological person dies, he or she ceases to exist *as a psychological person.* But since I think that living things (including psychological persons) are certain material objects, and I think that these material objects generally persist (as corpses) for at least a little while past their deaths, I am not prepared to accept any interesting version of the termination thesis.

At the outset, I mentioned that I had both good news and bad news. The good news is that most of us will survive death. Most of us will continue to exist after we die. The bad news is that though we will survive death, and will continue to exist after we die, each of us will then be dead. We will have no psychological experiences. We will just be corpses. Such survival may be of very little value.

Since this view about death and survival may seem a bit awkward at first, it may be useful to spell out in greater detail the materialist conceptual scheme of which it is a part. This is the topic of Chapter 7.

7

A Materialist Conception
of Death

A New Approach to Death

In the materialist view, death is something that happens to certain
material objects. Before they die, these material objects are alive.
After they die, these objects are dead. Thus, death marks a profoundly important border in the history of any such object. But
however important a border death may be for these objects, it does
not necessarily coincide with the border between existence and
nonexistence. In typical cases, according to materialism, formerly
living objects go on existing as corpses for a while after their
deaths. Eventually, they go the way of all flesh. They deteriorate
and finally go out of existence.

This way of thinking about death seems utterly natural to materialists. But to others it may appear strange. Therefore, it might be
useful to give a more detailed account of the materialist conception
of death.

For a philosopher in the analytic tradition, the most satisfying
sort of account would be a straightforward analytic definition of 'x
dies at t.' However, as I tried to show in Chapter 4, death is
enigmatic. I find that I cannot formulate such an analysis. Hence, I
will have to explain this conception of death in some other way.

The concept of death is intimately linked to a variety of other
concepts. I have already considered some of these related concepts. One closely related concept is the concept of life, which was
the focus of Chapters 2 and 3. Another is the concept of dying2,
which was the topic of Chapter 5. In Chapter 6 I briefly considered

the concept of being dead and the concept of a life, as well as a few other related concepts.

All of these concepts stand in various intimate relations to the concept of death. Some entail it; others are entailed by it; yet others can be defined by appeal to it; and others are incompatible with it. In light of this, it seems reasonable to expect that there are a number of fully general principles expressing conceptual linkages between the biological concept of death and these related concepts. It seems to me that it may be possible to gain deeper insight into the nature of death itself and its place in the materialist conceptual scheme by exploring some of the ways in which death relates to these other concepts. In this chapter, I formulate and discuss several such principles. Thus, although I will not be attempting to explain *what* death is, I will be attempting to explain *where* the biological concept of death is located in a certain materialist conceptual scheme.

The Lifeline

To have a convenient example for the application of these concepts, let us imagine some important moments in the history of a possible human being. Let us call this human being "Adam," and let us suppose that he was conceived at some moment, which we can call 't0'. Let us suppose that the story goes on as follows: Adam remained a fetus for nine months and then was born at t1. He developed normally, learning to walk and talk as children generally do. Much later, at t2, Adam became seriously ill. His condition deteriorated rapidly. Everyone said that Adam was dying. Fortunately, at t3, Adam was cured by the administration of a "miracle drug." Adam's life was uneventful for many years until t4, when he became seriously ill again. As before, his friends said he was dying. This time, however, there was no miracle drug. At t5 he fell into an irreversible coma. His heart continued to beat, and his lungs continued to function for several days. At last, at t6, Adam's heart gave out. He was pronounced dead. In accordance with Adam's wishes, the body was placed in an open casket so that Adam's friends could see him when they said their farewells. After the funeral, the body was cremated at t7.

We can plot some of these facts onto a chart, illustrating some of the highlights of the history of Adam:

t0	t1	t2	t3	t4	t5	t6	t7
Conception	Birth	Dying2	Recovery	Dying2	Coma	Death	Cremation

Death Itself, "a Death," and Being Dead

Let us begin by attempting to clarify two important concepts, each a near relative of the biological concept of death itself. The first of these is the concept of *being dead*.

It may at first appear that we can define 'dead' straightforwardly by appeal to 'dies' as follows:

> D1: x is dead at t =df. x died at some time earlier than t.

But suppose it is possible for something to live again after death; suppose that genuine revitalization is possible. In such a case, D1 would force us to say that the revived entity is at once living and dead. It would be living because it has been revitalized; it would be dead according to D1 because it died at some earlier time. This seems wrong to me. It seems to me that once it has been revived, such an organism would no longer be dead. It would then simply be alive again. Thus, I prefer to define 'dead' in this way:

> D1': x is dead at t =df. x died at some time earlier than t, and x has not been alive since then.

So the concept of being dead can be defined by appeal to the concepts of dying and being alive, together with the concept expressed by 'earlier than'.

The *death* of an entity is the event that consists in its dying. But since 'dying' is ambiguous, so is 'death'. As I see it, there are really (at least) *two* concepts of *a death*. On the one hand, we speak of an organism's death as the instantaneous event that occurs precisely when it dies—when it makes the transition from being alive to being dead. We may define this concept as follows:

> D2: e is the death1 of x =df. e is the event such that, necessarily, e occurs precisely when x dies.

As I tried to show in Chapter 5, there is also a process sense of 'dying'. I used 'dying2' to express this sense. Reflection on ordinary usage reveals that there is a corresponding process sense of 'death'. We use this sense when we say, for example, that someone's death was long, drawn-out, protracted, and the like. We may define this concept in this way:

> D3: e is the death2 of x =df. e is the event such that, necessarily, e occurs precisely when x is dying2.

Now we can say, without ambiguity, that someone's death2 lasted for six months, and finally ended with his death1.

These concepts can now be applied to the example involving Adam. Since Adam died at t6, we can say that his *death1* took place at precisely t6. Since he was dying2 from t4 until t6, we can say that his *death2* took place throughout the interval t4 to t6. Since he died at t6, and was never alive thereafter, we can say that Adam *was dead* at all times after t6.

There is a relatively trivial question about the moment of death1. In Adam's case, this is t6. What shall we say about Adam's vital status at t6? Was he alive at that fateful moment, or was he dead? Perhaps he was neither dead nor alive? Any choice here will generate some odd results. If we say that Adam was alive at t6, then we seem to be committed to the unintuitive view that Adam was still alive when he died; that his death occurred during his life. On the other hand, if we say that Adam was dead at t6, then we seem to be committed to the view that Adam was dead when he died; that his death occurred at a time when he was dead. In an extreme sort of case, this may generate the result that certain organisms die *at times when they do not exist!*

Although this is little more than an arbitrary choice on my part, I shall say that Adam was neither dead nor alive at t6. Rather, I shall say that Adam was alive right up to t6 and that he was dead at all times after t6. Thus, in this view, the moment of death itself is neither part of life nor part of death. Rather, the moment of death serves as a boundary between life and death. Since there is no such thing as "the last moment before t6," it then turns out that there is no last moment of Adam's life. Equally, since there is no first moment after t6, it also turns out that there is no first moment of Adam's death. This may seem odd, but I see no way to avoid some oddity here.[1]

Death and Life

In our effort to locate the biological concept of death in the materialist conceptual scheme, it will be useful to consider some of the conceptual relations between death and life. But before we do this, we must reach some agreement about certain of the facts of life. One of these concerns the temporal extent of a life. Consider Adam again. Precisely *when* was Adam alive?

According to the story I told above, Adam was conceived at t0, developed normally, and then was born at t1. These facts are not sufficient, by themselves, to determine when Adam began to live. Different people have different views. As I see it, Adam began to be alive at t0, when he was conceived. Although of course I cannot prove this point, there is a reason for saying that life begins at conception. It is this: there is a big difference between a living cell and a nonliving cell. Similarly, there is a big difference between unified collection of living cells and a unified collection of nonliving cells. In Adam's case, a certain living ovum was fertilized by a certain living sperm, thereby giving rise to a certain zygote. That zygote was properly formed, and was able to do the things that zygotes are supposed to do. It was in these respects unlike a zygote that was so defective that it could not function, or a zygote that has been preserved in formaldehyde or frozen in liquid nitrogen. Such zygotes would be nonliving. But in Adam's case, the zygote was as alive as any properly formed, properly functioning cell. So, like any such cell, it was alive.

I should hasten to point out that I have not claimed (nor will I claim) that the zygote was already a living *organism* or that it was a living *person.* Nor will I claim that it was capable of living on its own. I merely claim that, at first, it was just a living *cell.* Shortly afterwards, it became a living *pair of cells,* then a living *mass of cells.*

Normally, the fetus continues to live and grow throughout pregnancy. If it dies, there may be a miscarriage. If it dies shortly before birth, we say that it was stillborn. In Adam's case, there was no miscarriage and there was no stillbirth. The fetus did not die. It continued to be alive right through the time of birth. Once again, I have not said that it was a living organism or a living person during that period. (These points are discussed later.) I do say, however, that it was a living fetus. Hence, it was alive. Adam continued to be alive for many years, until he died at t6. At and after t6, he was not alive. After t6, he was dead. In light of all this, we can say that Adam began to be alive at t0 and continued to be alive until he died at t6.

Life and *death* are an interesting pair. Let us now consider some of the important relations in which these two concepts stand. Reflection on Adam's case suggests that they exclude each other, so that nothing can be both alive and dead at the same time. I think this is true:

Necessarily, nothing is both alive and dead at the same time.

There is a close connection between the definition of death proposed above in D1′ and this principle about the incompatibility of life and death. According to D1′, something is dead at a time only if it earlier died and *has not been alive since that time.* Hence, if something is dead at a time, it cannot also be alive. Thus, D1′ entails the incompatibility of simultaneous life and death.

Adam, who was alive at all times between t0 and t6, was dead at all times after t6. Thus, we are entitled to say:

Possibly, something is alive at one time, and dead at another time.

Once again, the truth of the principle is closely connected to the proposed definition of death. If D1′ is true, then every dead thing formerly was alive. So, since it is surely possible for there to be some dead things, the second principle is true. While a given object cannot be both alive and dead at the same time, it can be alive at one time and dead at another.

The second principle is an important element in the materialist view of death. In the materialist view, life is a property of certain complex material objects. In our present example, the living object is Adam's body, which is just an incredibly well-organized, constantly changing system composed entirely of physical parts. Around the time of death, this system begins to break down. Subsystems may fail; relationships between subsystems may be interrupted; elements may begin to deteriorate. The formerly living, complex material object, however, continues to exist for some time after death. In the case of Adam, that object continued to exist until t7, when it was cremated.

Thus, in the materialist conception, life and death are properties of material objects. Living zygotes, fetuses, human beings, and human corpses are equally material objects. The vital differences among these things are primarily due to their structures and capacities. At bottom, however, we are all just material objects.

Although living things generally die, this is not a matter of conceptual necessity. There are several ways in which a living thing might avoid death. It is conceivable that something might live forever without dying. More obviously, a thing might get out of life via one of the "deathless exits" (such as fission) discussed in Chapter 4. So, for all these reasons, the following is true:

> *Possibly, something is alive at a time even though it does not die at any later time.*

A corollary of this is the principle that it is possible for something to be alive at one time, even though it is never dead. Thus, materialists do not subscribe to the principle that death is inevitable. (But since it will not be easy for any human being to make use of deathless fission or fusion, and none of us will live forever, death is still *practically* inevitable *for us*.)

Although something can live without ever later dying, nothing can die without formerly living. This is a matter of conceptual necessity:

Necessarily, nothing dies at a time unless it was alive at some earlier time.

Similarly, nothing can be dead at a time unless it was alive at some earlier time. So one good thing about death is this: you cannot die or be dead unless you sometime lived.

I have claimed that nothing can die unless it lived earlier. This provokes a question about vital changes in the other direction: can a thing live if it died earlier? Consider this proposed principle:

Possibly, something is alive at a time even though it died at an earlier time.

Some people speak in such a way as to suggest that they think this principle is true. In Chapter 4 I mentioned that Jerry Lewis claimed to have died several times while undergoing open-heart surgery. He would surely insist that it is possible for a thing to live again after it has died.

So far as I can tell, none of the principles or definitions so far introduced here entails either that life after death is possible or that it is impossible. I find myself without clear intuitions on the question, and accordingly shall not commit myself. However, as I remarked earlier, I do have clear intuitions on a closely related principle. I think that this is true:

Possibly, something is alive at a time even though it ceased to be alive at some earlier time.

Anything that goes into suspended animation and then is reanimated is an example of a thing that is alive at a time even though it ceased (temporarily) to be alive earlier. Of course, nothing can cease *permanently* to be alive at a time and then come back to life.

Death and Existence

Adam was alive from t0 to t6. He existed throughout that time. Thus, whenever he was alive, he existed. Adam started being dead at t6 and will stay dead forever. It is clear that during at least some of this time (after cremation at t7) he did not exist. What is true of Adam seems to me to be true in general and of necessity. That is, life seems to entail existence, whereas death does not. In order to live, a thing must exist. However, a thing may be dead even though it does not exist. So we have two principles:

Necessarily, if a thing is alive at a time, then it exists at that time.

Possibly, a thing is dead at a time even though it does not exist at that time.

Being dead is an unusual property in this respect: it appears that a thing can be dead at a time even though it does not exist at that time. In this respect, being dead is quite different from dying2. Clearly, if a thing is dying2 at a time, it must exist then. But being dead, as contrasted with dying2, seems to be compatible with being nonexistent.

This suggests that being dead is a property that something can have at a time even though it is not "present" at that time. That would be odd. But reflection on the proposed definition, D1′, clarifies the situation. When we say, for example, that Adam is dead today, we are just saying that there was some time in the past, such that Adam died at that time, and he hasn't been alive since then. So, in a way, our statement does not entail that Adam has any "solid" properties today, just that there were some times in the past when he had some.

Some would surely say that I have understated the relation between being dead and being nonexistent. They would claim that being dead entails nonexistence. In other words, they would say that if a thing is dead at a certain time, then it must *not exist* at that time. This is reminiscent of the doctrine I dubbed the termination thesis in Chapter 6. I tried, by appeal to a variety of examples, to indicate how implausible it is. I will not repeat the examples here. I merely point out that (as I see it) during the period from t6 to t7, Adam's body existed but was dead. This shows that according to the materialist view, a thing may exist at a time when it is dead. So we have another general principle:

Possibly, a thing is dead at a time even though it does exist at that time.

Thus, in the materialist conceptual scheme, life entails existence—to be alive at a time, a thing must exist. But death entails neither existence nor nonexistence. Something may be dead at a time whether it exists then or not.

Deaths, Lives, and Histories

In a passage I mentioned earlier, Jay Rosenberg says that there is no possibility that a person's history might extend beyond that person's death.[2] For reasons I have already suggested, this claim does not mesh well with the materialist conception of death. In this connection, we should consider a closely related claim. This is the claim that there is no possibility that a person's *life* might extend beyond that person's death. These doctrines are more controversial than they may at first appear. In order to facilitate discussion of the two doctrines, it will be useful to try to explain what we mean when we speak of "the life" and "the history" of an entity.

Someone might say that the life of an entity is the period of time during which it is alive. But this has an obvious defect. If Adam and Eve start to live at the same moment, and cease to live at the same moment, then the period of time during which Adam lives is the same as the period of time during which Eve lives. Yet no one would want to say that Adam's life was Eve's life—that these two people "lived the same life."

We might instead think that the life of an entity is the property of being alive, as had by that entity. But lives have *duration,* whereas properties do not. Furthermore, this proposal seems to imply that we all have the same life—after all, the property of being alive is a universal, shared by all living things. The property of being alive that Adam had is the same as the property of being alive that Eve had.

I think it would be better to say that the *life* of an entity is an event—the smallest event that contains, as parts, all the events that happen to that entity during the time it is alive. This proposal gives clear sense to the notion that Adam's life started at some time (presumably t0) and ended at some other time (presumably t6); that it had duration; that it was distinct from Eve's life, even if it began and ended just when her life began and ended.

The *history* of an entity may correspondingly be thought of as the smallest event that contains as parts all the events that happen to that entity during the time it exists. Thus, Adam's history started when he began to exist and ended when he ceased to exist. I have claimed that Adam began to exist at conception at t0 and continued to exist (first as a living human being and then for a little while as a corpse) until he was cremated at t7.

Recall now that Rosenberg claimed that there is no possibility that a person's history might continue past that person's death. Anyone who accepts the materialist conceptual scheme will reject Rosenberg's claim. We maintain that Adam's history continued past his death at t6, and did not end until t7. My view is that in the vast majority of cases, a person's history continues for some period of time after his or her life ends.

I have to grant that the postmortem part of Adam's history was surely much less interesting than the part of his history that coincided with his life. From Adam's perspective, the postmortem part of his history might have been entirely worthless. I, for one, would not debate the point. I would insist, however, that if we want to give a complete account of the *history* of Adam (as opposed to the *life* of Adam) we should say a few words about his funeral.

Perhaps it will seem obvious that someone's *life* cannot extend beyond his or her death. But, as I suggested a few paragraphs back, this is not quite so simple as it may at first seem.

Let us provisionally suppose that it is possible to live again after being temporarily dead. To illustrate this sort of case, let us alter Adam's lifeline. Let us suppose that Adam died at t2 and then was reanimated at t3. If we assume that such a thing is possible, we will want to say that Adam was dead from t2 to t3, that he lived again from t3 until t6, and that he then died again at t6 and remained dead ever after.

We should note that if Adam's life followed this pattern, then it would be a "gappy" event—it would be an event that takes place for a while, then stops taking place, and then resumes taking place for a while. It would be like a trial that goes into recess over a weekend and then resumes on Monday.

This revised example illustrates one way in which "life after death" might be possible. For, at t4, Adam was alive even though he had died earlier at t2, and had been dead earlier from t2 to t3.

Since I do not know whether it is conceptually possible for something to live again after it has died, I do not know what to say about this example. However, anyone who thinks such a thing could happen will have to say that it is possible for a person's life to continue after his or her death. We all can agree, I think, that it is not possible for a person's life to continue after he or she ceases permanently to be alive.

Death and Humanity

Perhaps I have misunderstood the claims about histories and deaths. Maybe the point is really this: a person's history *as a human* cannot continue beyond that person's death. This proposal raises new problems: we have to consider what we mean when we speak of someone's history *as a human*.

We must begin by considering the concept of humanity. What do we mean when we say that something is *human?* Competent biologists, with appropriate equipment, can determine whether a cell is from an organism of the species *Homo sapiens*. By studying the DNA in that cell, such biologists can distinguish between a human cell and, for example, a chimpanzee cell or a cell from a dog or cat. If any such biologist had been given the opportunity to study the cells in the fetus that developed into Adam, he or she would have recognized those cells as human. Similarly, a competent biologist would have recognized the fetus itself as a *human* fetus, rather than one that would develop into a chimpanzee, dog, or cat. Since the zygote was formed from a pair of human gametes and developed normally, it was human from the start.

In light of all this, materialists hold that Adam began to be human at t0 when he began to live and exist. He continued to be human throughout his existence. This is *not* to say that he was a "human being" throughout his existence. Perhaps he was a human being only during some of that time—maybe starting at birth, or perhaps even later. But, as opposed to entities that are canine or feline, Adam was human.

What is the connection between humanity and life? Clearly, there were times when Adam was both human and alive. So humanity and life are obviously compatible. But it is equally obvious that life does not entail humanity; some living things are nonhuman. Furthermore, in the materialist view, humanity at a time does not entail life at that time. Adam continued to be human (as opposed to being feline or canine) after he died. If some cells were removed from the corpse and examined by a competent biologist, he or she would have been able to determine that those cells were *human*. Similarly, if the police find the rotting remains of some organism, they may bring it to the medical examiner for identification. The examiner may determine that the corpse is human (as opposed to being, for example, the remains of a sheep or goat). Thus, we should also accept this principle:

Possibly something is human and dead at a time.

A corollary of this is the principle that it is possible for something to be human and nonliving at a time. (I am inclined to suppose, however, that it is practically impossible for something to be human if it is *never* alive. Humanity at a time seems, not as a matter of conceptual necessity, but as a matter of practical necessity, to require life *at some time.*)

Now we can see the materialist answer to the question about whether someone's history *as a human* might continue past his or her death. It is pretty clear, I think, that Adam's history as a human did continue past his death. After all, he continued to exist as a human corpse after his death (until cremation) and he continued to be human (rather than, for example, canine). So his history as a human continued, too.

Death and Personality

A deeper and more controversial issue concerns the question whether it is possible for someone's history *as a person* to continue past his or her death. In effect, this raises the question whether there are, or can be, "dead people." Is it possible for a corpse to be a person? Closely related to this is the question when someone's history *as a person* begins. This is tantamount to the question whether fetuses are *persons*.

It seems to me that the debate about the personality of fetuses and corpses is largely empty and pointless. I suspect that different debaters use the term 'person' in different and confused ways, so that the doctrine warmly defended by some is conceptually unrelated to the doctrine just as warmly rejected by others. In some cases, I fear, the conceptual background is so confused that no particular doctrine is being affirmed or denied. In this sort of case, "define your terms" seems a good motto. Therefore, I will try to make a useful contribution by defining some terms.

We may start by taking note of what I have called "the biological concept of personality." At least some of the time, when we say that something is a 'person' all we mean is that it is a member of the species *Homo sapiens*. As I mentioned in Chapter 6, the biological concept of personality is not an ability concept. When we say that something is a biological person at some time, we do not indicate any psychological abilities or capacities that it then has. We merely indicate its location in our system of taxonomy; we allocate it to a certain biological species—*Homo sapiens*.

We can now formulate one version of the principle about histories "as persons" and death. That version makes use of the biological concept of personality:

Necessarily, no biological person's history as a biological person extends beyond his or her death.

Since I think Adam continued to exist and to be a biological person after he died, I think this principle is false. In Chapter 6 I presented some reasons for thinking that organisms retain their species membership after their deaths. I mentioned that a collection of dead butterflies still serves to instantiate a collection of butterfly species. Furthermore, if we want to investigate the anatomy peculiar to a certain species, surely it would be natural to dissect a dead member of that species. If the dead object were not a member of the species, how could dissecting it give information about the species?

In addition to the biological concept of personality, there is a psychological concept of personality. Roughly, we can say that something is a psychological person if it has self-conscious intelligence; if it is capable of purposive action; if it instantiates a sufficiently rich psychological profile. Since there are different degrees to which something might have self-conscious intelligence and these other psychological characteristics, it follows that the psychological concept of personality is a matter of degree—one entity may be more of a psychological person than another. One entity may be more of a psychological person at one time than it is at another.[3]

As I pointed out in Chapter 6, the biological concept of personality is independent of the psychological concept of personality. Something can be a biological person without being a psychological person to any degree. An example would be a severely brain-damaged human being—someone who is clearly a member of *Homo sapiens,* but who never develops any self-conscious intelligence. Another example would be a dead member of *Homo sapiens.* Consider again what happened to Adam between t5 and t6. He was terminally comatose. Therefore, he no longer had any self-conscious intelligence. Thus, he no longer was a psychological person to any (nonzero) degree, even though he continued to be a biological person.

In the other direction, I think we will want to say that something can be a psychological person to a high degree without being a biological person. An example of this would be a sufficiently self-conscious and intelligent dolphin or chimpanzee (if there are such) or a psychological person from another planet (again if there are such). Even if in fact all actual psychological persons are biological persons, we must still recognize that there is no need for things to be that way. Psychological personality is conceptually unrelated to biological personality.

It may seem at first that it is impossible for something to be a psychological person to any degree at a time if it is not alive at that time. Thus, we might be inclined to accept:

Necessarily, if something is a psychological person to any nonzero degree at a time, then it is alive at that time.

But further reflection may provoke doubts. Suppose someone were to develop a computer whose internal workings corresponded closely to the relevant internal workings of a human brain. Suppose, in particular, that the computer mimicked the parts of the brain that enable us to have self-conscious intelligence. Then, when turned on, the computer would be a psychological person to some nonzero degree. It would not be alive—at least, it would not exemplify what I have called 'the *biological* concept of life'.

A much less controversial point deserves to be made: it is surely possible for something to be a high-degree psychological person at one time and nonliving at another time. Adam was a full-fledged psychological person during most of his life. He was nonliving— even *dead*—during the period t6 to t7. Thus, according to the materialist view, we must accept:

Possibly, something is a high-degree psychological person at one time, and dead at another time.

I said earlier that I think that Adam, who was a psychological person, continued to exist for a time after he died. But Adam did not continue to exist *as a psychological person* after he died. When he died, he stopped having self-conscious intelligence and the other characteristics definitive of psychological personality. Perhaps this is how it must be:

Necessarily, no psychological person's history as a psychological person extends beyond his or her death.

It would be easy to imagine a case in which Adam's history as a psychological person would be "gappy." For example, suppose he fell into a coma at t2 and then regained consciousness at t3. In this case, it would be correct to say that he temporarily stopped being a psychological person between t2 and t3 when he was in a coma. This suggests a way in which our latest principle might be falsified. Suppose something is a psychological person. Suppose it dies, and thereby stops being a psychological person. Suppose (if this makes any sense) that it then comes back to life, and resumes being a psychological person. In this case, the individual's history as a psychological person would temporarily cease at the time of death, but then would resume at the time of revitalization. This case would show (if it is genuinely possible) that something can be a psychological person after a death. Of course, the example would not show that it is possible for something to be a psychological person at a time when it is dead.

In addition to the biological and the psychological concepts of personality, there is a *legal* concept of personality. Something is a legal person relative to some jurisdiction if, according to the laws of that jurisdiction, it is a bearer of legal rights, duties, and responsibilities. In the United States nowadays, living adult human beings are legal persons. However, it is clear that legal personality does not entail biological life, since corporations, trusts, foundations, and governmental entities are also legal persons, but these are not alive (in the biological sense of the term). Obviously, then, some legal persons are neither biological nor psychological persons. Furthermore, there are undoubtedly jurisdictions in which some biological and psychological persons are not legal persons. The question whether a given entity is a legal person in some jurisdiction is entirely a matter of convention. If the legislature decides to grant something legal personality, they can do it. In this respect, legal personality is different from biological and psychological personality, which are not matters of convention.

It should be obvious that it is possible for something's history *as a legal person* to extend beyond its death. If some legislature chooses to enact the appropriate laws, it can grant legal rights, duties, and responsibilities to dead bodies. The idea is not so farfetched. American courts have determined that dead human bodies deserve more respect than, for example, dead trees.

There is a respected tradition according to which there is also a *moral* concept of personality. Something is allegedly a moral person if it is the bearer of *moral* rights, duties, and responsibilities. It seems clear that something could be a moral person even though it is not a biological, psychological, or legal person. Corporations, assuming them to have moral responsibilities, would be moral persons but not biological or psychological persons. Some slaves might illustrate the fact that someone could be a moral person without being a legal person in any jurisdiction in which he or she lived.

So far as I can discern, there is no interesting connection between the moral concept of personality and the concepts of life and death. Corporations may be moral persons, but they are not (biologically) alive. Sufficiently lowly organisms may be alive, but they are not moral persons. If dead human bodies have the moral right to be treated with respect, then some dead things are moral persons. Thus, something's history *as a moral person* might extend beyond that thing's death.

Now, perhaps, we can understand why the debate about the personality of fetuses and corpses is so confused. There are several different things that might be at issue. Taken in one way, the question amounts to this: Are fetuses and corpses *biological persons?* I think that all human corpses are biological persons. I also think that, insofar as they are members of the human species, fetuses are biological persons.

I am reasonably confident that corpses are not *psychological persons* at all. The vast majority of human corpses were formerly full-fledged psychological persons, but death generally ruins the brain. The victim stops having any amount of self-conscious intelligence. So he or she stops being a psychological person.

I suspect that fetuses start out not being psychological persons at all, but gradually become psychological persons as they develop. Although it would be very hard to prove the point either way, it is reasonable to suppose that normal, healthy, eight-month-old fetuses have plenty of psychological experiences. If so, they are psychological persons to a significant degree. (This and related issues are discussed in Chapter 12.)

As I mentioned earlier, human corpses are already legal persons in the United States. Some jurisdictions have determined that fetuses have certain legal rights. For example, if a mugger attacks a pregnant woman and thereby causes the death of her fetus, he may be liable for manslaughter. Similarly, if the woman herself takes illegal drugs and thereby provides those drugs to the fetus, she may be liable for drug-related child abuse. Since such laws are at least possible, it is clear that there is no barrier to making fetuses legal persons.

As should be obvious, we are here drifting away from issues in metaphysics and toward issues in ethics. Rather than pursue this line of thought here, I prefer to call this discussion to a halt; it will be resumed in Part II.

A Materialist Way of Death

Let us now reconsider the place of death in the materialist conceptual scheme.

Suppose two previously independent material objects (an egg

and a sperm cell) fuse. A certain new material object comes into existence and is alive. Suppose that material object grows and develops steadily for a long time. Suppose it is alive up to some time, t, and then stops being alive. Suppose it is dead at all times after t. Then we may be sure that its death occurred precisely at t. If we use the term to express the biological concept of death, we may then say of this object that it died at t. Thus death, in this view, marks the boundary between a period of time during which a material object has been alive and a period of time during which it will be dead.

In order to be dead, an object must formerly have been alive. But no object can continue to be alive while it is dead. Many dead objects exist, so death is compatible with existence. But many other dead objects no longer exist, so death is also compatible with nonexistence.

So far as we know, every biological person eventually dies. Since, in the materialist view, these biological persons are their bodies, and in most cases the bodies continue to exist after they die and continue to be members of the human species, it would be correct to say that death does not necessarily mark the end of the history of an object as a biological person. A given biological person may continue to exist as a biological person after he or she has died.

But death is profoundly destructive. Brain cells are inevitably ruined by death. Thus, death (when it is permanent) does seem to mark the end of the history of an entity as a psychological person. Although a given psychological person may continue to exist for a time after death, he or she almost certainly will cease to be a psychological person when he or she dies. A rotting corpse no longer has self-conscious intelligence.

II

THE VALUE OF DEATH

One of my central claims is that death is a mystery. I have not claimed that death is a *phenomenological* mystery—that is, I have not claimed that death is mysterious because we cannot know how it feels to be dead. I assume that being dead does not feel like anything to the one who is dead. As I see it, the dead simply have no psychological experiences. I have been defending the view that death is a *conceptual* mystery—that it is impossible to formulate a fully satisfactory philosophical analysis of the concept of death.

Nevertheless, throughout Part I of this book, I have attempted to pull back the corners of the shroud so as to reveal something of death's nature. By discussing death's relations to *life, dying2, existence,* and other concepts to which it is closely related, I tried to mark out death's location in a materialist conceptual scheme. Thus, while I have not said *what* death is, I have tried to say *where* death is, conceptually.

In Part II I turn to the central axiological and normative issues concerning death. The central axiological (or "value-theoretical") question about death is the question whether death is an evil for the one who dies. It may seem obvious that death is a great evil for the one who dies, but Epicureans claim that this is impossible. Part II begins in Chapter 8 with a discussion of the Epicurean argument for this strange doctrine. I reject the Epicurean argument by appeal to a version of what has come to be known as "the deprivation approach." In Chapter 9, I try to develop my view about the evil of death by showing how it can be defended against a variety of objections.

In subsequent chapters, I turn to consideration of the central normative problems concerning death. After showing in Chapter

10 that there is a puzzle about the morality of killing, I try in Chapter 11 to solve that puzzle by developing a novel form of act utilitarianism. In Chapter 12 I extend my solution to a most perplexing sort of killing—the sort that occurs when an abortion is performed. And then in Chapter 13, I turn to moral problems concerning the killing of oneself. I claim that it is sometimes rational to welcome the Reaper.

Let us begin, then, by considering the ancient Epicurean argument for the notion that death cannot be a misfortune for the one who dies.

8

Epicurus and the Evil of Death

Let us begin our reflections on the axiology of death by asking an interesting (if somewhat grim) question: "What are the greatest misfortunes that can befall a person?" I suppose that most of us would list, among the great misfortunes, such things as these: suffering enormous pain, as for example if one is tortured or if one endures some terrible illness; suffering enormous injustice, as for example if one is imprisoned for years for a crime one did not commit or if one is subjected to racial or other unjustifiable discrimination; suffering great humiliation, as for example if one is discovered to be a worthless fraud, or if one is exposed as morally corrupt. There might be some disagreement about these claims, but I think there would be very widespread agreement that I have left out something I surely should have mentioned: death, especially premature death, is almost universally agreed to be one of the greatest misfortunes that can befall a person. Of all the great misfortunes mentioned so far, it is the only one each of us is sure to suffer.

In myth, literature, and art, death is represented as an ugly, menacing figure—the Grim Reaper. The Reaper has been feared and hated for as long as people have recognized his existence. Indeed, we think of the Reaper and what he represents as an especially mysterious, creepy evil—not something merely unpleasant. We find death so horrible that we avert our eyes in its presence; we rush to find a suitable blanket or coat to cover the body so that passersby will not see. In the case of a particularly unusual death, we may be at once fascinated and curious to learn more; but at the same time we are repelled and perhaps ashamed of ourselves for being interested in something so awful. Nothing, it would

127

seem, is more natural than to think that death is one of the worst misfortunes that can befall a person.

Yet there is a long-standing and respected philosophical tradition—Epicureanism—according to which all such attitudes are utterly irrational. Epicureanism was founded by the Greek philosopher Epicurus, who lived from 341 to 270 B.C. and taught in his school, the Garden, in Athens. Epicureans claim that they do not fear or hate death, and they tell us that they do not think that death is a misfortune for the one who dies. They think that ordinary people, who view death as one of the greatest of misfortunes, are in this wholly irrational. This is not just a matter of opinion with Epicureans. They think they can *prove* that death is not a misfortune for the one who dies. Let us look into this strange view.

Epicurus's Argument Against the Evil of Death

One version of one of the most famous arguments for this conclusion was presented by Epicurus in his "Letter to Menoeceus." The relevant passage is as follows:

> Become accustomed to the belief that death is nothing to us. For all good and evil consists in sensation, but death is deprivation of sensation. . . . So death, the most terrifying of ills, is nothing to us, since so long as we exist death is not with us; but when death comes, then we do not exist. It does not then concern either the living or the dead, since for the former it is not, and the latter are no more.

> . . . the wise man neither seeks to escape life nor fears the cessation of life, for neither does life offend him nor does the absence of life seem to be any evil. . . .[1]

In a passage that comes down to us as a mere fragment, Epicurus seems to present a highly compressed version of his argument about the evil of death. In that passage, he says:

> Death is nothing to us; for that which is dissolved is without sensation; and that which lacks sensation is nothing to us.[2]

Lucretius (99–55 B.C.) was a later advocate of Epicureanism and the author of a famous work, *De Rerum Natura* (or *On the Nature of Things*), in which he presents a somewhat inflated poetical statement of the main Epicurean doctrines. He offers what seems to be a slightly windy version of the same argument. It appears in this passage:

> Death therefore to us is nothing, concerns us not a jot, . . . For he whom evil is to befall, must in his own person exist at the very time it comes, if the misery and suffering are haply to have any place at all; but since death precludes this, and forbids him to be, upon whom the ills can be brought, you may be sure that we have nothing to fear after death, and that he who exists not, cannot become miserable, and that it matters not a whit whether he has been born into life at any other time, when immortal death has taken away his mortal life.[3]

While there are obviously important differences among these passages, and it might even be claimed that each of the longer passages contains several different arguments, it seems to me that there is one central argument that is pretty clearly present in all these passages. It is an interesting and puzzling argument. The general drift of the argument is fairly clear. It is based on the idea that once we are dead, we will feel no pain. From this, together with some subsidiary premises, Epicurus seems to derive the conclusion that death is no misfortune for the one who dies. I think that this argument provides the central backing for the Epicurean view about the evil of death.[4]

Let us begin by considering what the argument is supposed to prove. The conclusion of the argument is not entirely clear. It is stated in several different ways. Each is fairly vague: "Death is nothing to us"; "[death] does not concern [us]"; "[to the wise man] the absence of life does not seem to be any evil." In other passages, it appears that the point is that it is irrational to fear death; that the fear of death is empty and "vain." I shall provisionally understand the conclusion to be this:

5. Being dead is not bad for one who is dead.

Two preliminary points of clarification concerning the conclusion: First, let us distinguish between the process—sometimes long and painful—that leads up to death, and the state of being dead itself. As I tried to show in Chapter 5, it is not easy to define dying as a process (or, to avoid confusion, "dying2"). However, everyone will agree that while dying2, people always exist and are often in pain. On the other hand, once they are dead, people are never in pain, and perhaps they do not exist at all. In the passages I have cited, Epicurus does not attempt to show that there is nothing bad about *dying2*—the often painful terminal process that sometimes takes up the final days of life. Dying2 clearly can be a horrible experience, and the victim exists and sometimes suffers throughout. Rather, Epicurus seems to be talking about the state of being dead—the state one enters (if we can call it a state) after the process of dying2 has concluded; the state that takes place when we finally cease to be alive. This, he seems to be saying, is not bad for the one who undergoes it. Let us so understand the conclusion of his argument.

A second preliminary point is that the Epicureans surely do not mean to say that a person's death cannot be bad *for others*. One's friends may of course suffer as a result of one's death. I might suffer because my old friend is now dead. The Epicureans have nothing remarkable to say about this. The argument under consideration here is designed to show only that however bad it may be for others, being dead cannot be bad for the person who is dead. It must be admitted, of course, that if we were all convinced that death is not bad for those who are dead, then the burden of our own grief might be reduced a bit. I would be somewhat relieved if I came to believe that nothing bad has happened to my recently deceased friend. But this is a digression: the main point is that the argument purports to show that death is not a misfortune for the one who dies. With these points about the conclusion out of the way, let us turn to the premises of the Epicurean argument.

One premise in Epicurus's argument seems to be what I have called "the termination thesis." This is the doctrine that when a person dies, then he or she ceases to exist. This doctrine was the central topic of Chapter 6 above. I there tried to explain why I think it is false. However, it seems clear that Epicurus accepted this doctrine and used it as a premise in his argument, for he says near the end of the first quoted passage: "when death comes, then we do not exist." And he also says, in the same context, that the dead ". . . are no more."

Another of the premises is implicit in the claim that "that which is dissolved is without sensation." I take this to mean that once we have gone out of existence (become "dissolved") we have no sensations. Since pain and pleasure are types of sensation, Epicurus undoubtedly means to imply that the nonexistent do not suffer any pain or enjoy any pleasure. In the context of the argument under consideration, the relevant point is that if a person does not exist at a certain time, then he or she does not suffer pain at that time. Although Epicurus does not explicitly assert this premise in the "Letter to Menoeceus," he does state it elsewhere in corresponding passages, and in any case it seems implicit in the Letter. Lucretius seems to be appealing to this premise when he says that "he who exists not, cannot become miserable." Furthermore, it seems an obvious truth. Thus, I have no compunctions about considering it a suppressed premise here.

Another of the premises seems to be a form of *hedonism*, the doctrine that pleasure is the only thing that is good in itself for a person, pain the only thing that is bad in itself for a person. According to this view, other things, such as money or health, are good for a person only insofar as they are connected to his or her pleasure. Similarly, other things, such as poverty or illness, are bad for a person only insofar as they are connected to his or her pain. If these things were stripped of their connections to pleasure and pain, they would be value-neutral. Epicurus's hedonism comes out fairly clearly in his claim that "all good and evil consist in sensation." Remarks Epicurus makes elsewhere confirm that he was indeed a hedonist and that he was inclined to express his hedonism with statements like the one cited. It is not an accident that we describe delicious meals as "Epicurean delights."

I suspect that we naturally take hedonism to be a doctrine about pleasure—the doctrine that the only things that are good in themselves for a person are his or her own pleasurable experiences. But hedonists typically endorse the other side of the coin as well. They also accept the view that the only things that are bad in themselves for a person are his or her own painful experiences. Maybe the Epicurean point is that since being dead is not a painful experience, it therefore cannot be bad for a person. While I have some doubts about attributing this premise to Epicurus, I think it is suggested by his remarks, and in any case it may be instructive to consider a version of the argument in which it appears. So let us consider a preliminary version of the argument:

Epicurus against the evil of death—I

1. Each person stops existing at the moment of death.
2. If (1), then no one feels any pain while dead.
3. If no one feels any pain while dead, then being dead is not a painful experience.
4. If being dead is not a painful experience, then being dead is not bad for the one who is dead.
5. Therefore, being dead is not bad for the one who is dead.

Before turning to evaluation, let us briefly review the premises of the argument. The first premise is based directly on the termination thesis. There can be little doubt that Epicurus relied on it, since he explicitly says that "when death comes, then we do not exist."

The second premise is one that Epicurus does not explicitly state in the Letter but which he does state elsewhere. It seems in any case to be implicit in the Letter. Furthermore, it seems to me to be clearly true. It merely says that if we stop existing at the moment of death, then we don't feel pain while dead. Surely, no one will want to claim that nonexistent persons can feel pain!

The third premise is not explicitly stated in any of the passages but seems in any case to be true. Since the dead experience no pain, being dead cannot be a painful experience for those who are dead.

The fourth premise may seem to be a direct consequence of Epicurus's hedonism. If we assume (with Epicurus and Lucretius) that pain is the only thing that is bad in itself for a person, then we seem to be committed to the conclusion that since being dead is not a painful experience, it is not bad for the one who is dead. (I will consider an objection to this premise momentarily.)

When formulated as I have here formulated it, Epicurus's argument is logically valid. That is, in virtue of the logical form of the argument, if all the premises are true, then the conclusion must be true as well. Anyone who accepts all these premises but denies the conclusion contradicts him- or herself. So anyone who accepts all of these premises is committed to the Epicurean conclusion that being dead is not bad for the one who is dead. But, of course, we have yet to determine whether the premises are in fact true. Let us now turn to that project.

Difficulties for the First Version of the Argument

While I might want to raise various quibbles about various other premises, I want at the outset to focus on line (4), since it seems to me that this premise depends on a fundamental confusion. A central component of hedonism, as I formulated it above, is the view that painful experiences are the only things that are *intrinsically* bad for a person. That is, only pains are bad "in themselves" for a person. This view is consistent with the view that many other things can be bad for a person—so long as these other things are not *intrinsically* bad. Other bad things will be said to be *extrinsically* bad for a person. Thus, a hedonist surely can say that illness, poverty, injustice, and ignorance (to mention just a few obvious evils) are great evils for a person. But these things are not *intrinsic* evils according to hedonism. Their evil is derivative. They are evil only because they happen to be connected to pain.

To see the importance of the distinction, it may be instructive to recall some other Epicurean doctrines. Epicurus frequently insists that overindulgence in food or drink is on the whole a bad thing.[5] He realizes that such overindulgence might be quite pleasant. But since it inevitably leads to later pains, and these pains outweigh the immediate pleasures, the overindulgence is judged to be bad for the glutton—not intrinsically of course, since it is admitted to be pleasant. But extrinsically.

To sharpen this point, let us consider a case in which someone eats some tasty candy that has been contaminated with a slow-acting poison. Eating the candy is a pleasant experience. But it will cause serious pain later. A hedonist would not say that eating the candy is *intrinsically* bad for the person (because it is not a painful experience). Indeed, the hedonist will say that eating the candy is associated with many intrinsically good states. But the hedonist can give sense to the statement that it would be bad for someone to eat the candy; he can say that eating the candy is *extrinsically* bad for the person. It is extrinsically bad for the person by virtue of the fact that it is connected with later painful experiences—and these painful experiences will be intrinsically bad for the person.

So there is an important distinction between intrinsic badness and extrinsic badness. Now we must attempt to draw out the relevance of this distinction to the argument. Notice that line (4) says that since being dead is not a painful experience, it is not *bad* for the one who is dead. But what does this 'bad' in line (4) mean? We might take line (4) as a whole to mean that since being dead is not a painful experience, being dead is not *intrinsically* bad for the one who is dead. But then, to maintain the validity of the argument, we would have to take the conclusion to mean that being dead is not *intrinsically* bad for the one who is dead. But this is no news. Most of us who think that death is bad for the one who is dead do not think that death is bad in itself. We think that death is bad for a person because of what it does to him or her; death is bad somehow indirectly by virtue of what it does to us. Surely, no one who accepts hedonism would be inclined to say that death is intrinsically bad.

Furthermore, the claim that death is not intrinsically bad seems to have no bearing on the claim that we shouldn't fear death; or that death is "nothing to us"; since obviously lots of things that are not intrinsically bad are nevertheless worthy of being feared and are "something" to us. Consider eating poison, for example, or living in a country in which seething racial hatred is about to emerge. All of these things are bad for us, and worthy of our fear, but none of them is intrinsically bad. Once we are clear about the distinction between intrinsic and extrinsic badness, we will be happy to grant that death is not intrinsically bad. Our view all along has been that death is extrinsically bad for the one who is dead.

The second option is to take (4) to mean that since being dead is not a painful experience, being dead is not *extrinsically* bad for the one who is dead. If we understand (4) in this way, then we can understand the conclusion, (5), to be the claim that death is not extrinsically bad for the one who dies. That would be genuinely interesting and controversial, and it would support the further conclusion that death is not bad in any way for the one who dies. However, if we interpret (4) in this second way, it seems obviously false. Lots of things that are not painful experiences are nevertheless extrinsically bad for the one who undergoes them. Consider eating tasty but poisoned candy. Maybe death is like that. Maybe death, while not itself a painful experience, is connected to pain in such a way as to make it extrinsically bad.

My point, then, is this: 'bad' in line (4) of the argument is ambiguous. It might mean 'intrinsically bad'. But in this case the conclusion of the argument is uncontroversial. Most of us are willing to grant that death is not intrinsically bad. On the other hand, 'bad' in (4) might mean 'extrinsically bad'. In this case, (4) is clearly false. So the argument has to be revised.[6]

A New Version of the Argument

A natural reinterpretation of the argument might proceed by appeal to considerations such as these: Eating poisoned candy is bad for a person because it leads to, or causes, later pains. The same is true of gluttony or overindulgence. We might suppose that all extrinsic evils are like this. We might maintain that whenever something is extrinsically bad for a person, it is extrinsically bad for him or her because it leads to later pains. Since it will play an important role in the discussion to follow, let us take special note of this principle, which we can call "the causal hypothesis":

> CP: If something is extrinsically bad for a person, then it is bad for him or her because it leads to later intrinsic bads for him or her.

If CP is correct, then we can readily formulate a new version of the Epicurean argument for the conclusion that death cannot be extrinsically bad for anyone. Anything caused by someone's death must occur later than his or her death. But once he or she is dead, a person can never again suffer pains. Thus, a person's death cannot be the cause of any of his or her pains. Given CP, our new principle about the relation between intrinsic and extrinsic evil, it follows that death cannot be extrinsically bad for anyone. Let us attempt to reformulate the argument, making use of this line of thought.

Epicurus on the evil of death—II

1. Each person stops existing at the moment of death.[7]
2. If (1), then no one feels any pain while dead.
3. If no one feels any pain while dead, then death does not lead to anything intrinsically bad for the one who dies.
4. If death does not lead to anything intrinsically bad for the one who is dead, then death is not extrinsically bad for the one who is dead.
5. Therefore, death is not extrinsically bad for the one who is dead.

Once again, let us review the premises. Line (1) is just the termination thesis. It will not be debated here.

Line (2) seems obvious. If you do not exist at a time, you do not feel pain then. I will not debate (2) either.

Line (3) is a new premise. It is based directly on Epicurus's hedonistic thesis that pain is the only intrinsic evil for a person. Since pains are alleged to be the only intrinsic evils, and these cannot occur once a person is dead, death does not lead to any intrinsic evils for the one who dies. This seems plausible, once we grant the hedonistic assumption (and the assumption that we never live again after death). For present purposes, I grant both assumptions.

Line (4) is based on the causal principle, CP. According to that view, something is extrinsically bad for a person only if it leads to, or causes, things that are intrinsically bad for that person. So if death does not lead to, or cause, anything intrinsically bad for the one who dies, it cannot be extrinsically bad for the one who dies. That is what (4) says. It seems to make sense.

The conclusion of the argument is now the controversial and interesting claim that death is not extrinsically bad for the one who dies. Since I have already granted that death is not intrinsically bad for the one who dies, this conclusion is important. If it is established, we will be forced to agree that death is not bad in any way for the one who dies. I find that further conclusion unacceptable.

The Fallacy in the New Version

My own view is that this version of the argument is also fallacious. The fallacy is in line (4). As I see it, line (4) is based on a faulty conception of the relation between intrinsic and extrinsic evil. That faulty conception is embodied in the causal hypothesis itself, which says that in order to be extrinsically bad for a person, something must *cause* intrinsic evils for that person. I think this is an overly narrow view. Things can be extrinsically bad for a person for other reasons. Let us consider an example.

Suppose a young man is accepted by two colleges. We can call them College A and College B. After some reflection, he decides to attend College A. Suppose he spends four happy years at College A, but never studies any philosophy—because they do not offer any courses in philosophy at College A. Suppose he never learns anything about philosophy. Suppose, however, that he has outstanding aptitude for philosophy and that he would have enjoyed it enormously if he had been given the opportunity. He goes to his grave never realizing how much enjoyment he missed. If he had not gone to College A, he would have gone to College B, which offers many excellent philosophy courses. He would have become a philosophy major, and his life would have been much happier. In such a case, I would want to say that the fact that he went to College A was a misfortune for this young man. It's a pity; too bad for him. He would have been much happier if he had gone to College B.

For present purposes, one fact about this example is of crucial importance. It is this: although attending College A was bad for this young man, it was not in itself a painful experience, and it did not cause him any pain. Thus, the causal hypothesis is false. Some things are extrinsically bad even though they cause no pain.

Let us consider another example to illustrate the same point. Suppose a girl is born in a strange country—call it Country A. In Country A, they do not permit girls to learn to read and write. In this strange country, girls are taught to do laundry and raise children. Suppose this girl goes through life bearing children and washing laundry. Suppose she is reasonably satisfied, thinking that she has lived as a woman ought to live. She goes to her grave never realizing what she has missed. Suppose also that she had very considerable native talent for poetry—that she would have been a marvelously successful and happy poet if only she had been given the chance. I would want to say that it is a great pity that this woman had not been born in another country. I would say that something very bad happened to her, even though she never suffered any pain as a result.

These two examples illustrate the same point. Some things are bad for us even though they are not themselves painful experiences, and they do not lead to any painful experiences. In each case, as I see it, the thing that is bad for the person is bad for him or her because it deprives the person of pleasures he or she otherwise would have experienced. In the first example, going to College A did not cause our young man any pain. It was bad for him because he would have been happier if he had gone to College B. Similarly in the second example: being born in Country A did not cause the woman any pain. Still, it was very bad for her. She would have been much better off if she had been born elsewhere. Thus, we must reject the causal principle, CP. It is too restrictive.

How Death Can Be Bad for the One Who Dies

It is reasonable to suppose that there is some connection between intrinsic value and extrinsic value. We have seen that the connection cannot be the simple causal connection expressed by CP. My own view is that the connection is more accurately expressed by this principle:

> EI: Something is extrinsically bad for a person if and only if he or she would have been intrinsically better off if it had not taken place.

It should be obvious that EI generates much more plausible results in the two cases I have mentioned. Going to College A is extrinsically bad for the young man in the first example, according to EI, because his life would have contained more pleasure if he had gone elsewhere. The same holds true in the second example. Being born in Country A did not lead to any pain for the woman in that example. But she would have experienced more pleasure if she had been born elsewhere. So CP is false. EI is a more plausible view about the connection between intrinsic and extrinsic evil.

Now let us consider the application of my proposal to the case of death. Suppose a boy is undergoing minor surgery, and as a result of some foul-up with the anesthesia, he dies while unconscious on the table. His death is utterly painless, since it occurs while he is unconscious. Nevertheless, we might think his death is a terrible misfortune for him. My proposal (unlike CP) permits us to say this. We may imagine that he would have been quite happy on the whole for another fifty years if he had not died when he did. Then this boy's life contains less intrinsic value for him, measured hedonistically, than it would have contained if he had not died when he did. Therefore, according to my view (which is summarized in EI), this person's death is extrinsically bad for him even though it is not itself a painful experience, and it causes him no pain.

Notice what I am *not* saying. I am not saying that the boy's death is bad for him because it is a painful experience. That would be absurd. Death is not a sort of pain. Furthermore, I am not saying that his death is bad for him because it leads to, or causes, something intrinsically bad for the boy. I am assuming that pain is the only thing that is intrinsically bad for a person and that this boy cannot possibly suffer any pain while he is dead. So the evil of death cannot be explained in that way. What I am saying is that his death is extrinsically bad for him because his life is on the whole intrinsically less valuable for him than it would have been if he had not died when he in fact died. The evil of death is a matter of *deprivation;* it is bad for a person when it deprives him or her of intrinsic value; if he or she would have been better off if it had not happened.

Now let us return to the second version of Epicurus's argument. Take another look at line (4). It says:

4. If death does not lead to anything intrinsically bad for the one who is dead, then death is not extrinsically bad for the one who is dead.

In my view, this is where Epicurus went wrong. I think Epicurus has shown (given his hedonism) that nothing intrinsically bad happens to a person while he is dead. And I think it is also correct to say that death does not lead to, or cause, any painful experiences for the one who dies. But it is a mistake to conclude that death is not bad for the one who is dead. Death might be very bad for the one who is dead. If death deprives him of a lot of pleasure—the pleasure he would have enjoyed if he had not died—then death might be a huge misfortune for someone. More explicitly, death might be extrinsically bad for the one who is dead even though nothing intrinsically bad happens to him as a result. In my view, death would be extrinsically bad for him if his life would have contained more intrinsic value if he had not died then.

So my view is that Epicurus went wrong in thinking that all he had to prove was that nothing intrinsically bad happens to us once we are dead. He thought that it would follow that "death is nothing to us." Given the traditional causal conception of the connection between intrinsic and extrinsic evil, he would be right. But the traditional conception is mistaken. Things can be extrinsically bad even though they do not cause any intrinsic evil. Depriving us of intrinsic good can make something extrinsically bad as well. And that is why death is extrinsically bad. It is bad (when it is bad) because it deprives us of the intrinsic value we would have enjoyed if it had not taken place.

I would like to conclude this chapter by emphasizing some points of clarification.

1. It may appear that I am claiming that death is always bad for the one who dies. This is in fact not my view, and it is not entailed by my view. My view is that the badness of a given death depends on what would have taken place if that death had not taken place. Consider the case of some very old and unhappy person. Suppose that further life for this person will inevitably contain more pain than pleasure. Suppose he dies peacefully in his sleep. Then his death is not extrinsically bad for him. In fact, it is good for him. Such a death is extrinsically good for the one who dies, according to EI, because he would have been worse off if it had not taken place. His life, as a whole, would have contained more pain if he had lived longer. In such a case, as I see it, death is a blessing. I will consider this issue and its implications further in Chapter 13.

2. Since Epicurus tried to convince us that it is irrational to fear death, and I am denying some Epicurean views, it may appear that I am claiming that we should fear death, or that it is rational for us

to think of death as the Grim Reaper. This is not entailed by my view. Epicurus claimed that death is not bad for the one who dies. He also claimed that we should not fear death. I have debated the first point. I have argued that Epicurus was wrong about the evil of death. According to me, death is sometimes bad for the one who dies. So far as I can tell, nothing follows about whether we should fear death. Perhaps Epicurus was right about the fear of death. Maybe it is never rational to fear death, even though it is sometimes a great misfortune. Nothing I have said here commits me to any view on that topic.

But I am inclined to say this: if the fear of death makes your life worse for you than it would have been if you had not feared death, then the fear of death is also bad for you. You would be better off if you did not fear death. I would recommend, then, that if possible, you stop fearing death. No matter how bad death may be for you, you will be better off if you don't fear it.

3. I have claimed that in many cases, death is very bad for the one who dies. I have also been working within the framework of a hedonistic theory of value. Thus, it might seem that I am committed to the view that being dead is painful for the one who is dead.

Once again, nothing I have said here commits me to any such view. I agree with Epicurus that the dead suffer no pain. Being dead is not painful. Death itself does not lead to any pain. Nevertheless, in my view, death may be bad for the one who dies. It is bad, to repeat, precisely when it deprives the decedent of intrinsic value.

Perhaps there is something useful to be gleaned from Epicurus's remarks. There may be some people who fear death because they suspect that it will be a painful experience. Epicurus convincingly showed that any such person has an utterly irrational fear. Death—genuine death, that is, and not some other event that has been confused with death—will not be painful. If you fear death because you think it will hurt, then your fear is irrational. If possible, you should stop worrying about death. On the other hand, if you fear death and think it will be bad for you because you think it will deprive you of happiness, you might be right. In this case, I think, the fear of death has a perfectly rational basis.

I am by no means the first to have claimed that death can be bad for the one who dies. Nor am I the first to have claimed that the badness of death is primarily a matter of deprivation. The approach is well known.[8] However, many philosophers have claimed that the deprivation approach is unacceptable. They have presented a variety of arguments designed to show that it fails. These objections to the deprivation approach are the subject of Chapter 9.

9

More Puzzles About the Evil of Death

The Puzzles

Death is nothing to Epicureans. They do not fear or hate death. They do not view death as a misfortune for the one who dies. They think death is no worse for the one who dies than is not yet being born for the one who is not yet born. They say that ordinary people who look forward to their deaths with dismay are in this irrational. As we saw in Chapter 8, Epicureans think they can prove their views on these matters to be correct.

In his central argument for these conclusions, Epicurus says:

> So death, the most terrifying of ills, is nothing to us, since so long as we exist, death is not with us; but when death comes, then we do not exist. It does not then concern either the living or the dead, since for the former it is not, and the latter are no more.[1]

As I understand it, the argument is based on several principles. One is the termination thesis, according to which we cease existing when we die. Another is the doctrine that we cannot experience pain when we don't exist. And a final relevant principle is the hedonistic claim that "all good and evil consist in sensation"—pleasures and pains are the only intrinsic goods and evils that can befall a person.

When these principles are combined, we seem to be driven to the conclusion that neither the event of death nor the state of being dead is an evil for the person who dies and then is dead. Roughly, the reasoning is this: when we are in the state of being dead, we no longer exist and so cannot experience pain; a state is bad for a person only if it is painful for him or her; therefore, being dead is not bad for the one who is dead. Similarly, since we will cease to exist when we die, we will not experience any pain after death; an event is bad for a person only if it causes him or her to experience later pain; therefore, the event of a person's death is not bad for that person.

In Chapter 8, I attempted to show that these arguments are unsuccessful. I claimed that each argument is based on a failure to take due account of the distinction between intrinsic and extrinsic badness. I granted that being dead is not a painful experience. Perhaps this shows that being dead is not *intrinsically* bad for the one who is dead. Nevertheless, being dead still might be *extrinsically* bad for him or her. Suppose the one who is dead would have been happy if he or she had been alive. Then being dead deprives him or her of happiness and so is an evil. I also granted that the event of death does not cause, or lead to, later pains for the one who dies. Perhaps this shows that death does not *cause* evil for the decedent. Nevertheless, death might still be extrinsically bad for us because it *deprives* us of the goods we would have experienced if it had not taken place when it did.

This so-called deprivation approach is based on a novel conception of the relation between intrinsic and extrinsic value. According to this conception, something is extrinsically bad for a person to the extent that the person would have been intrinsically better off if it had not taken place. Many who have died would have been intrinsically better off if they had not died when they did. In all such cases, death was extrinsically bad for the one who died; being dead is extrinsically bad for them. Epicureans, I suggested, feel otherwise because they have a faulty conception of the relation between intrinsic and extrinsic evil.

The deprivation approach is not a novelty. Philosophers have been aware of it at least since the time of Epicurus.[2] However, many philosophers find it to be unacceptable. They think that there is something paradoxical, or incoherent, about the deprivation approach. One objection is this: if the deprivation approach is correct, then in many cases being dead is a misfortune for the one who is dead. This seems to imply that a misfortune can happen to a person at a time when the person no longer exists. But this seems impossible. Surely, someone has to be "present" at a time in order to suffer a misfortune then? The complaint seems reasonable. So we have our first puzzle: how can being dead be a misfortune for a person, if she doesn't exist during the time when it takes place?

According to the view proposed in Chapter 8, a person's death is bad for him to the extent that he is thereby deprived of goods. This seems to suggest that in order to find the precise degree of badness of a given death, we have to determine the amount of good and evil the decedent would have experienced if he had lived and compare this with the amount of good and evil he in fact does experience while dead. The badness of the death is the difference between these two values. So the proposed conception of extrinsic value seems to require that we make a certain comparison—a comparison between (a) how well off a person would be if he were to go on living and (b) how well off he would be if he were to die.

The second puzzle about the deprivation approach is that it appears that any such comparison is incoherent.[3] It seems to be, after all, a comparison between (a) the benefits and harms that would come to a person if he were to live; and (b) those that would come to him if he were to die. However, if he doesn't exist after his death, he cannot enjoy or suffer any benefits or harms after death. So there apparently is no second term for the comparison. There is no number that indicates the amount of pleasure minus pain that the dead person experiences while dead. So the required calculation cannot be performed.

Suppose we find some coherent way to formulate the view that a person's death is a misfortune for him because it deprives him of goods. Then we face another Epicurean question: *when* is it a misfortune for him? It seems wrong to say that it is a misfortune for him while he is still alive—for at such times he is not yet dead and death has not yet deprived him of anything. It seems equally wrong to say that it is a misfortune for him after he is dead—for at such times he does not exist. How can he suffer misfortunes then? As Epicurus said, death "does not then concern either the living or the dead, since for the former it is not, and the latter are no more."[4]

Another problem confronts the anti-Epicurean. If we can find a way to say that early death is bad for us because it deprives us of certain goods, then (whether we intended to or not), we probably will have found a coherent way to say that "late birth" also deprives us of certain goods—the goods we would have enjoyed if only we had been born earlier. Yet virtually nobody laments his late birth, or thinks it a misfortune that he wasn't born years or decades earlier. Lucretius presented a forceful statement of this puzzle. He said:

> Think too how the bygone antiquity of everlasting time before our birth was nothing to us. Nature therefore holds this up to us as a mirror of the time yet to come after our death. Is there aught in this that looks appalling, aught that wears an aspect of gloom? Is it not more untroubled than any sleep?[5]

So another puzzle that must be confronted is this: if early death is bad for us because it deprives us of the goods we would have enjoyed if we had died later, then why isn't late birth just as bad for us? After all, it seems to deprive us of the goods we would have enjoyed if we had been born earlier.

Axiological Preliminaries

These questions are troubling. Nevertheless, I think I can answer them. In order to make my proposed answers as clear and useful as possible, I will have to refine the fairly sketchy view presented in Chapter 8. It will be necessary to introduce some distinctions and some terminology. The first concept I must introduce is the concept of the intrinsic value for a person of a life.

There are several different ways in which a person's life might be evaluated. For example, we might want to know the extent to which someone's life benefitted others—how much better off are *we* in virtue of the fact that *he* lived? Thus, even if Mother Theresa does not get much out of life, we may want to evaluate her life by saying that it has been *good for us*.

A different sort of evaluation takes place when we ask how good someone's life is *for him*. When we ask this question, we seem to be asking, roughly, how much intrinsic value did this person receive throughout his life? How much of the things that are good in themselves fell to him? So, for example, if we think that hedonism is true, we may be asking, in effect, how much pleasure and pain this person experienced throughout his life.

It is important to note that when I speak of the value of a life for a person, I am *not* speaking of the amount of value that the person *thinks* he would get from that life; I am speaking of a certain objective value-theoretic fact about the life—a fact about which even the person himself might be mistaken. Thus, someone might think, near the end of his life, that his life had been full of things of great intrinsic value. He might be wrong.

If hedonism is true, then the value of a life for a person is determined in this way: first consider how much pleasure the person experienced throughout her life. Add it up. Then consider how much pain the person experienced throughout her life. Add it up. Then subtract the pain from the pleasure. The hedonic value of the life is the result. If hedonism is true, then the intrinsic value of the life for the person is equal to the hedonic value of the life.

In fact, I do not think that the value of a life should be determined in the simpleminded hedonistic way I have sketched. I am inclined to think that several other factors may contribute to determining how good a life is for a person. Later, in Chapters 10 and 11, I will present the outlines of my view. For now, however, I prefer to proceed on the pretense that hedonism is true. I have several reasons.

First and foremost, there is the historical reason. I am engaged in a debate with Epicurus about the evil of death. Epicurus was a hedonist. Some commentators have suggested that in order to answer Epicurus, we must reject his axiology—that his view about the evil of death is inextricably tied to his hedonism. I think this is a mistake. I want to show that even if we accept the Epicurean axiology, we can still reject his paradoxical conclusion about the evil of death.

A second reason for assuming hedonism is strategic. The central intrinsic value-bearing properties associated with hedonism are ones that a person can have at a time only if he is alive and conscious then. A person cannot experience pleasure or pain at a time if he or she is not alive then. I want to show how death can be an evil for the deceased even if this hedonistic axiology is assumed. Thus, I take myself to be trying to show that death may be an evil for a person even according to an axiology maximally hostile to this notion. If I succeed, it will be fairly easy to see how to extend the solution in the direction of more plausible axiologies.

A final advantage of the hedonistic axiology is its simplicity. If we assume that intrinsic value attaches only to experiences of pleasure and experiences of pain, and we assume that these are in principle subject to unproblematic quantification, then the determination of the value of a life for a person becomes quite straightforwardly a matter of simple arithmetic. To find the value of a person's life, just subtract the amount of pain that person suffers throughout her life from the amount of pleasure she enjoys throughout her life. Although the axiology is admittedly quite crude, its simplicity makes it especially useful for present purposes.

I should also point out that although I think the termination thesis is false (as I tried to show in Chapter 6), I am not going to debate it again here. I acknowledge that some people go out of existence when they die. (For example, consider a person standing at ground zero at the moment of a nuclear blast.) For present purposes, I will make the (for me incredible) assumption that everyone does the same. Once again, I do this in part for historical reasons—Epicurus seems to have accepted this view about death and nonexistence—and in part for strategic reasons. I want to make things hard on myself. I want to try to show how death can be bad for the deceased even on the assumptions (a) that things that affect the value of a person's life can happen to that person only at times when he exists; and (b) that death marks the end of existence for the deceased.

Things That Are Bad for People

The central question here is how a person's death can be bad for him. The claim that someone's death is bad for him is an instance of a more general sort of claim: the claim that something is bad for some person. It would be surprising if it were to turn out that we need two independent accounts of what is meant by statements to the effect that something is bad for someone: one account of the meaning of such a statement when the relevant object is something other than the person's death, and another account of the meaning of such a statement when the relevant object is the person's death.

Surely the statement about death ought to be nothing more than an interesting instance of the general sort of statement. So let us consider the more general question first, and then focus more narrowly on the specific case concerning death. What do we mean when we say that something would be bad for someone?

It seems to me that when we say that something would be bad for someone, we might mean either of two main things. One possibility is that we mean that the thing would be *intrinsically* bad for him. So if someone says that a state of affairs, p, is intrinsically bad for a person, s, he presumably means that p is intrinsically bad, and s is the subject or "recipient" of p. Given our assumed hedonistic axiology, the only things that could be intrinsically bad for someone would be his own pains. Thus, *Dolores suffering pain of intensity 10 from t1 to t3* would be intrinsically bad for Dolores.[6]

On the other hand, when we say that something would be bad for someone, we might mean that it would be *extrinsically* bad for him. At least in some instances, this seems to mean that he would be intrinsically worse off if it were to occur than he would be if it were not to occur; in other words, it means that the life he would lead if it were to happen is intrinsically worse for him than the life he would lead if it were not to happen. In this case, the thing itself might be intrinsically neutral. The relevant consideration would be the extent to which it would lead to or prevent or otherwise be connected with things that are intrinsically bad for the person. Consider an example. Suppose we are interested in the question whether moving to Bolivia would be bad for Dolores. Intuitively, this question seems to be equivalent to the question whether Dolores would be worse off if she were to move to Bolivia than she would be if she were to refrain from moving to Bolivia. Letting 'B' indicate the state of affairs *Dolores moves to Bolivia,* we can say this: B would be extrinsically bad for Dolores if and only if she would be intrinsically worse off if B were true than she would be if B were false. And this, in turn, seems to amount simply to the claim that B would be extrinsically bad for Dolores if and only if the value for Dolores of the life she would lead if she were to go to Bolivia is lower than the value for her of the life she would lead if she were not to go to Bolivia.[7]

Correspondingly, to say that a state of affairs would be extrinsically good for a person is to say that she would be intrinsically better off if it were to occur than she would be if it were to fail to occur. More exactly, it is to say that the intrinsic value for her of the life she would lead if it is true is higher than the intrinsic value for her of the life she would lead if it is false.

If we make use of our assumption that lives have numerical intrinsic values for individuals, then we can say precisely *how bad* or *how good* something would be for someone. Suppose that if Dolores were to move to Bolivia, the rest of her life would be a nightmare. Considering all the pleasures and pains she would ever experience, her life as a whole would have a hedonic rating of +100 points. Thus, the value-for-Dolores of the life she would lead if she were to move to Bolivia is +100. Suppose on the other hand that the value-for-her of the life she would lead if she does not move to Bolivia is +1000. Then she would be 900 units worse off if she were to move to Bolivia. That tells us precisely how bad it would be for her to move to Bolivia. The value-for-her of moving to Bolivia is −900. So the general principle says that to find the extrinsic value for a person of a state of affairs, subtract the value for him of the life he would lead if it is false from the value for him of the life he would lead if it is true.

In its most general form, then, the principle may be formulated as a principle about the extrinsic value (good, bad, or neutral) of states of affairs for persons. The extrinsic value of a state of affairs for a person is the result of subtracting the value-for-him of the life he leads if it does not occur from the value-for-him of the life he leads if it does occur. In other words:

D: The extrinsic value for *S* of *P* = the difference between the intrinsic value for *S* of the life *S* would lead if *P* is true and the intrinsic value for *S* of the life *S* would lead if *P* is false.

The Evil of Death

The application of these ideas to the case of death is straightforward. Recall the case of the boy who died while unconscious on the operating table (discussed in Chapter 8). Suppose we are wondering whether his death was bad for this boy. To find the answer, we must ask about the value for him of the life he leads if he dies when he in fact dies; and we must compare that value to the value for him of the life he would have led if he had not died then. If the life terminated by that death is worse for the boy than the life not terminated by that death, then his death on that operating table was extrinsically bad for him; otherwise, not.

Let's consider another typical example to see how this works in the case of one's own death. Suppose I am thinking of taking an airplane trip to Europe. Suppose I'm worried about accidents, hijackings, sabotage, etc. I think I might die en route. I think this would be bad for me. D directs us to consider the life I would lead if I do die en route to Europe on this trip, and to consider the value for me of this life. I see no reason to suppose that interesting parts of my past would be any different in that life from what they are in my actual life. So I assume that all my past pleasures and pains would be unaffected. The main difference (from my perspective) is that in that life I suffer some terminal pain and then a premature death and never live to enjoy my retirement. Let's suppose that that life is worth +500 to me—+500 is the result of subtracting the pain I suffer in that life from the pleasure I enjoy in it. Next, D directs us to consider the life I would lead if I do not die en route to Europe on this trip. The relevant feature of this life is that I do not die a painful and premature death in an airplane accident. Suppose in that life I do live to enjoy the fruits of my retirement. Let's suppose the intrinsic value for me of that life is +1100. Fairly simple calculations then yield the result that my death on this trip would be bad for me. More precisely, the result is that such a death would have a value of −600 for me. It would be a terrible misfortune.

We can see, then, that principle D calculates the extrinsic value of a state of affairs for a person by considering the sort of life he would lead if that state of affairs were to happen and comparing this to the sort of life he would lead if that state of affairs were to fail to happen. Thus, according to D, my death would be bad for me not because it would cause me to suffer pain, and not because it would itself be intrinsically bad for me. Rather, it would be bad for me because it would deprive me of 600 units of pleasure that I would have had if it had not happened when it did. More precisely, it would be extrinsically bad for me because the intrinsic value for me of the life I would lead if were to occur is much lower than the intrinsic value for me of the life I would lead if it were to fail to occur.

Some Proposed Answers

At the beginning of this chapter, I mentioned four puzzles about the evil of death. These were prompted by the Epicurean challenge. I will now attempt to answer those questions.

The first question was the question how, given that he doesn't exist after he dies, a person's being dead can be a misfortune for him. The simple answer is this: a state of affairs can be extrinsically bad for a person whether it occurs before he exists, while he exists, or after he exists. The only requirement is that the value of the life he leads if it occurs is lower than the value of the life he leads if it does not occur. It may be interesting to consider an example in which something bad for a person occurs *before* the person exists. Suppose my father lost his job shortly before I was conceived. Suppose that as a result of the loss of his job, my parents had to move to another town, and that I was therefore raised in a bad neighborhood and had to attend worse schools. I would have been happier if he had not lost his job when he did. In this case, the fact that my father lost his job was bad for me, even though I did not yet exist when it occurred. It was bad for me because the value-for-me of the life I would have led if he had not lost his job is greater than the value-for-me of my actual life (which, on the assumption, is the life I would have led if he did lose his job). The same may be true of cases involving things that will happen after I cease to exist (although, of course, such cases will illustrate *deprivation* of happiness, rather than *causation* of unhappiness).

It should be clear, then, that a person does not have to exist at a time when something extrinsically bad for him occurs. Given our hedonistic axiology, it would be correct to say that nothing *intrinsically* bad can happen to a person at a time unless he exists at that time. You cannot suffer pains at a time unless you exist then. However, even on the same axiology, the *extrinsic* value version of the thesis is not true. That is, it would not be correct to say that nothing *extrinsically* bad for a person can happen at a time unless he exists at that time. Perhaps some Epicureans have been misled because they failed to recognize the importance of the distinction between intrinsic and extrinsic value.[8]

The second puzzle concerns an allegedly illegitimate comparison. It may seem that I am maintaining that when a person's death is bad for him, it is bad for him because he is worse off being dead than he would have been if he had stayed alive. Yet this suggests that there is some degree of "bad-offness" that he endures while dead. However, since he doesn't exist while he is dead, he can have no degress of "bad-offness" then. The question, then, is this: does my answer presuppose an illegitimate comparison?

My answer presupposes no such comparison. I am not proposing that we compare the amount of intrinsic value a person receives during life to the amount of intrinsic value he receives while dead. I have assumed that the value for a person of a life is determined entirely by pleasures and pains that he feels during that life. Thus, the comparison is a comparison between the value for a person of one possible life (calculated entirely by appeal to what happens to him during that life) and the value for the person of some other possible life (also calculated entirely by appeal to what happens to that person during that life). I have provisionally agreed that nothing intrinsically good or bad can happen to a person at times when he does not exist.

In effect, then, my proposal is based on what has been called a "life-life comparison."[9] So, for example, consider the example concerning my imagined death en route to Europe. My proposal requires us to compare the value for me of two lives—the life I would lead if I were to die on the plane trip and the life I would lead if I were not to die on the plane trip. Since (according to our assumptions) the shorter life is less good for me, my death on that trip would be correspondingly bad for me.

The third puzzle was a puzzle about dates. I have claimed that a person's death may be bad for her because it deprives her of the pleasures she would have enjoyed if she had lived. One may be puzzled about just *when* this misfortune occurs. The problem is that we may not want to say that her death is bad for her during her life, for she is not yet dead. Equally, we may not want to say that it is bad for her after her death, for she does not exist then.

In order to understand my answer to this question, we must look more closely into the question. Suppose a certain girl died in her youth. We are not concerned here about any puzzle about the date of her death. We may suppose we know that. Thus, in one sense, we know precisely when the misfortune occurred. Nor are we concerned about the dates of any pains she suffered as a result of that death. We assume that there are none. The present question is rather a question about when her death is a misfortune for her. If Lindsay is the girl, and E is the state of affairs of *Lindsay dying at 4:00 A.M. on December 7, 1987,* then the question is this: "precisely when is E bad for Lindsay?" I have proposed an account of the evil of death. According to that account, when we say that E is bad for Lindsay, we mean that the value-for-her of the life she leads where E occurs is lower than the value-for-her of the life she would have led if E had not taken place. So our question comes to this: "Precisely *when* is it the case that the value-for-Lindsay of the life she leads in which E occurs is lower than the value-for-her of the life she leads if E does not occur?"

It seems clear to me that the answer to this question must be "eternally." For when we say that her death is bad for her, we are really expressing a complex fact about the relative values of two possible lives. It seems clear that if these possible lives stand in a certain value relation, then (given that they stand in this relation at any time) they stand in that relation not only when Lindsay exists, but at times when she doesn't. If there were a God, and it had been thinking about which possible life to give to Lindsay, it would have seen prior to creation that E would be bad for Lindsay. In other words, it would have seen that the value-for-Lindsay of the life in which E occurs is significantly lower than the value-for-Lindsay of the relevant life in which E does not occur. And it would have seen this even though Lindsay did not yet exist at that pre-creation moment.

A final puzzle concerns the fact that we feel that early death is a greater misfortune for the prematurely deceased than is "late birth" for the late born. Why is this?

Suppose Claudette was born in 1950 and will die somewhat prematurely in 2000 as a result of an accident. We may want to say that her premature death will be a misfortune for her. Consider the life she would lead (call it L2) in which she does not die prematurely. Suppose that in L2 she lives happily until 2035. Since she has thirty-five extra years of happiness in L2, the value for her of that life is higher than the value for her of her actual life (or L1). D yields the result that her premature death is extrinsically bad for her. But now consider the claim that Claudette suffered an equal misfortune in not having been born in 1915. This fact seems to deprive her of thirty-five happy years too—the years from 1915 to 1950 when she was in fact born. Yet we feel uncomfortable with the idea that her late birth is as great a misfortune for Claudette as her premature death. Why is this?

Consider the state of affairs of *Claudette being born in 1915.* Call it "B." In Claudette's actual life B is false. Consider the life she would lead if B were true. (In other words, consider what would have happened if Claudette had been born 35 years earlier.) Call this life L3. I see no reason to suppose that Claudette lives any longer in L3 than she does in her actual life. Any such change in life span strikes me as being superfluous. I am inclined to suppose that the value for Claudette of L3 is slightly lower than the value for her of her actual life—after all, in L3 she probably endures hard times during the Great Depression, and maybe even catches measles, whooping cough, and other diseases that were rampant in those days. The twenties and thirties were not such fabulous decades for children. If she has just fifty years to live, she's better off living them in the second half of the twentieth century, rather than thirty-five years earlier.

I think the reply to Lucretius's challenge is thus based on an asymmetry between past and future. When we are asked to consider what would happen if Claudette were to die later, we hold her birth date constant. It has already occurred, and we tend to think that unnecessary differences in past history are big differences between lives. Thus, it is more natural to suppose that if she were to die later, it would be because she lives longer. On the other hand, when we are asked to consider what would have happened if she had been born earlier, we do not hold her death date constant. Instead, we hold her life span constant, and adjust the death date so as to accommodate itself to the earlier birth date.[10]

Someone might claim that I have made an unfair comparison. They might want to insist on holding life spans constant. They might say that Claudette would be better off living longer if the extra time is tacked on to the end of her life. They might say that Claudette would not be any better off if the extra time were tacked on to the beginning of her life. (That is, if she were born in 1915 instead of 1950 but lived until 2000 anyway.) The question is vexed, since it is hard to discern values for Claudette of the relevant possible lives. My own inclination is to say that if she lives eighty-five happy years in each life, then the value for her of the one is equal to the value for her of the other. In this case, I can't see why anyone would think it would be better for her to have the thirty-five years tacked on at the end of her life rather than at the beginning. When the comparison is fair, principle D generates the correct results.

Conclusions

I have claimed that there is nothing paradoxical or incoherent about the idea that death may be bad for the one who dies. My explanation of the evil of death is a version of the traditional view that death is bad for the decedent (when it is bad for him) primarily because it deprives him of the goods he would have enjoyed if he had lived. But the deprivation approach generates further puzzles. In this chapter I have attempted to formulate coherent answers to four such puzzles. I have attempted to provide my answers within a fundamentally Epicurean framework. I have assumed that hedonism is true, and I have assumed that people go out of existence when they die. I have attempted to show that even if we grant these implausible assumptions, we can still answer these objections to the deprivation approach. There is nothing incoherent about the naive view that death can be an evil for the deceased.

Thus, I have attempted to show that if we formulate our account properly, we can provide satisfactory answers to these puzzling questions: "How can death be bad for the deceased if she doesn't exist when it takes place?", "When is death bad for the deceased?", "Is there an illegitimate comparison between values accruing to the living and values accruing to the dead?", and "Why is early death worse than late birth?"

Since I have claimed that death can be bad for the one who dies, it may seem that I am now in a position to explain why it is wrong to kill people. But that too turns out to be a bit of a puzzle. It is the topic of Chapter 10.

10

Utilitarianism, Victimism, and the Morality of Killing

"Thou Shalt not Kill"

One of the most widely accepted and intuitively plausible moral principles is "Thou shalt not kill." I take this to mean (or to imply) that it is morally wrong to kill people. It is hard to think of a moral principle with greater immediate credibility. Surely, if any moral principle is true, some version of this one is. Nevertheless, moral philosophers seem to stumble when they attempt to explain or justify this most obvious of moral truths. Utilitarians in particular are in this matter embarrassed, but they are not alone. There is plenty of embarrassment for moral philosophers of all persuasions. This, as I see it, is one of the most notorious scandals of moral philosophy. Moral philosophers have not managed to explain why it is wrong to kill people.

In this chapter, I first devote a little attention to the formulation of the puzzle, and then I attempt to explain why some traditional normative theories apparently fail to account for the wrongness of killing. The first of these theories is a standard version of hedonic act utilitarianism. The second is a theory according to which the wrongness of killing is explained by appeal to the harm it does to its victim. Before turning to the answers, let us consider the question a bit more closely.

It might appear at the outset that we could formulate our question straightforwardly as follows:

Q1: Why is it wrong to kill people?

And it might furthermore appear at the outset that the question is clear enough to permit immediate consideration of some proposed answers. This would be a mistake.

We must at the outset distinguish between *moral* normative appraisal and *legal* normative appraisal. Killing people, under ordinary circumstances, is legally wrong virtually everywhere in the world. It is legally wrong because virtually every jurisdiction has established a law prohibiting killing under ordinary circumstances. I suspect that killing people has been made illegal at least in part because it is so widely felt that it is terribly *morally* wrong to kill people. I am not here directly concerned with the question "Why is it legally wrong to kill people?" The question here is about morality, not law. So we must understand the question to be this:

Q2: Why is it morally wrong to kill people?

It is widely believed that there are "societies." Furthermore, it is widely believed that virtually all of these societies have moral codes—sets of moral principles accepted throughout the society. It is, finally, also widely believed that virtually every society has a moral code that includes a prohibition against killing other people (or at least against killing other members of the society) under ordinary circumstances. This generates an interesting sociological question: "Why has virtually every society adopted a moral code that includes a prohibition against killing?"

However interesting this question may be, it is not the question under consideration here. I do not mean to be raising an empirical question, to be answered by appeal to the scientific methods of sociology, psychology, or sociobiology. Rather, I mean to be raising a philosophical question. I mean to be asking why killing people is morally wrong, not why people have adopted moral codes according to which killing people is morally wrong.

Quite a large part of the philosophical literature on the wrongness of killing seems to me to be marred by a confusion of two importantly different questions. One is a question about the *prima facie* moral wrongness of killing; the other is a question about the *all-in* moral wrongness of killing. Although we may not use this term to express it, we are all familiar with the concept of all-in moral wrongness. If some act of killing is all-in morally wrong, then that act is, from the moral perspective, just plain wrong—that act ought not to be performed. To perform that act would be to do something morally impermissible, something that violates a correct moral principle, something that would not be morally right to do.

On the other hand, 'prima facie morally wrong' is a technical term brought into moral philosophy primarily through the efforts of W. D. Ross.[1] To say that an act of killing is prima facie morally wrong is *not* to say that it appears at first glance to be wrong, nor is it to say that the act is in fact wrong. Ross attempts, in several different ways, to explain what the term does mean. In one passage, he says that an act is prima facie wrong when it has some morally important feature in virtue of which it "tends to be wrong."[2] He goes on to say that any act that has that feature, and that has no other morally relevant feature, would be all-in morally wrong. Ross makes it clear that a single act might be prima facie morally wrong and yet at the same time also prima facie morally obligatory. Thus, for example, suppose a criminal promises to "rub out" a certain enemy. Killing the enemy would be prima facie morally wrong (according to Ross) because it is injurious to the enemy. At the same time, the very same act would be prima facie morally obligatory (according to Ross) because it would be the keeping of a promise.

It is important to recognize that the concept of prima facie moral wrongness (or "PF-wrongness" as I shall say) is vastly weaker than the concept of all in moral wrongness (or "AI-wrongness"). Ross himself points out that virtually every interesting and controversial act is both PF-wrong and PF-obligatory.[3] That is, every such act has some features that tend to make acts wrong and other features that tend to make acts obligatory. So, from the fact that some act would be PF-wrong we cannot infer that it would be AI-wrong; from the fact that it would be PF-obligatory, we cannot infer that it would be AI-obligatory. Facts about the act's PF-normative status, by themselves, do not generate any conclusions about whether it would be AI-right, or AI-wrong, or AI-obligatory to perform the act.

Another important difference between PF-normative statuses and AI-normative statuses is that the PF statuses are always matters of degree, whereas AI-normative statuses seem not to be matters of degree. Ross uses the term 'stringency' to indicate the strength, or intensity, of the PF obligation or prohibition to perform an act. So, while two acts might both be PF-wrong, the PF prohibition against the first might be more stringent than the PF prohibition against the second. Similarly, while two acts might be PF-obligatory, the PF obligation to perform one might be stronger, or more stringent, than the PF obligation to perform the other. This gives Ross the basis for his fundamental moral principle, which is formulated near the end of the following passage:

> It is obvious that any of the acts that we do has countless effects, directly or indirectly on countless people, and the probability is that any act, however [PF] right it be, will have adverse effects . . . on some innocent people. Similarly, any [PF] wrong act will probably have beneficial effects on some deserving people. Every act, therefore, viewed in some aspects, will be prima facie right, and viewed in others, prima facie wrong, and [all-in] right acts can be distinguished from [all-in] wrong acts only as being those which, of all those possible for the agent in the circumstances, have the greatest balance of prima facie rightness, in those respects in which they are prima facie right, over their prima facie wrongness, in those respects in which they are prima facie wrong.[4]

I think it would be accurate to say that in this passage, Ross affirms his fundamental principle about all-in moral rightness. He apparently means to affirm that an act is all-in morally right if and only if no alternative has a greater balance of PF rightness over PF wrongness. Perhaps the same point could be made by saying that, according to Ross, an act is all-in morally right if and only if no alternative is a more stringent PF obligation. In any case, Ross clearly wants to claim that the AI-moral normative status of an act is determined by the stringency of the PF-normative status of the act, as compared with the stringencies of the PF-normative statuses of its alternatives. So Ross was interested in PF-normative statuses because he thought he could explain AI-normative statuses by appeal to them.[5]

We can see, then, that a Rossian might very well be interested in the question whether killing is PF-wrong. For suppose it could be shown that every killing is PF-wrong. And suppose further that some method could be devised by means of which we could determine the relative stringency of the PF-wrongness of various acts of killing. Then, by appeal to this information and similar information about alternatives, we could formulate a general Rossian principle about the circumstances in which killing is all-in morally wrong. Abstractly, the principle would be that an act of killing is AI-morally wrong if and only if some alternative is a more stringent PF obligation.

On the other hand, suppose we are unwilling to accept anything quite like Ross's view about the relation between PF-normative statuses and AI-normative statuses. Suppose we are dubious about the concept of "tendency to be right"; or about the notion of "relative stringency"; or about the principle that AI-right acts are precisely those that maximize stringency of PF obligation. Then I can see no reason for us to concern ourselves about the question whether killing is PF-wrong. For, even if we could establish beyond the shadow of a doubt that every killing is PF-wrong, this result would have no relevance to the question whether killing is morally right or wrong. Since, in the absence of some linking principle such as the one endorsed by Ross, conclusions about PF-normative status are divorced from conclusions about AI-normative status, it is hard to understand why a non-Rossian would want to exert himself over the question whether killing is PF-wrong. Such results, no matter how conclusive, would have no bearing on what we should do, or why we should do it.

I am interested in questions about the all-in normative status of killing. I want to understand why killing people is all-in morally wrong. I am not a Rossian. Thus, I am not interested in the question whether every act of killing is PF-wrong. In any case, these reflections on Ross and the concept of PF wrongness indicate a further sharpening of the question. I mean to be considering this question:

Q3: Why is it all-in morally wrong to kill people?

(From now on, I will again use 'right', 'wrong', etc., in the ordinary way, to express all-in moral rightness, all-in moral wrongness, etc. I will have nothing further to say about prima facie normative statuses.)

A final preliminary comment: we have reached the point at which it appears that the central question here should be: "Why is it all-in morally wrong to kill people?" This would most naturally be taken as a question about each individual act of killing; it would be the question why each such act is all-in morally wrong. But the question presupposes that each such act is all-in morally wrong, and that is by no means a plausible presupposition. Some acts of killing (e.g., a killing in self-defense when the killer must either kill or be killed) are at least arguably morally permissible. Indeed, some acts of killing seem to be morally obligatory (e.g., the killing of a deranged mass murderer who can be stopped in no other way). So the question must be reformulated.

A natural revision would be this: we could focus on that subset of killings that includes all and only morally wrong killings. We could ask why those acts of killing are morally wrong. In other words, we could formulate our question this way:

> Q4: Why is it all-in morally wrong to kill another person, in any instance in which it is all-in morally wrong to kill another person?

A remaining possible difficulty should be mentioned. Q4 seems to be based on the presupposition that there is precisely one explanation that serves to explain why it is wrong to kill a person in every case in which it is wrong to kill someone. But a "pluralist" might say that different cases require different answers. Perhaps in one case it is wrong to kill someone because it unjustifiably shortens his life; in another case it is wrong to kill someone because doing so will lead to riots and ultimately to the destruction of property and innocent lives; in yet another case it might be wrong to kill someone because some of the evidence given at his trial was perjured.

In spite of the fact that the question could be further sharpened by taking account of this latest point, I propose to stick with Q4. I have two main reasons: first, in what follows I will be presenting critical discussions of several popular views about the morality of killing. According to each of these, there is a certain feature that is shared by every morally wrong act of killing—and this feature serves to explain, in every case, why the act of killing is morally wrong. Thus, none of the theories to be discussed here is pluralist. They all accept the presupposition that stands behind Q4. Secondly, the theory I eventually defend is also "nonpluralist." I accept the presupposition, too.

Let us then turn to a consideration of one of the simplest of serious answers to our question.

Hedonic Act Utilitarianism and the Morality of Killing

According to one of the simplest and most attractive normative theories, whether an act is morally right or not depends entirely on how good or bad its results would be, compared with the results that could have been produced by doing something else instead. According to this view, whenever any act is morally wrong, it is wrong because its results are worse than the results that would have been produced by some alternative. Furthermore, according to the most popular version of the theory, the standard used to evaluate results is *hedonic*—one outcome is better than another if and only if it contains a greater balance of pleasure over pain than the other. This view is *hedonic act utilitarianism*. Before we look into its implications for killing, we must clarify the theory.

Let us assume that whenever a person confronts an interesting moral choice, there are several actions available to her. Each of these is something she can do on that occasion. However, the actions are incompatible with each other, so that she cannot do more than one of them. Finally, whatever she does on that occasion, it must be selected from that group of options. Let us say that these actions constitute the person's "alternatives" on that occasion.

Each of the alternatives would lead to certain consequences— things that would happen if the alternative in question were to be performed. Among these consequences are pleasures and pains that would befall the agent, her victim (if any), bystanders, and others who would be affected by the act. For each alternative, therefore, there is some total amount of pleasure that would be experienced if that alternative were performed. This is not just the pleasure that would be experienced by the one who performs the act. It is the total amount of pleasure that would be experienced by all those who would be affected by the act. Similarly, there is some total amount of pain that would be suffered by all those affected if that alternative were performed. The "hedonic utility" of an alternative is the total amount of pleasure it would produce minus the total amount of pain it would produce.

When we say that an alternative "maximizes hedonic utility," what we mean is that no alternative has greater hedonic utility; in other words, no alternative would produce a greater balance of pleasure over pain for all affected than it would. Or, to put the same point in perhaps simpler terminology, when we say that an alternative maximizes hedonic utility, what we mean is that nothing else the agent could have done instead on that occasion would have made a greater contribution to the world's net balance of pleasure over pain.

So the first theory to be considered here is hedonic act utilitarianism, and it may be formulated as follows:

HAU: An act is morally right if and only if it maximizes hedonic utility.

According to hedonic act utilitarianism (HAU), whenever it is morally wrong to kill someone, it is morally wrong precisely because killing that person fails to maximize hedonic utility; in other words, it is wrong because there was, among the alternatives available to the killer, some other act that would have produced a greater balance of pleasure over pain for all affected persons. Or, to put it more simply, HAU says that when killing is wrong, it is wrong because it makes the world a less pleasant place. Thus we have our first answer to the question about the morality of killing.

HAU-K: An act of killing is morally wrong if and only if it fails to maximize hedonic utility.

In some cases, HAU-K seems to generate suitable results. Here is an example. Suppose a popular, amusing young man works as a clerk at a convenience store. Suppose he is alone in the store one night when a holdup man enters, displays a handgun, and demands all the cash. Suppose the clerk quickly hands over all the money. The holdup man is about to leave the store when he realizes that the clerk will be able to identify him. He reflects on his alternatives. They are as follows:

a1: Shoot and kill the clerk.
a2: Shoot and wound the clerk.
a3: Threaten the clerk, but don't shoot.
a4: Apologize for the whole business, and return the money.

We cannot determine the implications of HAU-K unless we know the relative hedonic utilities of the alternatives in the example. Let us therefore assign some plausible utilities. We start with a1. If the holdup man were to kill the clerk, quite a few people would suffer pain. The clerk himself might endure some pain for a few moments before dying; his friends and family would suffer the pains associated with their grief; other convenience store clerks would suffer the pains of fear—they would be more inclined to worry about their own safety. If the holdup man has any conscience, he too might suffer some pains as a result of a1. These would be the pains of remorse, as he reflects on his miserable behavior. Furthermore, of course, if the holdup man is later apprehended and convicted, he will suffer further pain in jail or perhaps even as he awaits execution on death row. Let us agree, then, that the hedonic utility of a1 is very low—we can use -250 to express this value.

There is no reason to suppose that any of the other alternatives would have such a low hedonic utility. a2 would be pretty painful, since it would lead to the pain associated with being shot, but it would not lead to the pains of grief and fear, and it would be followed (after a brief delay) by all the happiness that the clerk would experience throughout the rest of his life. a3 would be even less painful, since if it were performed, no one would be shot or killed. A4 would clearly lead to the smallest amount of pain. If a4 were performed, no one would be shot or killed; no one would have to live in fear; no one would go to the electric chair. It is the least painful of the holdup man's options.

But the essential fact here is that a1 would not maximize hedonic utility. Surely, some other alternative (probably a4) would make a greater contribution to the world's pleasure/pain balance. Hence, HAU-K implies that it would be morally wrong for the holdup man to kill the clerk. This seems to me to be a satisfactory outcome. HAU-K tells us, in this case, which I call "the case of the popular store clerk," that killing the clerk would be morally wrong; and it furthermore tells us that it would be morally wrong because it would fail to maximize hedonic utility. This may seem plausible.

We can now see that hedonic act utilitarianism provides a straightforward answer to our fundamental question. According to this theory, it is morally wrong to kill another person whenever doing so fails to maximize hedonic utility. So, whenever it is wrong to kill, it is wrong precisely because the potential killer could have made a greater contribution to the world's pleasure/pain balance by doing something else—something that would not involve killing. It is important to take note of the fact that hedonic act utilitarianism implies that it is sometimes morally right to kill another person. According to this theory, it is right to kill when killing would maximize hedonic utility.

Why HAU Fails to Explain the Wrongness of Killing

It has long been recognized that theories relevantly like HAU generate wholly unacceptable results in other cases involving killing.[7] We can see how this can happen if we consider a variant of our first example. The variant is another case in which some potential killer has the option of killing some potential victim. But the new case differs from the first example in certain important ways. Each of these differences is designed to decrease the amount of pain that would be caused by killing.

We noted above that killing the store clerk in the first example has relatively low hedonic utility in part because the clerk was a well-liked person. If he were killed, his many friends would suffer the pains of grief. So let us alter this aspect of the example. Let us instead suppose that the potential victim is a shy, unpopular fellow, with no friends or family. We can imagine that he is a homeless vagrant who wanders inconspicuously from town to town. If he were killed, no one would miss him. Killing him, therefore, would not cause any third party to suffer the pains of grief.

We also assumed in the first example that the clerk himself would suffer some pain as a result of being shot. This pain contributed to the low utility of killing in the first example. Let us therefore change the example in such a way as to avoid this pain, too. Let us suppose now that the killer is a very accurate marksman, and that if he were to shoot the vagrant, he would kill him instantly—the vagrant would die so fast that there would be no time for him to feel any pain.

We can also change the example by supposing that the killer is remorseless and cold-hearted. He would not feel even the slightest twinge of regret about killing the vagrant. Thus, his act would not generate any pain of remorse. On the contrary, we can suppose that he will derive some malicious pleasure from his act of wanton cruelty. While we are at it, we might as well also suppose that the killer will never be caught, and will never suffer any punishment as a result of the crime.

In order to decrease the hedonic utilities of the alternatives to killing, let us assume that the vagrant is not a happy person. Let us assume that he gets very little pleasure out of his dismal existence. Thus, continued life for him will add only a tiny amount to the worldwide balance of pleasure over pain. We can assume that the killer would get more pleasure from killing him than the vagrant would get from continuing to live. Let us call the revised example "the case of the unhappy vagrant."

Let us now consider the hedonic utilities of the alternatives in the new example. In this example, killing the vagrant has a relatively high hedonic utility. The act would cause some pleasure for the killer, and (we may suppose) no pain for anyone. Thus it would have a positive hedonic utility. We can suppose it would be $+50$. Wounding the vagrant would obviously cause a lot of pain for the vagrant, and would not give pleasure to anyone. We can give it a -50. Simply leaving him alone would not be bad, but would also fail to give anyone any significant pleasure. Only the vagrant himself would enjoy this. Give it a $+10$. In this case, HAU generates the conclusion that it would be morally obligatory for the killer to kill the vagrant. The result is so obviously wrong that we may safely conclude that hedonic act utilitarianism fails to account properly for the wrongness of killing.

Theories Based on Harm to the Victim

Utilitarianism says that killing is all in wrong (when it is wrong) because it makes the world as a whole worse. And traditional hedonic utilitarians calculate the value of the world as a whole simply by adding up all the pleasures and pains that would be experienced by everyone. The pleasures and pains experienced by the victim are not given any special treatment. This may seem to be the core of the difficulty. Surely, what makes killing wrong (when it is wrong) must be something about the harm it does to the victim. Indeed, it may appear that a killing that harmed its victim would be wrong even if by some accident it happened to make the world as a whole better. R. E. Ewin stated this point dramatically when he put it this way:

> To think of the wrongness of killing somebody in terms of whether or not it will upset somebody else is to miss completely the somewhat obscure point. The Common Moral Consciousness is quite clear that the reason why it is wrong to kill somebody has something to do with him, not with his mother or maiden aunt.[8]

This is the intuition behind harm-to-the-victim theories of the wrongness of killing. According to these theories, the normative status of an act of killing is determined entirely by its impact on the victim—benefits and harms to third parties are irrelevant.

This sort of view has been defended by many moral philosophers. For example, in a recent article in *The Journal of Philosophy,* Don Marquis says:

> What primarily makes killing wrong is neither its effect on the murderer nor its effect on the victim's friends and relatives, but its effect on the victim. The loss of one's life is one of the greatest losses one can suffer. The loss of one's life deprives one of all the experiences, activities, projects, and enjoyments that would otherwise have constituted one's future. Therefore, killing someone is wrong, primarily because the killing inflicts (one of) the greatest possible losses on the victim.[9]

In order to provide a clear focus for the discussion of this view, let us take a moment to formulate it clearly. Every act of killing has a "victim"—a person who gets killed if the act is performed. Instead of considering the total impact of an act of killing, we could concentrate exclusively upon the impact it will have on its victim. That is, we could consider just the pleasures and pains that would be experienced by the victim of that particular act of killing, if it were performed. Then, to make useful comparisons among alternatives, we could similarly focus, in the case of each alternative to an act of killing, on that alternative's impact on the same person—the one who would be the victim if the killing were performed. Let us say that if we evaluate alternatives in this way, we are ranking them according to their "victim value," rather than according to their total hedonic utility.

Clearly then, if a happy person is killed in some brutal manner, the victim value of the killing may be seriously negative. The victim will suffer a substantial amount of pain while dying and very little pleasure (if any). If the victim would otherwise have lived happily for many years, he is vastly worse off being killed. Thus, the victim value of such a killing will be much lower than the victim value of letting him live.

So, going back to the example concerning the store clerk, we can see that killing him would have a lower victim value than would letting him live, because his life would have contained a much greater balance of pleasure over pain if he had been permitted to live. Obviously, in this example, the clerk fares much better if the holdup man does not kill him. In this case, the clerk gets to live out the rest of his life, which we may suppose will contain quite a lot of pleasure.

According to harm-to-the-victim theories, what is true in this example is universally true. Whenever it is all-in wrong to kill someone, killing that person is all-in morally wrong because it harms the victim; in every such case there is, among the alternatives available to the killer, some act that would have better consequences for the person who would be the victim if the killing were performed. That is, there is something else that the potential killer could do that would lead to better consequences *for the potential victim*. We can state this view about the morality of killing as follows:

HV: An act of killing another person is all-in morally wrong if and only if it fails to maximize victim value.

According to this theory, what makes killing someone morally wrong is the harm done to the victim, and harm is assessed hedonically. So we can restate the answer to our fundamental question in this way: whenever it is all-in morally wrong to kill another person, it is wrong to kill that person because killing him will make him worse off with respect to pleasure and pain than would some alternative.

This hedonic version of the harm-to-the-victim theory generates results that are different from those generated by HAU, and in many cases the results generated by this new theory are far more plausible than those generated by HAU. For example, in the case of the unhappy vagrant, this theory seems to imply that it would be wrong to kill the vagrant. It explains the wrongness of the killing by appeal to the fact that the vagrant himself would be better off if he were allowed to continue to live. Furthermore, according to the hedonic version of the theory, the vagrant is better off because his life will contain a more favorable balance of pleasure over pain if he lives than it will if he is killed. This sort of explanation appears to be consistent with something that sensitive moral judges might say.

And Why They Fail, Too

Unfortunately, harm-to-the-victim theories generate morally unacceptable results in a wide variety of cases. Two sorts of case are especially striking.

The first problem for HV arises from the fact that this theory pays no attention to benefits and harms that will befall individuals other than the potential victim of the killing. In some cases, benefits to third parties are large enough to outweigh harms to the victim. Consider, for example, a case in which a vicious serial murderer has been cornered. Suppose he has taken some hostages and is threatening to kill them unless he is permitted to escape. A police marksman with a high-powered rifle is in a position where he can shoot and kill the murderer. It is certainly possible that the marksman's alternatives might be just these:

a1: Shoot and kill the murderer.
a2: Allow the murderer to escape.

And it furthermore might be the case that the world as a whole would be vastly better off if the marksman were to select a1. For it might be the case that if he were allowed to escape, the serial murderer would go on to engage in dozens of brutal murders, whereas if he were killed on the spot, no further harm would come to anyone. In such circumstances, it is reasonable to suppose that it would be morally permissible to kill the murderer.

However, a theory such as HV requires that when we calculate the obligations of the police marksman, we must disregard all harms and benefits that would befall third parties. We must focus exclusively on harms and benefits that would befall the victim—in this case, a vicious killer himself. Clearly, the killer himself might be much happier if allowed to escape. So the victim value of a1 might be much lower than the victim value of a2. If so, HV tells us that it would be morally wrong for the marksman to kill the murderer; and it would allegedly be wrong despite the fact that if it is not done, he will proceed to kill dozens of innocent third parties. Surely, this is a mistake. In such a case it would be morally right to kill, even though it would be harmful to the victim.

A second sort of case deserves notice. There are plenty of people whose lives contain on balance more pain than pleasure. For example, consider a well-loved woman who endures the chronic pain of some disease such as arthritis. Suppose that in spite of her pain, she wants to go on living, in part because others depend on her. Suppose her doctor has the choice of:

a1: administering a drug that will kill her painlessly.
a2: allowing her to continue to live in pain.

If HV were true, it would be morally obligatory for the doctor to kill his patient, simply because killing her has a higher hedonic victim value than does allowing her to live. But this result is absurd. If she wants to go on living, and others love her and depend on her, it would be monstrous for the doctor simply to take matters into his own hands and terminate her life. Thus we have a second sort of case in which HV generates incorrect moral conclusions.

Harm-to-the-victim theories such as HV seem to me to have two main defects. First, they go wrong because they utterly ignore effects on third parties. In some cases, harm to the victim must be weighed against benefits and harms to others. Sometimes, as in the case involving the serial murderer, it is morally right to kill someone even though he would be better off if allowed to live. Second, our hedonic version of the theory goes wrong because it evaluates harm to the victim entirely by appeal to pleasure and pain. In the example involving the arthritis victim, we saw that it is sometimes morally wrong to kill a person even though continued life for her would contain more pain than pleasure. Perhaps if there were some other way of evaluating benefit and harm, the theory could be made to generate less offensive results. Although other theories have been put forward, perhaps this will suffice to show that there is a problem about the morality of killing. Straightforward hedonic versions of act utilitarianism and victim-valuism clearly fail to explain why it is wrong to kill. In the next chapter, I develop and defend a novel theory that seems to me to be much more plausible.

11

Why Killing Is Wrong

According to the view I will present and defend in this chapter, killing another person is all in morally wrong (when it is wrong) because it makes the world worse; and such killings make the world worse primarily because they unjustly deprive their victims of intrinsic goods that they would have enjoyed if they had not been killed. The theory is a version of act utilitarianism. It differs from hedonic act utilitarianism axiologically—that is, it employs a different method of evaluating outcomes. Pleasures and pains are not the only relevant factors. According to my proposal, outcomes are to be evaluated by appeal to a theory of value that assigns a fundamental place to considerations of *justice*. Justice, in turn, is measured by appeal to the extent to which people get the other intrinsic goods (such as, perhaps, pleasure and life) that they deserve. Since the theory is fairly complicated, it may be a good idea to approach it gradually, by consideration of some preliminary approximations. We start with a part that is already familiar—a component of act utilitarianism.

Ideal Act Utilitarianism

Hedonic act utilitarianism can be split into two components. One is a view about the evaluation of outcomes. According to this view, outcomes are to be evaluated strictly by appeal to the amounts of pleasure and pain that they contain. An outcome is better if and only if it contains a greater overall balance of pleasure over pain. This is the *hedonic* component of hedonic act utilitarianism.

The other component is the part that says that it is morally right to perform an act if and only if no alternative would have a better outcome. This component says, roughly, that it is the relative *goodness* or *badness* of the results that determines the *rightness* or *wrongness* of an action. This is sometimes castigated as the view that "the ends justify the means." It is also known as "ideal act utilitarianism."

When ideal act utilitarianism is combined with hedonism, we get hedonic act utilitarianism. But ideal act utilitarianism can be combined with other value theories so as to generate other, nonhedonic versions of act utilitarianism. Let us consider one fairly simple (and fairly implausible) way in which this can be done. This theory is based on the idea that life itself is the only intrinsic good. I call it "vitalistic act utilitarianism." So far as I know, no one has ever defended it in print. But a number of people have suggested that killing is wrong because life itself is a good, and it is wrong to reduce the world's supply of this good. This intuition stands behind vitalistic act utilitarianism.

Vitalistic Act Utilitarianism

Sometimes people say that "life is sacred." Perhaps they mean that life is good in itself—good, that is, regardless of what it contains. Someone might go on to say that more life is always better than less, again regardless of what it contains. Furthermore, one could say that nothing else is good in itself.

These views generate a view about the evaluation of outcomes. According to this view, one outcome is better than another if and only if it contains more life than the other. This would be "vitalism" in value theory—the view that life itself is the only intrinsic good.

Here's one specifically "humanistic" way to develop vitalism: first we introduce the concept of "individual length of life." A person's individual length of life in an outcome is the total number of years that person lives in that outcome. Next we introduce the concept of "universal length of life." The universal length of life of an outcome is the sum of the individual lengths of life of all the people who would exist if that outcome were to take place. In other words, the universal length of life of an outcome is the number you get if you add together all the numbers representing the individual lengths of life of all the people who would exist if the outcome were to take place.

According to this universal, humanistic form of vitalism, the value of an outcome is entirely determined by its universal length of life; one outcome is better than another if and only if the one contains a greater universal length of life than the other. When we combine this vitalistic axiology with ideal act utilitarianism, we get "vitalistic act utilitarianism". According to vitalistic act utilitarianism, the normative status of each act is determined by the relative size of its outcome's universal length of life. In other words:

> VAU: an act is morally right if and only if its outcome maximizes universal length of life.

According to VAU, we determine the normative status of an action in this way: first we figure out what the alternatives are; then, for each alternative, we figure out how many people would exist if it were performed and how long each of them would live. Then, for each alternative, we add up the individual lengths of life, so as to yield each alternative's universal length of life. If one alternative has highest universal length of life, it is the one we morally ought to perform; if some are tied for first place, each of them is permissible; if an alternative fails in this way to maximize universal length of life, it is judged to be morally wrong. It is forbidden.

Someone might suppose that vitalistic act utilitarianism explains why it is wrong to kill people. The explanation would be simple: it is wrong to kill people because killing them reduces the total amount of human life that gets lived. According to VAU, it is always wrong to reduce the total amount of human life that gets lived. This theory says that our moral obligation is always to maximize this value.

Thus, VAU has this implication concerning the morality of killing:

> VAU-K: An act of killing is morally wrong if and only if it fails to maximize universal length of life.

VAU-K generates plausible results in the cases we have so far considered. In the case of the happy clerk, VAU-K says that it would be wrong to kill the clerk. The explanation is simple: the outcome of killing the clerk contains less life (by the number of years robbed from the clerk by killing him) than each alternative. Hence, according to VAU-K, it would be wrong to kill him. Similarly, in the case of the unhappy vagrant, VAU-K says that it killing would be wrong. In this case the reasoning is the same. If the vagrant is killed, then fewer years of human life get lived. Thus, this outcome is condemned by vitalism, and the act ruled morally wrong by VAU-K.

But it should be obvious that in other cases VAU yields preposterous results. One sort of difficulty arises from the fact that, in any case in which a person's alternatives have no impact on total length of life, VAU says that it makes no moral difference what the person does—each alternative is morally permissible. So, for example, if Jones has the choice of (a) torturing Smith steadily for the next five years; or (b) not torturing him, and if Smith would live just as long in either case, and if there is no third party whose length of life would be affected by Jones's choice, then VAU says that it would be morally permissible for Jones to torture Smith.

Another sort of difficulty arises when a person is in a position to affect the size of the population. In the simplest case, VAU seems to imply that we have a moral obligation to have as many children as possible, no matter how miserable they would be. Our obligation to produce more children continues up to the point where there are so many children that they begin to crowd each other out and thereby shorten their lives.

Reflection on another case helps to emphasize the difficulty. Suppose the Commandant of Condoms is required to select a birth control policy for his nation. Suppose that under one of his choices, the population would become enormous—but because of overcrowding, each person would be miserable. Suppose that under another of his choices, the population would remain relatively modest—but each person would be quite happy. According to VAU, the Commandant of Condoms morally ought to maximize total length of life, regardless of the impact on the level of happiness of the people. So, in the imagined case, the Commandant's duty would be to enforce the policy that would lead to the largest possible population, even though each person would be much less happy.

It should be obvious, then, that there is something profoundly wrong with the purely vitalistic axiology on which VAU is based. Life may be good, but it cannot be the only good. We must not be so obsessed with quantity of life that we forget entirely about quality of life.

Hedono-vitalistic Act Utilitarianism

The fundamental idea behind utilitarianism is that we ought to behave in such a way as to produce the best outcome. In its most popular form, utilitarianism evaluates outcomes by appeal to a hedonic axiology. We have seen that this theory—HAU—generates unacceptable results concerning killing. Similarly for vitalistic act utilitarianism. A natural reaction to these difficulties would be to propose some sort of combination of hedonism and vitalism. That is, we could consider a value theory according to which the value of an outcome is determined by some combination of the amount of pleasure in that outcome and the amount of life in that outcome. Then, perhaps, we will be able to say that other things being equal it is wrong to kill because that reduces the amount of life that gets lived; and furthermore, other things being equal, it is wrong to torture, because that reduces the amount of pleasure that gets experienced. And finally, perhaps, we will be able to say that it is wrong to overpopulate the world with miserable people because, while it does increase the amount of life that gets lived, it more seriously decreases the amount of pleasure that gets experienced.

It is important to notice that I am not proposing the view that an act is morally right if and only if it maximizes *both* hedonic utility and universal length of life. That would be an absurd view, for in some cases no act available to the agent maximizes both of these values. For example, in a case already mentioned, the Commandant of Condoms had his choice of population policies. One would maximize hedonic utility; the other would maximize universal length of life; no alternative available would maximize both. We cannot require the Commandant of Condoms simultaneously to maximize both values, since this is something he cannot do. So we have to be careful about how we formulate the theory.

According to the theory I want to discuss, there are two main sources of positive intrinsic value. Thus, this view is a form of pluralism in axiology. The theory agrees with hedonism in saying that pleasure is intrinsically good. It also agrees with vitalism in saying that life is intrinsically good. I therefore call the view "hedono-vitalism."

Hedono-vitalism is based on the idea that the intrinsic value of an outcome is entirely based on how much pleasure and life it contains. In some cases, one outcome contains lots of life but little pleasure, while another outcome contains lots of pleasure but little life. It must be possible in every such case to find some total that represents the combined value of the life and pleasure in that outcome. Presumably, we are to add the value of the life to the value of the pleasure, so as to indicate the value of the "life + pleasure" in that outcome. Thus, for the theory to make any sense, it must be possible to compare the value derived from an amount of life with the value derived from an amount of pleasure; it must be possible to add together values thus derived from life with values derived from pleasure; and so on. Yet it might seem that life and pleasure are like apples and oranges—their values are incommensurable, and it makes no sense to speak of the maximization of their sum.

I think, however, that certain considerations suggest that values of amounts of life can be weighed against values of amounts of pleasure. Let us look into this.

There are many circumstances in which a person is forced to choose between added life and added pleasure. Whenever a person gets pleasure from engaging in a life-threatening activity, she confronts such a choice. Suppose, for example, that a certain woman really enjoys smoking. Suppose, furthermore, that she knows that if she smokes, she will contract lung cancer and will die young. So if she quits smoking, she will live longer, but she will be less happy. (To simplify the example, we can suppose that she will commit painless suicide shortly after contracting cancer, so there is no extra added pain on this alternative.) We might ask, in a case such as this, "How much extra pleasure would it be reasonable to exchange for (say) a one-year reduction in lifespan?"

Hedono-vitalism presupposes that there is a precise answer to any such question. In other words, hedono-vitalism presupposes that there is a precise rate of exchange between pleasure and life, so that for any amount of either of these valuable items, there is some amount of the other that is just as valuable. If this is right, then it makes sense to speak of the total intrinsic value of the life + pleasure in an outcome.

Hedono-vitalism also presupposes that nothing else has any intrinsic value. Thus, according to this theory, the intrinsic value of an outcome is determined entirely by consideration of the amount of life it contains and the amount of pleasure it contains.

When we combine our new hedono-vitalistic theory of value with ideal act utilitarianism, we get a new normative theory— "hedono-vitalistic act utilitarianism," or HVAU. It is this:

> HVAU: An act is morally right if and only if it maximizes the combination of hedonic utility and universal length of life.

This new theory has some clear and interesting moral implications. Consider a case in which someone faces several alternatives that will have no effect on universal length of life. No matter what he does, just as many people will live and each of them will live just as long. Suppose furthermore that these alternatives will produce different amounts of hedonic utility. Then, in order to maximize the combination of universal length of life and hedonic utility, it is necessary merely to maximize hedonic utility. So, in this sort of case, HVAU yields exactly the same results as hedonic act utilitarianism, for in this sort of case considerations of universal length of life become irrelevant.

A corresponding point holds true in the case in which a person faces a bunch of alternatives that have the same hedonic utility—in order to maximize the combination of hedonic utility and universal length of life, one needs only to maximize universal length of life. In this sort of case, HVAU yields the same normative result as vitalistic act utilitarianism, for in this sort of case considerations of hedonic utility become irrelevant.

There are other cases in which HVAU generates clear results. One is the case in which the alternatives that maximize hedonic utility also maximize universal length of life. So if one of my choices would make people most happy and would also make them live longest, then HVAU says that it is the one I ought to perform. In this sort of case, HVAU agrees with *both* HAU and VAU. Unfortunately, there are some cases in which the implications of HVAU are indeterminate. Since we have not formulated any clear principles concerning the rate of exchange between life and pleasure, it is impossible to determine the implications of HVAU in cases in which alternatives produce varying amounts of life and pleasure, and no alternative that maximizes one of them also maximizes the other. To see the problem more clearly, recall the case of the Commandant of Condoms who was thinking of introducing a birth-control policy. Suppose one policy would yield a population of one million, each living seventy-five years. Suppose also that these people would be miserable—each barely scraping by. Suppose the other policy would yield a population of five hundred thousand, each living seventy-five years, but suppose each member of this smaller population would be very happy. Clearly, the first policy maximizes universal length of life, and we can suppose the second policy maximizes hedonic utility. In the absence of a principle concerning the rate of exchange, we simply cannot tell which maximizes the combination of these values. This is a defect in hedono-vitalistic act utilitarianism, and it makes it harder to figure out the theory's normative implications in certain cases.

In spite of this difficulty, hedono-vitalistic act utilitarianism generates clear results in some cases, and some of these results are clearly more attractive than those generated by HAU or VAU. Consider, for example, the case in which Jones has the choice of (a) torturing Smith; or (b) not doing so. Assume that neither alternative has any effect on universal length of life. Then, as we saw earlier, vitalistic act utilitarianism says (absurdly) that it makes no moral difference which Jones does. HVAU, on the other hand, says that it would be wrong to torture, because it would generate needless pain.

Similarly, consider the case (discussed above in Chapter 10) in which some homeless vagrant is destined for a life of minimal pleasure. No matter what we do for him, he is not going to experience any significant amount of pleasure in the rest of his life. Furthermore, he is entirely friendless, so that if he were killed, no one would miss him. Finally, the killer is utterly remorseless and a very good marksman—he won't feel so much as a pang of regret if he kills the vagrant, and the vagrant will die so quickly that he will feel no pain. Hedonistic act utilitarianism seems to imply that, in a case such as this, it is morally permissible for the killer to kill the vagrant. This is an absurd consequence. Hedono-vitalistic act utilitarianism does not have this implication. Since the vagrant will have a shorter life if he is killed, HVAU says it would be wrong to kill him, even though he will experience very little pleasure during the rest of his life. Since life itself is an intrinsic good according to this theory, the consequence in which his life is longer is correspondingly better—sufficiently better to insure that it would be wrong for the killer to kill the vagrant (so long as the life spans of others remain unchanged).

Problems for HVAU

In spite of the fact that HVAU generates plausible results in some cases, and is indeterminate in a large range of important cases, I think we know enough about the theory to see that it is false. Let us consider an example that brings out the difficulty.

Suppose a rich man has a serious heart condition. Unless he gets a heart transplant, he will die within six months. He sends his butler out to the nearest convenience store. The butler is not on a shopping trip. His mission is to kill the clerk and return with the body. They plan to remove the clerk's heart and use it to replace the ailing heart of the rich man. A surgeon has agreed to perform the operation for an enormous fee.

Suppose the scheme is very carefully worked out. Suppose furthermore that if they were to kill the clerk and use his heart for transplantation, the rich man would live much longer and would be very happy. He would enjoy a lot of pleasure in the extra years he would then experience. Of course, the clerk would die young. On the other hand, if they do not kill the clerk, then the clerk would live much longer, but (we will assume) he would enjoy relatively little pleasure. In this case, the rich man would die promptly.

In a situation such as this, it might turn out that hedono-vitalism implies that it would be better to kill the clerk. For it might turn out that the total amount of pleasure + life that would take place if the clerk were killed is greater than the total amount of pleasure + life that would take place if he were allowed to live. This would be undeniable in the extreme case in which the amount of pleasure that would be enjoyed is greater if the clerk dies and the rich man lives, *and* the amount of life that gets lived would also be greater if the clerk dies and the rich man lives.

Hedono-vitalistic act utilitarianism implies that in a case such as this, it would be morally obligatory for the butler to kill the store clerk. The obligation arises from the fact that the outcome of that act contains a greater balance of the combination of life and pleasure than does any alternative. This result should strike the reader as morally outrageous. Surely, no sane person thinks that it is obligatory to kill a person whenever doing so will maximize the combination of life and pleasure. Furthermore, I think that there is a certain aspect of the situation that every sane person would point to as the source of the difficulty. We all would say that it would be wrong in such a case to kill the clerk, and it would be wrong because it would be so *unfair*. There would be a huge *injustice* involved in taking life and pleasure (no matter how little) away from the clerk, merely so as to give it to the rich man. This is the central intuition behind the view I mean to defend, "justicism." We now turn to the development of that view.

Justicism

According to hedonism, a state of affairs is better if it contains more pleasure. According to vitalism, a state of affairs is better if it contains more life. According to hedono-vitalism, a state of affairs is better if it contains more pleasure + life.

But another option would be to say that the value of a state of affairs depends not on the raw amounts of pleasure and life it contains, but on the quality of the "fit" between the amounts of pleasure and life people receive and the amounts of these goods that they deserve. So, in this view, if people deserve a lot of life and pleasure, and they get a lot of life and pleasure, then that is very good. On the other hand, if they deserve no life and pleasure, but get a lot of each, then that may be fairly bad.

Let us consider the sort of case that serves to emphasize the difference between justicism and hedono-vitalism: suppose a fixed amount of life and pleasure is going to be enjoyed. Suppose some people deserve a lot of life and pleasure, whereas others deserve nothing. In such a case, justicism implies that the total value of the state of affairs depends crucially on how the goods are distributed. If the deserving people get the life and pleasure, while the undeserving people get nothing, then things are exactly as they should be. The whole state of affairs is quite good. On the other hand, if the deserving people get nothing, while the undeserving people get to enjoy all the life and pleasure, then things are not as they should be. The goods have been distributed unfairly. The whole state of affairs is much worse, *even though the total amount of life and pleasure is exactly the same.* Hedono-vitalism, as we have seen, implies that so long as the same amount of life gets lived, and the same amount of pleasure gets experienced, the value of the whole state of affairs remains the same—no matter who lives and who gets the pleasure. I think justicism is the more plausible theory.

In order to flesh out this view, we must say something about the concept of *desert.* Specifically, we must give some attention to the factors that affect the amount of life and pleasure that a person deserves. There are several such factors. Let us briefly consider two here. (A third factor will be introduced in Chapter 12.) First, how much an individual deserves depends in part on how much he or she has already experienced. Consider a case in which just one person will be able to experience some pleasure. Suppose person A has already experienced enormous amounts of pleasure, whereas person B has experienced nothing but pain. Suppose they are otherwise relevantly similar. It is reasonable to think that it is more important to give this new pleasure to B—that by virtue of the small amount B has so far experienced, B is "more deserving." So, even though they contain the same amount of pleasure, the outcome in which B experiences the pleasure is better than the outcome in which A experiences it.

Something similar seems to happen in the case involving not pleasure, but life itself. We may agree that something very bad happens when an old person dies—even if his death is quite painless. Yet many would hold that something even worse happens when a young person dies. Perhaps this intuition is based in part on the notion that the old person has already enjoyed his fair share of life, whereas the young person has been short-changed. If we accept this sort of view, we will say that the amount of life that a person deserves depends at least in part on how much life he or she has already experienced.

A second important factor is past behavior. Consider another case in which just one person will be able to experience some pleasure. Suppose person A has behaved miserably throughout his life, whereas person B has behaved admirably. Suppose they are otherwise relevantly similar. So far, they have enjoyed equal amounts of intrinsic good. It is reasonable to think in this case that it is more important to give this new pleasure to B—that by virtue of his admirable past behavior, B is more deserving of the new pleasure. Once again, though the outcomes contain equal amounts of pleasure, the one in which B gets it is better than the one in which A gets it.

We can generalize the intuition behind justicism. We have been assuming that the important intrinsic goods are life and pleasure, while the important intrinsic evil is pain. Some might quarrel about this. They might say that pleasure is really intrinsically worthless; they might say instead that knowledge or freedom (for example) is intrinsically good. In order to present a view that will be most widely acceptable, let us simply bypass the difficult question about what is intrinsically good. Let us instead focus more abstractly on the class of "primary intrinsic goods"—things, whatever they may be, other than justice, that are intrinsically good. (I shall continue to write as if the primary intrinsic goods are in fact pleasure and life, but I do this merely for illustration. The reader is invited to supply his or her own axiological intuitions.)

Now we can say that a person's "individual justice level" in an outcome is the degree to which the amount of primary intrinsic goods he or she gets in that outcome "fits" the amount he or she deserves in that outcome. We can abbreviate this by saying that an individual's justice level in an outcome is the quality of the fit between his "desert level" and his "receipt level" in that outcome. So if I deserve a lot of intrinsic goods and get much less in a certain outcome, then my individual justice level in that outcome is quite low. If I deserve a lot and get a lot, then it is high. If, perhaps because I have already had too much and have behaved miserably, my desert level is negative, but nevertheless my receipt level is positive and quite high, then my individual justice level is low. In this case, I have gotten much more than I deserve. In general, we can say that an individual's justice level in an outcome is highest when what he gets is closest to what he deserves; the value drops off when he gets less than he deserves, and fails to increase when he gets more than he deserves.

Next we can say that the "universal justice level" of an outcome is the sum of the individual justice levels in that outcome. Roughly, the idea is that the universal justice level of an outcome is supposed to be an overall rating that reflects the degree of "fit" between what individuals get in that outcome and what they deserve in that outcome.

Justicism in axiology is the theory that the intrinsic value of an outcome is entirely determined by the universal justice level of that outcome. Thus, according to this view, one outcome is intrinsically better than another if and only if the extent to which individuals get the primary intrinsic goods more closely approximates the extent to which they deserve to get those goods in the one than it does in the other. We determine this degree of approximation by finding the sum of the individual justice levels in that outcome.

Justicized Act Utilitarianism

When we combine justicism with ideal act utilitarianism, we get the view that our moral obligations are determined by the universal justice levels of the outcomes of our alternatives. Loosely, the idea is that we ought to behave in such a way as to maximize the fit between desert levels and receipt levels. We can call this view "justicized act utilitarianism." It can be stated as follows:

JAU: An act is morally right if and only if it maximizes universal justice level.

The theory assigns normative statuses to acts in the following way: first, we must consider all the alternatives to the given act. What else could the agent have done instead? For each alternative, we must consider how much of the primary intrinsic goods (whatever they may be) each person would get if it were performed. We must compare this amount with the amount of primary intrinsic goods that people would in that case deserve, so as to determine how closely each person's receipt level approximates his desert level. Then, for each alternative, we must find the sum that indicates the overall quality of the fit between desert levels and receipt levels in that outcome. That is the universal justice level of that outcome. According to JAU, an act is morally right if no alternative has a greater universal justice level.

Let us reconsider some examples in order to see how this theory is supposed to explain the morality of killing.

The Popular Store Clerk. In the case of the popular store clerk (discussed in Chapter 10), a holdup man was thinking of killing a popular, amusing young convenience store clerk. JAU implies that it would be wrong for the holdup man to kill the clerk. The explanation is straightforward. If the clerk lives, he gets to enjoy the life and pleasure that he deserves. Of course, the holdup man may get to enjoy less pleasure in this outcome. However, that's not bad at all, since the holdup man does not deserve any pleasure. His misery in this outcome does not significantly reduce the total extent to which people get the intrinsic goods they deserve. Therefore, according to justicism, this is a very good outcome.

On the other hand, if the popular store clerk is killed, he does not get the life and pleasure that he deserves. This is extremely bad. Similarly, the clerk's many friends do not get to enjoy his company if he is killed. This also serves to decrease the value of this outcome. The holdup man may get some added pleasure, but since he does not deserve it, that only makes the outcome as a whole worse. So we can see that justicism entails that it would be much worse to kill the clerk, and so it would be morally wrong. This is as it should be.

The Vagrant. The fact that JAU yields an acceptable result in the case of the popular store clerk is not terribly remarkable. Hedonistic, vitalistic, and hedono-vitalistic act utilitarianism yield the same result in that fairly straightforward case. The case of the friendless vagrant is more challenging. Recall that this case is like the first, except that the vagrant is both unhappy and unpopular—he is not going to enjoy much pleasure if he lives, and no one will miss him if he is killed.

Nevertheless, JAU entails that it would be wrong to kill him. It would be wrong primarily because it would deprive him of many years of life that he deserves. If the vagrant is twenty years old, and deserves to live to the age of seventy-five, then killing him is extremely bad—it robs a deserving person of fifty-five years of life. This is quite obviously a huge injustice, and so it is condemned by justicism. Admittedly, if the vagrant lives, his life will not be filled with pleasure; nor will he spread any pleasure among his friends and neighbors, since he is assumed to be boring and friendless. But since life itself is assumed to be a primary good, justicism implies that it is better if the vagrant lives as long as he deserves to live, no matter whether his life is pleasant or not.

Vicious Serial Murderer. In connection with harm-to-the-victimism, I discussed the case of a vicious serial murderer. A police marksman had the choice of (a1) killing this murderer; or (a2) allowing him to go free. We stipulate that if he goes free, the murderer will kill many innocent third parties. If we evaluate outcomes entirely by consideration of the harms and benefits that befall the *victim,* then we have to say that the marksman morally ought not to kill the murderer, because the murderer (in this case, he is the victim) fares better if allowed to go free.

JAU yields vastly more plausible results in this case. JAU bases its decision on consideration of the extent to which *everyone* gets treated justly in each outcome. If the marksman kills the murderer, then the murderer gets what he deserves—no more pleasure; no more life. Similarly, the murderer's potential victims also get what they deserve—full, happy lives. On the other hand, if the marksman fails to kill the murderer, no one gets what he deserves. The murderer himself gets to live (and kill) another day. He does not deserve this, so it is bad. All his further victims are robbed of the life and happiness they deserve. These are further evils. Therefore, allowing the murderer to go free is vastly worse, according to justicism, than killing him. JAU therefore entails (correctly) that the marksman morally ought to kill the serial murderer, even though the murderer will be worse off if this is done.

Arthritis Victim. Some hedonistic versions of victimism seem to imply that the doctor in this example (discussed above in Chapter 10) morally ought to kill the old lady, simply because the remainder of her life contains more pain than pleasure. This seems to be a defect in such theories—especially if the old lady wants to live and if others love her and depend on her in various ways.

Justicism, on the other hand, asks us to consider the fit between desert levels and receipt levels in each outcome. If the old lady is killed, she gets neither further pleasure nor further life, each of which (we may assume) she deserves. So this is very bad. Her friends, who depend on her and want her to live, are robbed of the pleasures she would bring to them. Since they deserve these pleasures, this is also quite bad. On the other hand, if the old lady continues to live, she will at least get the life she deserves (if not the pleasure), and this will be fairly good. Her friends will also have the opportunity to enjoy her company, which they deserve. This too is quite good. Hence, JAU implies that the old lady should be allowed to live, even though continued life will contain more pain than pleasure. Once again, this result seems to me to be more plausible than the result generated by hedonic victimism.

Involuntary Heart Transplant. In this example (discussed above), a rich man is dying of heart disease. He needs a transplant. He sends his butler to the local convenience store to kill the relatively unhappy clerk, whose heart will be used for transplantation. Hedono-vitalism seems to imply that it would be better for the clerk to die, since the rich man will be happier and will live just as long as the clerk would have lived. But surely it cannot be morally obligatory for the butler to kill the clerk.

Justicism generates correct results in this case. If the clerk is killed, he is not robbed of much pleasure—his life would not have been very happy in any case. But he is robbed of fifty-five years of life that he deserved. This is extremely bad. So he gets less of the primary goods than he deserves. The rich man gets extra happiness and life, but since he has gotten these primary goods by killing an innocent person, he does not deserve them. Thus, there is nothing good about his enjoyment of these primary goods. On the whole, then, killing the clerk seems to be quite bad, because it deprives some people of primary goods that they deserve, and it supplies other people with primary goods that they do not deserve.

On the other hand, if the clerk is not killed, things are not as bad. The clerk gets to live the life he deserves, which is good. Admittedly, he does not get to enjoy as much pleasure as he deserves, and that is not so good. The rich man suffers the misfortune of early death, and that is bad too—especially if he deserves in this outcome to live a full life. However, I think we can see that justicism implies that this outcome is on the whole better than the outcome of killing the clerk. The central difference is that in this outcome at least one person gets some of the primary goods he deserves. On the other hand, if the clerk is killed, no one gets what he deserves. So JAU implies that it would be wrong to kill the clerk. This seems right.

I think that further reflection on the cases so far discussed will reveal that JAU generates acceptable results in every case. It therefore seems to provide a plausible answer to the fundamental question about the wrongness of killing. It tells us that it is all-in morally wrong to kill people (when it is wrong) because such killings make the world worse. And they make the world worse primarily because such killings degrade the quality of the fit between desert levels and receipt levels. In typical cases, the harm to the victim is crucial. Generally, killing the victim robs him of added life or pleasure that he deserves. This may be sufficiently bad to outweigh any good produced by killing him. So the wrongness of killing is fundamentally a matter of injustice.

But the theory acknowledges that sometimes it is morally right to kill another person. According to the version presented here, it is right to kill another person whenever doing so enhances the fit between desert and receipt. In the case of the serial murderer, deserving people get more of the life and pleasure they deserve if this madman is killed, and one who deserves less gets less—and so JAU directs the marksman to kill the murderer. Once again, this seems right. Justice requires that this vicious killer be killed.

Any theory that purports to explain the morality of killing must confront a variety of extremely difficult cases. JAU has already been exposed to some of these. But there are even harder cases. One of the hardest is the case of abortion. When a fetus is aborted, something dies. It is not clear that the thing that dies is a person, or even that it is a human being. Perhaps it is only a part of a human being. However, according to JAU, *every* act must be evaluated by appeal to the same standard: the extent to which individuals get to enjoy the primary goods that they deserve. Hence, whether abortion involves killing a person or not, every act of abortion is evaluated by JAU. We will have to consider the implications of the theory for this most controversial sort of killing.

In connection with our consideration of the morality of abortion, we will consider the morality of conception. Whenever a couple confront the decision whether to conceive a child or not, they face something approximating a life-or-death decision. If they conceive, an extra person will live. If they do not conceive, that extra person will not live. (Of course, the extra person will not in that case *die*. It is not entirely clear that he will be "deprived" of life, but he surely will not get to live the life he otherwise would have lived, and that is in some respects like dying.) Thus, we have to consider the implications of our theory for questions of conception; and we have to consider whether these implications are acceptable.

All of these thorny topics are discussed in Chapter 12.

12

Abortion and the Failure to Conceive

It sometimes appears that the quality of our thought on a topic is inversely proportional to the intensity of our emotions concerning that topic. The abortion debate seems to me to be a case in point. Those who are profoundly committed, one way or the other, on the question of the morality of abortion sometimes defend their view with blatantly irrational arguments. So, for example, some advocates of freedom of choice may assert that "a woman has a right to do whatever she wants with her own body." If we sit down in a cool moment to reflect dispassionately on this slogan, it will take about four-tenths of a second to realize that it is obviously false. Consider a fat woman who is annoyed by the whimpering of her neighbor's baby. She could use her body to smother and kill that infant. Surely, except perhaps under the most bizarre of circumstances, she has no right (legal or moral) to do this with her body.

On the other side, those who abhor abortion sometimes say that where life and death are concerned, it is always wrong to "play God." Presumably, they are suggesting a general principle from which it would follow that it is always wrong to act in such a way as to alter God's plans for the size and composition of the population. Presumably, they think that aborting a fetus would in this way thwart God's will. Yet many such people are fertile and married. Each night, when they go to bed, they must either attempt to conceive a child or not. Whatever they do, their behavior will affect the size and composition of the population. Suppose they conceive a child one night. Then they have acted in such a way as to bring a child into existence—a child who would not have existed if they had refrained on that occasion from intercourse. Are they then "playing God"? Suppose they don't conceive a child. Surely then they are "playing God," since, as a result of their decision, some child who would have existed in fact does not exist.

Someone might say that God decides when the couple will conceive a child, and so they are merely doing His will. Of course, it is then open to the advocate of abortion to say that God decides when a fetus shall be aborted, and so abortionists are also only doing God's will.

In order to gain any insight here, we must reject all such slogan-mongering and appeals to emotion. My aim in this chapter is not to affect legislation, or to rally supporters, or to rouse the reader to political action. Rather, it is to attempt to lay out the rationale behind what I take to be a fairly reasonable position about the morality of abortion.

Two features of the literature about the morality of abortion surprise me. One is this: writers often write in such a way as to suggest that abortions are morally homogeneous—that is, they seem to assume that every abortion has the same moral normative status as every other abortion. Thus, some say that every abortion is morally wrong; others say that every abortion is morally indifferent. But it seems to me that it would be far more reasonable to start without any such assumption. Surely we ought at least to consider the possibility that some abortions are morally permissible, whereas others are morally wrong. (Of course, it might be best to have laws that would give all abortions the same *legal* status. That is another question entirely, and one about which I shall have very little to say.)

The second surprising feature of much of the literature on abortion is this: a great deal of it is divorced from reflection on morality in general. Thus, some writers argue vigorously for some view about the morality of abortion, without considering the more general moral principles from which these particular principles would follow. This seems to me almost as pointless as advocating a moral principle concerning how to behave on Tuesdays. Surely, if the principle is to have rational backing, it must be derived from something more general, something that has independent intuitive appeal.

In Chapter 11, I presented and defended a moral principle about killing. According to that principle, killing is all-in morally wrong (when it is wrong) primarily because it makes the world worse;

some other act open to the agent would have had better results. I suggested that the results should be evaluated by appeal to "justicism"—the view that the value of an outcome is entirely determined by the extent to which individuals who exist in that outcome get what they deserve of the primary intrinsic goods. In the case of morally wrong killings, what generally makes the outcome worse is the fact that the killing deprives the victim of life and pleasure that he or she deserves.

This view about killing is a direct consequence of a fully general moral principle—the principle according to which we should always behave in such a way as to make the world as good as we can possibly make it. According to the proposal discussed in Chapter 11, we make the world best when we maximize the quality of the fit between desert levels and receipt levels. This view (with certain refinements) seems to me to be approximately correct. It also has implications for abortion.

My aim in this chapter is to draw out some of these implications, and to attempt to explain why they seem reasonable to me.

Three Examples

In order to provide some focus for the discussion to follow, I want to begin by presenting three examples. The examples are intended to highlight the special features of abortion, by contrasting it to actions otherwise relevantly like it, but differing from it precisely in that these other actions are not *abortions*.

The Murder Example. A young couple have a five-year-old daughter. They are annoyed by the constant whimpering of their child. They decide to kill the child in some painless manner. Due to unusual circumstances, they could get away with it. Furthermore, the parents would feel no remorse. Indeed, they would be happier with the child out of the way.

Let us suppose furthermore that if the child had been permitted to live, she would eventually have outgrown her annoying behavior. She would have gone on to lead a long and happy life.

The Abortion Example. A woman discovers that she is pregnant. She and her husband fear that they would be annoyed by the constant whimpering of their child, if it should be born. They decide that the fetus will be aborted. They do this, and are happier.

Let us furthermore suppose that if the fetus had been permitted to develop and to be born, it would have turned out to be a healthy girl. She would have whimpered quite a lot during infancy, but would eventually have outgrown this annoying behavior. She would have gone on to lead a long and happy life.

The Nonconception Example. A young couple are about to engage in sexual intercourse. They fear that if the woman were to become pregnant, and were to bear a child, that child would whimper a lot, and they would be annoyed. They discover, to their dismay, that no suitable contraceptive devices are available. Accordingly, the couple agree to avoid sexual intercourse on that occasion. So they take separate cold showers instead, and the woman does not become pregnant.

As in the previous example, let us furthermore suppose that if the woman in this example had become pregnant on that occasion, she would later have given birth to a healthy girl. That girl would indeed have whimpered annoyingly during infancy, but would eventually have outgrown the habit. She would have gone on to lead a long and happy life.

The examples are intended to be alike in certain important respects. In each case, the young couple are able to determine whether a certain person gets to live out a long and happy life. If they behave in one way, the child will live seventy-five years and will be reasonably happy. If they behave in another way, the child will not live seventy-five happy years.

The central differences among the examples arise from the "age" of the child at the time of the choice. In the murder example, the parents face this choice at a time when their victim is already five years old; in the abortion example, they face this choice at a time when their "victim" is still a fetus—some would say that she is not yet a person at this time. In the nonconception example, they face the choice at a time when their potential victim does not yet exist. Otherwise, the three examples are intended to be very much alike.

In spite of their similarities, the three examples will surely elicit sharply divergent moral intuitions. Every morally sensitive person will agree that killing the five-year-old in the murder example would be a moral outrage; most will agree that failing to conceive her in the nonconception example would be morally permissible.

On the other hand, morally sensitive people will surely disagree about the abortion example. Some, perhaps noting the similarities to the murder example, will view the abortion as a moral outrage. Others, perhaps noting the similarities to the nonconception example, will view it as morally indifferent.

But it seems to me that the most plausible view is that the abortion example is too vague to be evaluated. It might be felt that if the abortion were to occur during the first week of pregnancy, it would be more like failure to conceive, and not very bad. On the other hand, if it were to occur during the eighth month of pregnancy, it would be more like murder, and accordingly horrendous. If it occurs during the middle of pregnancy, its badness is a function of its date: the later it occurs, the worse it becomes. Since the proposed date of the imagined abortion has not been specified, some would say that we don't know enough about the example to reach a moral conclusion.

Let us briefly consider how these cases would be treated by some of the normative theories we have considered. Hedonistic act utilitarianism tells us that the morally right act is the one that maximizes hedonic utility—in other words, according to this theory, we ought always to behave in such a way as to produce the greatest balance of pleasure over pain.

We have assumed that the daughter in the murder example would go on to lead a long and happy life if she were allowed to live. Let us assume (quite reasonably I think) that her happiness would be sufficient to outweigh any pains to her parents caused by her whimpering. Then, if the case is otherwise unremarkable, HAU implies that it is morally wrong for the parents to kill her; morally obligatory for them to allow her to live. This follows from the assumption that the world will contain more pleasure if she lives than it will contain if she dies. No one could quarrel with this outcome.

HAU has similar implications for the abortion example. Recall once again that the child would lead a long and happy life if she had the chance to live it, and that her happiness would outweigh any pains she would produce. In this case, the hedonic utility of aborting the fetus (at any stage of development) is much lower than the hedonic utility of letting it develop into this child. HAU implies that it would be morally wrong to abort the fetus. Someone might think that this provides a plausible basis for an argument against abortion.

However, HAU seems to have precisely the same implications for the nonconception example. Assuming once again that if the couple were to conceive a child, it would be a healthy girl who would lead a long and happy life, HAU implies that it would be morally wrong for the parents to fail to conceive her; morally obligatory for them to cause her to live. Just as in the previous cases, this follows from the assumption that the world will contain more pleasure if she lives than it will contain if she does not live. Very many people would quarrel with this outcome. Can the mere fact that she would be happy if she were to exist make it morally obligatory to bring this girl into existence? Surely it is far worse to kill an already living child than it is to fail to conceive her in the first place. Hedonic act utilitarianism draws no such distinction.

Vitalistic act utilitarianism evaluates actions by appeal to the amount of human life their outcomes contain. According to this theory, we ought always to act in such a way as to maximize the amount of human life.

In the murder example (given natural assumptions about alternatives) VAU tells us that it would be morally obligatory for the parents to allow their daughter to live. Since the girl lives much longer in that outcome than she does if she is killed at age five, and all other life spans remain constant, the total amount of life is greater (by seventy years) if the parents let her live. VAU them implies that it is their moral obligation to let her live. Once again, this seems reasonable.

Vitalistic act utilitarianism might seem to provide a rationale for the view that abortion is generally wrong. In the abortion example, VAU seems to imply that it is the moral obligation of the parents to see to it that the fetus is not aborted. This is the immediate consequence of the stipulated fact that the total amount of life is greater (this time by about seventy-five years) if she lives than it is if she is aborted.

But "pro-lifers" should not view this as an interesting argument for their position. Given the same natural assumptions about alternatives, VAU yields the very same result in the nonconception example. If the parents conceive a child, she will live for seventy-five years. If they don't, all other life spans will be unaffected. Hence, the total amount of life would be greater (again by about seventy-five years) if the parents conceive the child. VAU implies that it is their moral obligation to bring her into existence. This result seems much less reasonable, since the evil involved in killing an already existing child seems to be *greater* than the evil (if any) done by failing to create her in the first place. Yet if vitalism were true, the reverse would be the case. Since killing the five-year-old deprives her of only seventy years of life, whereas failing to conceive her deprives the world of seventy-five years of life, vitalism says that murder is *less evil* than failure to conceive. This result casts further doubt on VAU, and hence shows that we have no reason to be impressed by its implications for abortion.

Since they seem to me to be pretty obvious, I shall not review the implications of hedono-vitalistic act utilitarianism for these cases.

It may appear, then, that these examples illustrate a stumbling block for every form of utilitarianism. The difficulty seems to be that utilitarianisms are unable to make any sense of the important difference between the case in which someone is killed and the case in which someone never exists in the first place. In both cases, utilitarianism is committed to the view that the normative status of the act is determined by considering the value of the outcome, compared with the values of the outcomes of the alternatives. If we evaluate outcomes by adding up pleasures and pains, then the timing of the act becomes irrelevant. It makes no difference whether we kill the child at age five or prevent her existence entirely. If the hedonic utilities are the same (as they are supposed to be in the examples presented here), the normative status of the acts must be the same. The same is true if we evaluate outcomes by adding up amounts of life, and if we evaluate them by adding up amounts of life + pleasure.

It may appear, then, that utilitarianisms of all forms diverge in a most serious way from some of our firmest moral intuitions concerning killing and failing to conceive. If this is right, then we have no reason to be interested in what utilitarianism tells us about abortion. Since the theory generates clearly unacceptable results in some cases, its results in other, more complicated cases, are of no value. There is no reason to suppose that they might be true.

However, it seems to me that any such harsh evaluation of utilitarianism would be premature. In Chapter 11, I presented and defended a form of utilitarianism that yields interesting and plausible results in a wide variety of examples involving killing. I think that (with some refinements) this theory will be seen to yield interesting and plausible results in the current examples involving killing and nonconception. In light of this success, I think it may be worthwhile to consider what this theory tells us about abortion. Perhaps we can all agree that the theory serves to regiment one family of moral intuitions about abortion. Some may even agree that it serves to articulate the truth about the morality of abortion.

Justicism, Murder, and the Failure to Conceive

According to the normative theory presented in Chapter 11, an action is morally right if and only if it maximizes what I called "universal justice level"—the extent to which the amount of primary intrinsic goods received by individuals approximates the amount of such goods those individuals deserve. For purposes of illustration, I have been assuming that life and pleasure are the main primary intrinsic goods.

Since it tells us always to maximize the good, the view is a form of act utilitarianism. However, it is neither hedonistic nor vitalistic. It does not require us to maximize either pleasure or life. Instead, it requires us to maximize a form of justice. It tells us to behave in such a way as to insure that pleasure and life (or whatever else may be primarily intrinsically good) are distributed as fairly as possible. Those who deserve the primary intrinsic goods are to get, insofar as possible, as much as they deserve; those who deserve none are to get none. The more closely these aims are approximated, the better the outcome.

It should be obvious, then, that "justicism" entails that the killing of the five-year-old would be a horrendous evil. An innocent child is fully deserving of her allotted seventy five years of life and happiness. If the parents deprive her of this—even if they kill her painlessly—they commit a huge injustice. On the other hand, if they allow her to live in peace, she will at least get the life she deserves. In our example, we stipulate that she also will get the happiness she deserves. Since the child's continued existence is assumed to have no detrimental impact on the extent to which others get what they deserve, the value of letting her live, as calculated by justicism, is vastly greater than the value of killing her. So JAU does not permit this sort of killing.

The fact that JAU generates plausible results in this example is hardly cause for rejoicing; every other theory we have considered yields the same results in this relatively straightforward example. What may be more interesting is that JAU yields far more plausible results in the nonconception example. Here JAU diverges from other forms of utilitarianism, which seem to imply that failure to conceive is just as bad as murder. JAU does not have this implication.

According to justicism, in order to determine the value of an outcome we must consider the extent to which the individuals who exist in that outcome get the primary intrinsic goods that they deserve in that outcome. Clearly, if a certain individual does not exist in a certain outcome, she neither deserves anything nor gets anything in that outcome. Her welfare (or lack thereof) has no impact on the value of the outcome. We might say, somewhat paradoxically, that she does not even contribute a "zero" to the calculations—she has no individual justice level at all in that outcome, since she never exists in that outcome.

As we have seen, hedonism and vitalism imply, in our examples, that it would be *better* for the parents to kill the child at age five than it would be for them to fail to conceive her in the first place. In each case, this follows from the fact that if the child lives five years, she gets at least some of the primary intrinsic goods, whereas if she never exists at all, she gets none. Justicism does not have this paradoxical implication. According to justicism, it is far *worse* for the parents to kill the girl. This follows from the stipulated facts that (a) if they kill her, she gets much less life and pleasure than she deserves, and this is a great evil. On the other hand (b) if she never exists, she neither deserves nor gets any life or pleasure. This is assumed to be valueless.

In light of this, JAU makes it morally permissible for the parents to refrain from conceiving this girl. Although the girl would have been happy if she had existed, no injustice is done to anyone who exists if she never exists. This, according to justicism, is the relevant factor. Indeed, it would be better, according to this theory, for the parents to conceive some other child—one whose existence would make a greater overall contribution to the extent to which individuals get the primary intrinsic goods they deserve.

It is clear, then, that even though JAU is a form of act utilitarianism, it does not have the defect shared by HAU, VAU, and HVAU. By virtue of crucial features of its method of evaluating outcomes, JAU implies that killing (in the cases under consideration here) is much worse than failing to conceive. Since JAU generates results that are intuitively plausible in the murder example and the nonconception example, we have reason to be curious about the implications of the theory for the abortion example. Let us then consider the normative consequences of JAU for abortion.

Justicized Act Utilitarianism and the Problem of Abortion

According to JAU, the normative status of any act is determined by the value of its outcome, compared with the values of the outcomes of its alternatives. Values of outcomes, in turn, are determined by the quality of the fit between the desert levels and the receipt levels of the individuals who exist in those outcomes. Abortion is no exception. According to JAU, the normative status of any proposed abortion is determined in exactly the same way.

I have constructed the abortion example in such a way that values accruing to third parties are virtually negligible. We assume that others would deserve and get primary goods at about the same rate, whether the abortion is performed or not. Thus, the fundamental question that must be confronted here concerns just the fetus itself. What share of good or evil is contributed to the world by virtue of its abbreviated existence? We know that the fetus gets only a few weeks or months of life; similarly we can reasonably assume that it gets at best a tiny amount of pleasure. The value of this short existence, then, depends crucially on how much life and pleasure it deserves. Shall we say that the fetus, like the murdered child, deserves a full and happy life? If so, the abortion is worse than the murder of a five-year-old. Indeed, given this view, we seem to be committed to saying that the *earlier* the abortion takes place, the *worse* it is. After all, on this view, earlier abortions deprive fully deserving individuals of *more* of the primary goods. This strikes me as being seriously counterintuitive.

Shall we say instead that the fetus deserves nothing, and hence that its abortion is morally indifferent? This seems to imply that even if we abort the fetus ten minutes before it would have been born, nothing has been deprived of goods it deserves, and so no evil has been done. This too I find impossible to accept. Some sort of compromise must be found.

Earlier, in Chapter 7, I suggested that certain forms of *personality,* or the quality of being a person, are matters of degree. According to one variant of this view (the variant based on the concept of *psychological* personality), the fetus starts out being not a person at all, and that it gradually becomes "slightly personal." As its intellectual and emotional capacities increase, the fetus becomes "more personal." Then, around the time of birth, it becomes a full-fledged person. We might want to consider the idea that the amount of life and pleasure that the fetus deserves at a time depends on how "personal" it is at that time. This would explain why it is not bad at all to abort a day-old fetus but monstrous to abort an eight-month-old fetus.

The basic insight behind this proposal seems to me to be worthy of consideration, but I am not happy with the choice of terminology. I think we confuse the issue and induce needless ambiguity, when we use the word 'person' in this context. One obvious problem is that the term is not ordinarily used to express a property that comes in degrees. Some surely will not be comfortable with the notion that one entity is "more a person" than another. Another difficulty is that the term 'person' seems to me to be ambiguous. As I indicated earlier, I think the term can be used to express at least four different concepts.[1] First, it can be used to express *biological personality,* which I take to be the concept of a human organism. Second, it can be used to express *psychological personality,* which I take to be the concept of an entity with self-conscious intelligence and other psychological characteristics. Third and fourth, it can be used to express the concepts of *legal* and *moral* personality. Since the term is thus multiply ambiguous, I think it would be more fruitful to approach the issue from some other angle.

Suppose two landowners own adjacent parcels of land. Suppose that a nearby nuclear dump has leaked and has contaminated the land beyond repair. Since a government agency was responsible for the contamination, the government has agreed to purchase the land, in each case for a "fair price." Now the question arises: how much do the landowners deserve for their parcels?

The landowners originally paid equal amounts for the parcels. The parcels are identical in size and shape. They also are identical in current market value—each is worthless. It might appear that if the government compensates the landowners equally, it will have compensated them fairly. But there is more to the story.

Let us suppose that one landowner is merely a speculator. He bought the land years ago and has never set foot on it. His plan was simply to "sit on it" until a likely buyer offered a sufficiently high price. The other landowner is a tree farmer. He plowed and cultivated the land; he installed drainage, removed boulders and trees, increased fertility. Let us suppose that he planted a crop of trees, which (were it not for the nuclear contamination) would be ready for harvest only after the passage of several more years. As I see it, the tree farmer deserves more for his land than the speculator deserves for his; this is a simple matter of justice. Furthermore, as I see it, the difference in desert is due to the fact that the farmer made a greater investment, in the form of planning, materials, equipment and labor, than did the speculator. Since the farmer put so much more into his parcel of land, fairness requires that he should get more out of it when the govenrment buys it back.

Something like this may apply to people and their lives. It seems to me that, other things being equal, a person deserves more out of her life if she has "put more into it." Perhaps the point can be illustrated by appeal to an example. Suppose there are two young women. Suppose they are of approximately equal age, and suppose they had approximately equal natural gifts and opportunities. Suppose that one of them has sacrificed and studied and practiced and has developed her talents so that now she is about to begin her career as a scientist, whereas the other allowed her talents to rust—she made nothing of herself.

In these circumstances we might want to say that the first woman has "invested" more in her life than has the second; she has "put more into it," and has not yet had an opportunity to reap the rewards of her investment. Consider now the injustice that would take place if these two women died prematurely. Although obviously a great injustice would occur in each case, there is some plausibility to the notion that the injustice would be greater in the case of the first woman, since, by early death, the she loses a life in which she has made a greater investment.

We can extend this idea to the case of a fetus. We can say that a day-old fetus has not yet had any opportunity to make a very big investment in its life. It has not yet exerted any efforts, undertaken any training, undergone any pains, or even endured any boredom in anticipation of later returns on investment. So far, it has done just about nothing with its life. In virtue of its minuscule investment, it deserves relatively little.

On the other hand, an eight-month-old fetus probably has made a much greater investment. She has endured the boredom of a long, claustrophobic, underwater captivity. She has exerted energy and other resources to the tasks involved in growth and development. Though she has made a substantial investment, she has not yet had an opportunity to enjoy the benefits of her prenatal labors. In light of the fact that she has made a significant commitment to her future life, it is reasonable to maintain that she is fully deserving of the opportunity to enjoy that life. To abort her now would be to perpetrate a huge injustice upon her.

In general, and barring unusual circumstances, I would say that a fetus's investment in its life steadily increases from conception to birth. Obviously, I am not suggesting that each fetus exerts itself with the intention of thereby developing into a mature human being. I suspect that most fetuses (especially during their first few months) haven't the slightest notion of what they are doing, or what the eventual payoff will be. The suggestion is rather that they engage in activities that have a point only insofar as they help to bring the fetus closer to maturity; if the fetus endures these activities for eight long months and then is killed, her efforts are deprived of their point, and she suffers a serious injustice. If the injustice is serious enough, aborting the eight-month-old fetus may be as bad as killing a child.

This rather lengthy discussion of investment and desert may have obscured my main point. Thus, I should restate it. As I see it, a particular abortion is morally right if and only if it maximizes universal justice level—the quality of the "fit" between the amount of primary intrinsic good individuals deserve and the amount they get. If other individuals deserve and get approximately the same share of primary goods whether the abortion takes place or not, then the normative status of an abortion will depend upon its impact on the aborted fetus. Since a day-old fetus has made just a tiny investment in its life, it does not yet deserve much from life. Hence, the injustice involved in aborting it may be relatively small. This evil may fairly easily be counterbalanced by some good that would be enjoyed by the mother, or some other person. On the other hand, since an eight-month-old fetus has made a substantial investment in its life, it fully deserves the opportunity to continue to live. To kill it would be as great an injustice as killing a child. It could not easily be counterbalanced.

This approach does not entail that abortions are morally homogeneous. There are some circumstances in which it would be morally permissible to abort a fetus. Let us consider some of these. Suppose some fetus is badly deformed. Its deformities are so severe that it will surely die shortly after birth. Nothing can be done to make its life long or happy.

In such a case, an evil is done to that fetus if it is aborted. It deserves to live and to be happy. If it is aborted, it will not live and it will never be happy. However, if it is not aborted, it will make an even greater investment in its life. It will struggle and suffer. But its suffering will be pointless, since it will die without reaping any of the rewards of its labors. This will be an even greater injustice. Its parents will surely also suffer pains they do not deserve as they watch their child decline and die. Therefore, although every abortion involves some evil, less evil is done if this fetus is aborted— indeed, in a tragic case such as this, the earlier the abortion, the less bad it will be.

Suppose a girl is raped and becomes pregnant. She has thus endured a terrible experience which she surely did not deserve. That was a great evil. If the fetus is permitted to come to term, and to be born, the girl will suffer further undeserved pain. Indeed, whether she keeps the baby or gives it up for adoption, it is inevitable that she will be further victimized. She fails to enjoy certain pleasures she deserves; she suffers certain pains she does not deserve. This makes the world much worse.

On the other hand, if the fetus is promptly aborted, less evil is done. Admittedly, some further evil is done. The fetus, which deserves a chance to enjoy the primary intrinsic goods, will get none. But if the fetus is aborted early enough, it may be killed at a time when it has not yet made any significant investment in its life. Thus, it may not yet have a very significant claim on that life. If so, the injustice it suffers is relatively small. Once again, it should be aborted; the earlier the better.

The "Right to Life"

It may appear that when I say that some fetus deserves a chance to enjoy the primary intrinsic goods, I am merely saying that the fetus has a "right to life." The appearance is of course heightened by the fact that I have suggested that life is one of the primary intrinsic goods. However, this appearance is seriously misleading. There are important differences between the view proposed here and typical views involving the alleged "right to life."

One difference is this: according to some views about the right to life, it makes no sense to say that one individual has more of the right to life than another, or that the right to life comes in various degrees. However, as I have developed the notion, it does make perfectly good sense to say that one individual deserves the primary intrinsic goods more than another. We are already familiar with the notion that desert is a matter of degree and that justice requires distributions of goods in accordance with desert.

A huge fraction of the literature on abortion is concerned with the question *when* an individual first comes to have the right to life. Obviously, if this right is an "all or nothing" property, then there must be a precise moment when the fetus (or the child) first comes to have it. But, as has so often been pointed out, no moment seems fully appropriate. Neither conception, nor quickening, nor viability, nor birth is sufficiently unproblematic.

On the other hand, since desert admits of degrees, my proposal confronts no such difficulty. It is open to me to say that as the fetus grows and develops, the extent to which it deserves a full and happy life steadily increases. I have no reason to suppose that there is some moment prior to which the fetus deserves nothing, and after which the fetus fully deserves a full life. This accords well with the intuitive notion that the badness of abortions gradually increases through time so that, other things being equal, later abortions are worse than early ones.

A closely related difference is this: those who appeal to an alleged right to life often have a hard time explaining the basis for this right. What justifies the claim that a certain individual has this right? Is it merely the fact that it is capable of living? Why does that give it the right to live? My view, on the other hand, is based on concepts already familiar from our thought about justice. Other things being equal, if an individual puts more into something, he or she deserves more out of it.

Those who speak of the right to life sometimes seem to suggest that if an individual has the right to life, then it is absolutely morally wrong to deprive that individual of life. Thus, this right seems to be absolute. The implication is that once an individual has the right to life, no further considerations could possibly lead us to conclude that it might be permissible for that individual to be killed. Yet we are all familiar with tragic cases in which we want to say both that the fetus has some claim on life, but that this claim conflicts with the claims of the mother, or other interested parties. If, instead of framing the issue in terms of an absolute right to life, we frame it in terms of varying degrees of deservingness of the primary goods, we can accommodate our intuitive sense that conflicting interests must be weighed.

Others who appeal to the alleged right to life do not view it as absolute. They seem to acknowledge that this right may conflict with other rights, such as for example, the alleged right to privacy. However, in the absence of some general theory about the weighing of conflicting rights, the claims about rights seem to have no direct bearing on the fundamental question concerning what morally ought to be done in such cases. My own claims about desert are not in this way isolated from normative theory. As I see it, outcomes are to be evaluated by appeal to the extent to which the individuals who exist in them get the primary goods they deserve in them. What we morally ought to do, then, depends on the values of the outcomes. In this way, relative degrees of desert play a crucial role in a normative theory concerning how we ought to behave.

In light of these important features, I think it is fair to say that the view proposed here is significantly different from any view based on the notion that there is a "right to life."

Advantages of This View

The approach advocated here has many advantages. (a) One of the greatest of these, as I see it, is that this view about the morality of abortion is the immediate consequence of a fully general view about the morality of action of all sorts. We start with the fundamental utilitarian insight that the right act is the one that maximizes the good. Then, by paying careful attention to relatively clear cases involving killing and failing to conceive, we elicit an appropriate conception of the good. On this view, the value of an outcome is directly proportional to the extent to which individuals who exist in that outcome get the primary intrinsic goods they deserve in that outcome. We then apply this view to the much more confusing puzzle about abortion. So the present theory is not just an ad hoc, localized view about abortion. It is the result of applying a fully general normative theory—one that generates plausible results in a wide variety of less controversial cases—to this most perplexing issue.

(b) Another advantage of my proposal is that it enables us to say that aborting a fetus is wrong (when it is wrong) for precisely the same reason that killing a child is wrong (when it is wrong).[2] In each case, the act is wrong because it makes the world worse; and in each case, the act makes the world worse because it decreases the extent to which individuals get the primary intrinsic goods they deserve. In typical cases of both sorts, the individual who suffers the greatest injustice is the individual who is deprived of a life. Surely, this is consistent with our best intuitions on the matter.

(c) However, my approach does not commit me to the view that failing to conceive a child is just as bad as aborting it prenatally or killing it postnatally.[3] We can go on to say that failing to conceive is generally not wrong, primarily because failing to conceive does not make the world worse. If a couple fails to conceive a child who would have been happy, no individual is thereby doomed to get less of the goods than she deserves. Since the deprived child simply does not exist in the relevant outcome, there is no victim. No one suffers injustice. Hence, according to my view, the world is not made worse by failure to conceive. This constitutes another advantage of the proposal.

(d) Some theories about abortion make essential use of obscure and controversial concepts. Some appeal to the notion that fetuses are "persons"; others claim that they have "the right to life." Unlike all such views, my view is not based in any way on the notion that fetuses are "persons," or that they have "the right to life." These concepts play no role in my theory.

Earlier (in Chapter 7) I distinguished several concepts of personality. These are (1) biological personality; (2) psychological personality; (3) legal personality; and (4) moral personality. I claimed that the various concepts are logically independent, since something could be, for example, a biological person without being a psychological person. Furthermore, I suggested that these concepts have different structures. Some (e.g., psychological) are matters of degree. Others (e.g., legal) may be absolute. Some (e.g., legal) are conventional. Others (e.g., psychological) are not.

However, in my discussion of abortion I have not appealed in any way to any of these concepts of personality. The crucial concept here is *desert*. An individual may deserve a full and happy life whether that individual is a person or not. What matters most is the magnitude of that individual's investment in its life. (I should perhaps acknowledge that the concept of *desert* is slightly slippery. In my view, however, it is less slippery than, for example, the concept of a right to life.)

(e) Some views imply that abortions are morally homogeneous. This seems to me to be most implausible. Although every abortion involves some evil, in some cases the abortion seems to be the lesser of possible evils. In other cases, it seems a huge evil. My view entails that different abortions may have different moral normative statuses. Generally, earlier abortions are less bad than later ones. Generally, abortions of more seriously deformed fetuses are less bad than abortions of healthy fetuses. Generally, it is morally wrong to abort a well-developed, healthy fetus for some frivolous reason. However, of course, different cases must be evaluated separately. In each case, the moral normative status of an abortion depends on the value of the outcome of that particular abortion, compared with the values of its alternatives. This, it seems to me, accords well with our reflective moral intuition.

I should perhaps again emphasize that my view has no direct consequences for legislation. It implies neither that abortion should be legally permitted nor that abortion should be legally prohibited. However, since earlier abortions are generally much less bad than later ones, this view seems to me at any rate to *suggest* that it might be best for the law to permit early abortions, but to prohibit late ones. Similarly, and for reasons that have been discussed above, the view suggests that it might be best for the law to permit abortions (even fairly late ones) in cases in which the resulting child inevitably would lead a horrible life. Equally, it suggests that rape victims should be permitted to have abortions. However, the theory itself is not a legal proposal. It is a theory about the *moral* normative status of abortions. I leave the investigation of the *legal* puzzle to others.

(f) Perhaps one of the most significant virtues of my proposal is that it provides a coherent framework for further discussion and debate. It seems to me that advocates of widely divergent views about abortion can accept the general structure I have proposed. Instead of wrangling fruitlessly about whether fetuses are "persons," or whether they have "the right to life," it would surely be more productive to agree at the outset that different abortions may have different normative statuses, and that in general, an abortion is morally permissible if and only if it makes the world better. Furthermore, it might be useful to agree at the outset that an abortion will make the world better only if contributes to the extent to which all affected individuals get the primary intrinsic goods they deserve.

With these as agreed starting points, the debate can focus more productively on the real issues: how much has a tiny fetus invested in its life? How much does it therefore deserve? What other individuals will be affected by the abortion? How much have they invested in their lives, and how much of the good do they deserve? How will the abortion affect the extent to which these others receive the goods they deserve? What are the alternatives in this particular case; and how good or bad would they be?

13

The Morality and Rationality of Suicide

Welcoming the Reaper

There are certain circumstances in which a visit from the Reaper is anticipated not with foreboding, but with a hopeful sense that suffering will soon be ended. Consider, for example, the case of an elderly man who has lived a rich and satisfying life. Suppose that his wife died years earlier, and his children are now grown and entirely independent. No one relies on him for emotional or financial support. Suppose he has contracted a painful, incurable, fatal disease. Suppose this disease has debilitated the old man, so that he is no longer able to perform any worthwhile sort of work. He is no longer useful either to himself or to others.

Let us imagine that this man sees no point in engaging in a lengthy, agonizing, and ultimately unsuccessful battle against this disease. Instead, he prefers simply to put his affairs in order, write some notes to his children and his few remaining friends, and then to kill himself—perhaps by taking an overdose of sleeping pills, and then settling down in his car, with the motor running, in the tightly closed garage.

Very many people, I suppose, would see nothing wrong with the old man's choice. Of course, we all would be saddened to learn that this man was placed in such unpleasant circumstances. No reasonable person could maintain that it is, on the whole, a good thing that this man has been put in a position in which death seems preferable to further life. However, given that he is in this situation, many of us would say that his method of dealing with it cannot be faulted either from the perspective of morality or from the perspective of rationality. This man's choice appears to be neither immoral nor irrational.

Nevertheless, a number of philosophers have argued that the choice of suicide is never rational. No matter how miserable one's situation, the decision to terminate one's life is, according to these philosophers, always irrational (or at least "arational"). Other philosophers have argued that such a decision must always be immoral. I take it that their point is that it is always morally wrong to commit suicide. Let us consider the arguments.

Three Arguments for the Immorality of Suicide

There are three classic arguments apparently designed to show that it is always morally wrong to commit suicide. Each of these was formulated by St. Thomas Aquinas[1] (though others, both earlier and later, have also defended them).[2]

Aquinas presents the three arguments in the following passage from *Summa Theologica:*

> Suicide is completely wrong for three reasons. First, everything naturally loves itself, and it is for this reason that everything naturally seeks to keep itself in being and to resist hostile forces. So suicide runs counter to one's natural inclinations. . . . Second, every part belongs to the whole in virtue of what it is. But every man is part of the community, so that he belongs to the community in virtue of what he is. Suicide therefore involves damaging the community. . . . Third, life is a gift made to man by God, it is subject to him who is *master of death and life.* Therefore, a person who takes his own life sins against God. . . . God alone has authority to decide about life and death.[3]

None of these is a particularly impressive argument. Let us briefly consider how they are supposed to work and why they are so unpersuasive. The first argument seems to have two premises. One of these states that every act of suicide "runs counter to natural inclinations." The other states that every act that "runs counter to natural inclinations" is morally wrong. Since they make use of the vague expression "runs counter to natural inclinations," one cannot be sure precisely what these premises mean. Thus it will be impossible to refute either of them conclusively. Nevertheless, it is fair to say that each premise *seems* false, or at least quite dubious. In the natural course of events, lemmings commit mass suicide by leaping off cliffs and falling into the sea. This is a quite remarkable phenomenon, but there is no good reason to insist that when they do this, the lemmings are doing something that "runs counter to their natural inclinations." In fact, when they commit mass suicide they seem to be doing precisely what they are naturally inclined to do. Thus, it is not clear that all who commit suicide thereby do something that runs counter to their natural inclinations.

Furthermore, and perhaps more relevantly, quite a few people apparently are naturally inclined to kill themselves. Some of these people admittedly are suffering from depression. Perhaps their decisions run counter to their natural inclinations. But others, perhaps facing circumstances like those of the old man described above, seem to be naturally inclined to take their own lives. So, in spite of its obscurity, I have my doubts about the first premise.

In connection with the second premise, consider what happens when you go for a medical checkup involving close scrutiny of parts of your body that are not normally exposed to strangers. You allow the doctor to treat you in ways that seem, in some important sense, to "run counter to natural inclination." Yet no reasonable person would want to say that all such behavior must be morally wrong. So the second premise is open to serious question, too. Since both premises are apparently false, the first argument fails.

The second argument is based on the notion that whenever a person commits suicide, he thereby damages some community of which he is part. Apparently, the point here is that by committing suicide, he deprives his community of his good works. This allegedly shows that every act of suicide is morally wrong. I see no reason to suppose that the premise is true. Surely there are some cases in which a person is so incapacitated that he is no longer able to make a worthwhile contribution to the welfare of others. Perhaps the old man described above is so debilitated by his disease that he can't even do a tiny bit of volunteer work at the hospital. In other cases, while it might be possible for someone to make some contribution to the welfare of others, the costs to himself in continued suffering might very substantially outweigh the benefits to others. On balance, it might simply be too much to ask of him. Thus, I am convinced that the second argument fails, too.

The third argument seems to rely on the notion that certain decisions should be left up to God. In particular, decisions about the date of a person's death should never be made by the person himself.

In his essay "On Suicide," David Hume attempted to refute this argument.[4] If there is a God, and it is responsible for the creation of this world, then, ultimately, God is responsible for absolutely everything that happens. Thus, whether a person commits suicide or struggles valiantly to keep himself alive, he is usurping God's will to exactly the same extent. In an interesting passage, Hume asks a rhetorical question. According to the argument under consideration, we "rebel against God" if we commit suicide. Hume asks:

> Why [is it] not impious, say I to build houses, cultivate the ground, or sail upon the ocean? In all these actions we employ our powers of mind and body, to produce some innovation in the course of nature; and in none of them do we any more. They are all of them therefore equally innocent, or equally criminal.[5]

Hume's point is that suicide is no different from any other "innovation in the course of nature." Either they all involve rebellion against God, or none of them does. No one would want to say that every action, no matter how trivial, involves a rebellion against God. Why should we think that suicide is different?

In light of the views defended above in Chapter 11, my own position on the morality of suicide should be clear. I claimed that there is one moral standard applicable to every act. As I see it, morality requires us to make the world as good as we can make it. We make the world better when we maximize the extent to which individuals get the primary intrinsic goods they deserve. I pointed out that this view about morality in general entails a view about the morality of killing. It is morally right to kill a person whenever doing so makes the world better; whenever doing so is a necessary condition for the maximization of what I called 'universal justice level'. Under all other circumstances, killing is wrong.

Suicide is a special sort of killing in which the killer and the killed are the same individual. On my view, suicide is no exception to the general principle about killing. Suicide is morally permissible when it makes the world better. And I think there are circumstances in which suicide does make the world better. Consider the old man discussed above. He has a number of options, including suicide. Provided that no other person would thereby be deprived of primary intrinsic goods that he or she deserves, and provided that he himself either no longer deserves or no longer will be able to get such goods, it surely might be the case that he makes the world better by removing himself from it. If so, justicized act utilitarianism implies that it would be morally permissible for him to kill himself. Of course, in any case in which the would-be suicide has some better option, suicide would be morally wrong. Suicides are not normatively homogeneous. Some are right, some are wrong. It all depends on the circumstances. This seems to me to be a plausible view about the morality of suicide.

It may be possible to sketch, in fairly rough terms, some of the implications of this view about suicide. According to this approach, suicide is morally permissible when it maximizes the quality of the fit between the amounts of primary intrinsic goods people deserve and the amounts of such goods they get. If a person is very old and has already had all the life and pleasure he deserves, and his death will not harm any other deserving individual, then it may be permissible for him to take his own life.

The case of a younger person is more difficult. He may still deserve lots of life and pleasure. If he kills himself, he will not have the opportunity to enjoy these. However, if he is certainly not going to be able to enjoy the primary intrinsic goods he deserves in any case—perhaps because of irreversible illness—and his death will not harm any other person, then it may be permissible for him to kill himself.

There are some cases in which a healthy young person, fully deserving a long life, may commit suicide. If, by killing himself, a person insures that many others get to enjoy intrinsic goods that they would otherwise not be able to enjoy, then it may be permissible for the young person to kill himself. An example may be provided by the case of a soldier who, in time of war, sacrifices himself in order to insure the welfare of his comrades.

But all such generalizations are extremely speculative. In order to reach a firm decision about the morality of some proposed suicide, one would have to know what alternatives are available to the one who proposes to kill himself. One would also have to know the outcomes of all these alternatives. One would have to know, for each outcome, the extent to which those who exist in it deserve the primary intrinsic goods, and the extent to which they get these goods. When we are ignorant of these crucial details, we are not qualified to announce firm conclusions about the morality of suicide.

Let us turn, then, to a consideration of the question whether suicide is always *irrational*.

An Argument for the Irrationality of Suicide

There are several different things that might be meant by saying that someone's behavior is "irrational." Prominent among these is the idea that neither the person himself nor anyone else would be able to explain his behavior by showing that he had good reasons for behaving as he did. Thus, suppose we find someone behaving in a way that "makes no sense" to us—for example, we find him eating dead worms from a rusty bait bucket. We think he must be crazy. We ask him why he is doing this. He is unable to provide any explanation. We ask his friends what he is trying to achieve. They shrug their shoulders. They don't get it either. We conclude that his behavior is completely irrational.

In "Suicide and Rationality," John Donnelly seems to claim that suicides are in this sense irrational. He briefly describes the case of some miserable person whose fortunes are at an all-time low. This person is contemplating suicide. Donnelly says:

On the brink of such an act, some philosophers would argue that the agent in question could justify his contemplated action by arguing that "I would be better off dead than alive" or something similar, such as "I will take my life and finally attain some consolation in death." But this type of reply is senseless inasmuch as it presupposes that a corpse can be the subject of various *psychological* predicates.[6]

Donnelly's point is plausible: if the person succeeds in killing himself, he will not subsequently have any psychological experiences. After death, he will not be *happy* to any degree and will not be *consoled*. Accordingly, it would be absurd for him (or for anyone) to attempt to rationalize his action by saying that he will be happier dead, or that death will bring him consolation. It would be, as Donnelly says, as nonsensical as it would be to say that some cadaver is "at peace with the world."[7]

If a would-be suicide really thinks that he will be happier dead, and gives this "reason" for proposing to kill himself, then he is confused. His rationale is, as Donnelly suggests, hopelessly muddled. Donnelly mentions some other equally unacceptable proposed explanations. He concludes that there is simply no way in which the behavior of the suicide can be shown to be reasonable, in the relevant sense.

I think Donnelly has overlooked some plausible interpretations of the remarks about being "better off dead." Obviously, it would be a mistake to suppose that the old man described above would be *happier* dead. However, the sick old man might think of his choice as a choice among several possible lives. He might recognize that, since he has already lived out the initial eighty-year segment of his life, he has no further choice with respect to that. No matter what he does now, the life he ultimately turns out to have led will have to start with that combination of events. However, he might think that he does still have some choices with respect to the life he leads. One possible life ends with suicide in the eightieth year; another ends with disease-caused death in the eighty-fifth year. The second possible life is just like the first up to the eightieth year, but differs from the first in that it contains a painful and unhappy five-year-long terminal segment. The first life ends with suicide in the eightieth year, and has no such painful terminal segment.

If asked to explain why he chooses suicide, the old man might say that he prefers the shorter life to the longer; that he thinks it is better, from a self-interested point of view, for him to live the eighty-year life rather than the eighty-five-year life. If he wanted to make use of the terminology introduced earlier in Chapter 9, he might say this: "Since I suffer five years of uncompensated pain the longer life, the value-for-me, measured hedonically, of the longer life is much lower than the value-for-me, measured in the same way, of the shorter life. But I will get to live the life that is better for me only if I commit suicide now. For this reason, I choose suicide." It seems to me that if he explains his behavior in this way, he gives a perfectly good reason for committing suicide. Nothing in this explanation presupposes that the elderly man will continue to have psychological experiences after death, or that he will be "happier dead than alive."

I should emphasize the fact that this rationale is not in any way based on a comparison between the painful five-year segment in the longer life and some corresponding but painless five-year segment occurring after the suicide in the shorter life. The elderly man does not compare how it goes for him in the next five years in one life with how it goes for him in the next five years in the other life. The life that ends with suicide does not have another five-year segment. I am not suggesting that we compare the value-for-him of this imaginary post-mortem segment of the suicide life with the value-for-him of the five-year segment of the non-suicide life. I am suggesting that we compare the value-for-him of the shorter life as a whole with the value-for-him of the longer life as a whole. This sort of comparison seems to me to be conceptually unproblematic, as I tried to show above in Chapters 9 and 10.

Some remarks in Donnelly's paper suggest that he may be thinking that one serious trouble with suicide is that it involves a choice between two options (life and death) when one of these options (death) is unalterably shrouded in mystery. The would-be suicide cannot know enough about death to make a reasoned choice between these options.[8] This sort of argument is somewhat more explicitly developed by Philip Devine in *The Ethics of Homicide*. Let us consider what Devine has to say.

An Epistemic Argument Against the Rationality of Suicide

Devine recognizes that "rational" has several senses. In one sense, a "rational choice" is one made calmly and deliberately. Devine acknowledges that, in this sense, the choice of suicide might be rational. But he dismisses this as largely irrelevant, since someone might make a "blatantly foolish or even pointless" decision in this calm and deliberate way.[9]

Another sense of 'rational' is more relevant to present concerns. In this sense, when we assess a decision as "rational," we mean to indicate something about the quality of prior knowledge and reasoning that went into the decision. At a minimum, we mean to indicate that the person who made the decision had adequate knowledge of the various options among which he was choosing. As Devine says, " . . . a precondition of rational choice is that one knows *what* one is choosing, either by experience or by the testimony of others who have experienced it or something very like it.'[10]

But by its very nature, death allegedly precludes any such prior knowledge. Assuming that each of us dies at most once, no one has the benefit of past personal experience to serve as a guide when contemplating suicide. No one can say, "Last time it worked out well. I shall try it again." Similarly, since no one returns from death with first-hand reports of what it is like, we cannot make use of testimonial evidence. No one can say, "All my dead friends reported that it worked out well for them. I shall try it, too." Devine alludes to these epistemic difficulties by saying that the choice of death "presents itself inevitably as a leap in the dark."[11]

In virtue of this alleged "opaqueness of death"[12], Devine concludes that the choice of suicide can never be rational. He insists that "human beings characteristically find themselves in profound imaginative and intellectual difficulty when they attempt to envisage the end of their existence."[13] How can a choice be rational, he seems to ask, when the chooser cannot even imagine the thing he is choosing?

So Devine is apparently relying on two premises here. According to the first, anyone who chooses death does not know what he is choosing. According to the second, it is never rational to choose something, if you do not know what you are choosing. The conclusion is that the suicide, who chooses death, must be making an irrational choice.

But each premise is open to serious question. According to the first, those who choose death do not know what they are choosing. They cannot even imagine what death will be like.

Since I have claimed that death is an enigma, it might appear that I am committed to accepting this premise. However, this would be a mistake. Even though I cannot formulate a satisfactory philosophical analysis of the concept of death, I think I do know what it will be like for me to be dead. Here's what it will be like: I will be lying cold and inert on a slab; I will appear greyish and pale; a kindly doctor will be saying, "Alas, poor Feldman, I knew him well." Of course, I do not imagine that I will be *feeling cold* or *feeling tired* or *hearing the doctor saying these grim words.* I am confident that I will be having no psychological experiences whatsoever.

So the first premise is apparently wrong. If I choose death, I do know (in what seems the relevant way) what I am choosing.

Sometimes we make rational decisions even though we do not know precisely what we are choosing. Suppose I am a contestant on a television game show. Suppose I have answered some questions correctly, and now I have a choice: I can either (a) take my modest cash prize (let us assume it is ten dollars); or else (b) take a chance on the mystery prize. I have no idea what the mystery prize is, but I have good reason to suspect that it might be something worth thousands of dollars.

In these circumstances, I might decide to risk my modest winnings on the mystery prize, even though (in some sense) I do not know what that prize is. I think this decision, under the circumstances, might be "reasonable." If my evidence suggests that it is likely that the mystery prize will be quite valuable, then it is even more appropriate to say that my choice is "reasonable." If so, the example shows that we can make rational decisions concerning choices, even in cases in which we do not know *what* we are choosing.[14] Thus, I suspect that both of Devine's premises are mistaken. We sometimes do know what we are choosing when we choose death; we can sometimes rationally choose an option even when we do not know what we are choosing.

"Calculative Rationality" and Suicide

Devine hints at yet a third concept of rationality while discussing some examples that are alleged to refute his thesis. He admits that there might be a sense of 'rational' in which it would be correct to say that the choice of death in these cases is rational. But he goes on to say:

[B]ut if so their rationality is not of the calculative sort. We are dealing, that is, not with a situation concerning which rational men will exhibit a range of estimates, but with a situation in which one man's estimate is as good as another, because what is being done is a comparison with an unknown quantity.[15]

I want to focus on the idea that there is a "calculative" sort of rationality, and that the choice of suicide cannot be rational in this way.

There is a well-established tradition according to which one concept of rational choice can be explicated by appeal to the notion of "expected utility." An example may help to introduce the concept. Suppose I have some disease. Suppose it can be cured either by surgery or by drugs. Suppose it sometimes goes away without any treatment. My doctor cannot tell me in advance precisely what will happen to me, but he can tell me the likelihood of various outcomes for each option.

Suppose the doctor tells me this: surgery is very expensive, but it will almost certainly work. There's a 1 percent chance that it will fail. Drugs are much less expensive, but they are also less certain. There's a 20 percent chance that they will fail. Hoping for spontaneous remission is of course free. But there is only a 5 percent chance that it will work.

In order to calculate the expected utility for me of each course of action, it will be helpful to draw up a little chart. On the chart, we list the three main courses of action (surgery, drugs, no treatment). For each course of action, we list the main possible outcomes (cure, no cure), the likelihood of the outcome given the course of action, and the values for me of the outcomes. Our chart then looks something like this:

Course of Action	Outcomes	Likelihood (%)	Value for me
Surgery	cure	99	100
	no cure	1	−50
Drugs	cure	80	110
	no cure	20	−40
No treatment	cure	5	115
	no cure	95	−35

A cure with no treatment is more valuable for me (115 points) than a cure with drugs (110 points) or a cure with surgery (100 points) simply because the cure with no treatment would be free, whereas a cure with surgery would be very expensive and a cure with drugs would be fairly expensive. Similar considerations also explain why no cure is worse for me if I undergo surgery (-50 points) than it would be if I take no treatment (-35 points).

To find the *expected utility* for me of surgery, we calculate as follows: multiply the value-for-me of each possible outcome of surgery by the likelihood of that outcome given surgery. Add the products. Thus, in this example, we multiply 99 by 100 (giving 9900) and 1 by -50 (giving -50). We then add these products, yielding an expected utility for me of surgery of 9850. Similar calculations for the other options yield the result that drugs have an expected utility for me of 8000 and no treatment has an expected utility for me of -2750.

Under these circumstances, it would be rational (in this calculative sense) for me to opt for surgery, because it maximizes expected utility for me. In other words, when we take into account the values-for-me and likelihoods of all the possible outcomes of each option, we find that the option that is most reasonable for me to choose, given my limited knowledge, is surgery. Of course, surgery might fail. I might turn out to be in the unfortunate 1 percent. But still my choice would have been rational in the relevant sense.

Devine suggests that suicide cannot have rationality "of the calculative sort." I suspect that he means that suicide cannot maximize expected utility for any person. If this is his view, I think he is mistaken. I think the choice of suicide might maximize expected utility for some person, and I think the calculations are in principle feasible.

Consider again the elderly man mentioned at the beginning of this chapter. He might think that his main options are (a) suicide; and (b) continued life. He might also think that the possible outcomes of suicide are (a1) bliss in heaven; (a2) torment in hell; and (a3) no further experience of any sort—we can call this "oblivion." He might think that the possible outcomes of continued life are: (b1) misery followed by eventual death; and (b2) miraculous recovery and happiness. His chart might look like this:

Courses of Action	Outcomes	Likelihood %	Value for him
Suicide	Heaven	1	+1000
	Hell	1	−1000
	Oblivion	98	0
Continued life	Misery	99	−500
	Miracle	1	+500

In this case it is clear, I think, that if the elderly man chooses suicide, his choice is perfectly rational (in the calculative sense). After all, the expected utility for him of suicide is zero, whereas the expected utility of continued life is −49,000. I think the calculations in this case are neither more nor less problematic than corresponding calculations that would be made in other, entirely uncontroversial cases.

I have claimed that under certain circumstances suicide can be the rational choice (in several senses of 'rational'). I should emphasize that I am certainly not suggesting that suicide is *always* a rational choice. For purposes of contrast, we can consider the case of a teenager suffering from clinical depression. He might feel miserable, and he might be obsessed with thoughts of suicide. He might be overwhelmed by the desire to take his own life. Yet since clinical depression can quite often be treated successfully by the careful administration of certain drugs, and since even if not treated it often clears up in less than a year, it would be horribly *irrational* (in several senses of the term) for the depressed teenager to opt for suicide. The value-for-him of a short, suicidal life is vastly lower than the value-for-him of a longer life in which he seeks appropriate medical treatment and is cured. Similarly, provided that he gets some reliable information about the success rates of various antidepressant drugs, the expected utility for him of suicide will also be lower than the expected utility for him of continued life.

Thus, in spite of the fact that I have claimed that there are circumstances in which a visit from the Reaper is to be welcomed, it should be clear that I do not advocate suicide for everyone who feels despondent. Furthermore, I think it would be grotesquely irresponsible for anyone simply to allow a depressed but otherwise healthy friend to kill himself. A depressed would-be suicide is probably not capable of estimating the values-for-himself and probabilities of various outcomes. He might think that continued life promises little. We might know better. We might know that there is a good chance that with appropriate treatment he will soon begin to feel better and that he will probably go on to live a long and reasonably happy life. Nothing I have said here should be taken to imply that in such a case, we are simply to allow the depressed person to kill himself if he so chooses.

Euthanasia

Suppose the elderly man mentioned above is extremely weak. Suppose also that his garage doors are rusty and hard to operate. He is unable to close these doors without help. Suppose I am a neighbor of this man, and I understand his circumstances. Finally, suppose he asks me to help him close the doors, so that he will be able to kill himself. What should I do? Could it be morally right for me to help this man to commit suicide?

My answer to this question must be hedged with "ifs." We first must consider whether the world as a whole will be better with this old man out of it. The relevant consideration is the extent to which everyone gets the primary intrinsic goods he or she deserves. It might be that the universal justice level is higher if I help my neighbor kill himself than it would be if I were to refuse. *If* this is the case, then it seems to me that morality permits me to help this man kill himself.

However, even in this case, it does not follow that my action would be *legally* permissible, or even that it ought to be legally permissible. It might be that the law ought to be written in such a way as to make it legally wrong for me to help the old man kill himself. This may seem paradoxical, so I should explain.

Although some suicides help to make the world better, others do not. Others involve net decreases in the extent to which people get the primary intrinsic goods they deserve. In very many instances, those who might be present at the scene would not be able to tell with any assurance whether a particular suicide is one of the good ones or one of the bad ones. All sorts of considerations might cloud their judgment. They might be confused in part because they love and sympathize with the would-be suicide, and he is begging for their assistance. In an altogether different sort of case, they might be confused because the would-be suicide is a burden to them, and they stand to inherit millions if he dies.

It would be a bad idea to frame a law in such a way as to allow us to assist all and only those sucides that make the world better. The problem is that we often cannot tell whether a particular suicide is of this "optimific" sort. We would then be unable to determine whether the law permits or prohibits a certain course of action. It would be a terrible law. In this situation, it might turn out to be best simply to rule that all such attempts at euthanasia are legally prohibited. *If* this is the case, then the law ought to be written in this way. There ought to be a law saying that we must not help the old man commit suicide.

In this sort of case, helping the old man might turn out to be morally required but legally prohibited. I hope that I will never face a dilemma of this sort. But if it should happen, I hope that I will have the courage to do what morality requires.

14

Epilogue

Some confrontations with death are so sudden and so immediately terminal that the one who is thus confronted has no time to reflect on what is happening. Before he can gather his wits, he is dead. The opportunity for reflection is forever lost.

In other cases, however, we confront death more indirectly. He may enter our home, and we may feel a cold shiver as he brushes past, but he has not come for us. In such cases, after death has done his damage, there may be plenty of time for reflection. When thus indirectly confronted by death, many reactions are possible. Some of course will be overcome by grief or anger. Others may be moved to embrace the consolations of religion. Still others may want to immerse themselves in art or literature devoted to death.

But for philosophers there seems to be no alternative: we must try to *understand* death. We ask again the ancient philosophical questions about death, and we struggle again with the philosophical puzzles prompted by their apparent answers. That is what I have done in this book.

The central conceptual question about death is easily asked: "What is death?" I have struggled with this question, and I have concluded that death is a mystery. Although it seems at first that death is just the cessation of life, this "standard analysis" cannot be correct. I tried to show that variations of the standard analysis are also mistaken. I have been unable to formulate a satisfactory philosophical analysis of the concept of death. Nevertheless, I have attempted to sketch the outlines of a materialist conceptual scheme involving death itself and several other closely connected concepts. I have attempted to explain how death relates to life, to dying2, to existence, to personality, and to certain other concepts. Thus, I have attempted to come to grips with the nature of death by showing where death is, conceptually speaking.

In addition to these conceptual questions about the nature of death, there are also ethical and value-theoretical questions about death. One of the deepest of these is prompted by the old Epicurean view that death cannot be an evil for the one who dies. I have tried to show that the Epicurean argument for this conclusion fails. Even if the dead cannot experience anything *intrinsically* bad, death still might be *extrinsically* bad for them.

Going beyond this somewhat negative conclusion, I tried to show that we can make good sense of the naive notion that death is generally a great misfortune for the one who dies. My view is a variant of the deprivation approach, according to which the evil of a given death is primarily a matter of *loss*—a person's death is bad to the extent that it deprives him or her of goods. This helps to explain our sense the death of a young person is generally worse than the death of a very old person who has already enjoyed a full, rich life. The loss suffered by the young person is greater than that suffered by the old person.

Given this account of the evil of death, it naturally follows that some deaths are good for the one who dies. Again, it depends on what would have happened to the decedent if he had not died when he did. When the life as a whole I would have led if I had continued to live is worse for me than the life as a whole I would have led if I die now, then it is best for me to die now. My death, in this sort of case, is a blessing for me. This naturally gives rise to a number of questions about causing death.

It seems perfectly obvious that it is morally wrong to kill people in most ordinary circumstances, and yet it is not easy to explain precisely why this is so. For a utilitarian, the explanation seems especially difficult. Yet I have attempted to show that if we calculate the values of outcomes properly and give due weight to considerations of investment and desert, we may be able to solve this puzzle too. As I see it, what makes killing wrong is what makes any wrong act wrong—it makes the world worse than it needs to be. If we determine the value of the world by considering the quality of the fit between the amounts of primary intrinsic goods individuals receive and the amounts they deserve, this form of utilitarianism may generate plausible solutions to a number of puzzles about the morality of killing. Abortion, suicide, and euthanasia are controversial and problematic forms of killing. Nevertheless, it seems to me that my view about the morality of killing in general can readily be extended so as to yield sensible views about the morality of these sorts of killing, too.

It surely will appear to some readers that I have made these questions more complicated than they need to be. These readers may have felt impatient with my plodding style. Perhaps they would express their complaint by insisting that it would have been easier to answer the questions more directly, without all the distinctions and definitions.

While I appreciate the importance of getting to the heart of the matter, I nevertheless think that there is good reason to insist on patience. In the preface to *Principia Ethica,* G. E. Moore remarked:

> It appears to me that in Ethics, as in all other philosophical studies, the difficulties and disagreements, of which its history is full, are mainly due to a very simple cause: namely to the attempt to answer questions, without first discovering precisely *what* question it is which you desire to answer.

The relevance of Moore's remark to the present case should be obvious. Suppose a beloved friend has died. Suppose we are moved to reflect on the nature and value of her death. We may want to understand this monster that has destroyed our friend, and we may want to reassure ourselves that our friend is now safe from harm. We may thus ask what death is, and whether a person can survive it; if it is truly a great evil, or whether it can sometimes be a benefit to the one who dies. Other questions, as puzzling and as widely debated as these, may trouble us, and we may spend time and energy trying to find answers.

As I see it, these questions are puzzling in large part because they are so obscure and ambiguous. We hardly know what 'death' means. We may be using 'people' in several different senses when we ask whether *people* can survive death. We may have no clear conception of what we mean when we say that someone has been 'injured' by something, or that someone has 'survived' something.

Thus, no matter how eager we are to locate answers to these questions, our efforts are premature and doomed to failure if we don't understand the questions.

Some may prefer to grapple with these questions in some other way. They may be satisfied merely to savor the sounds of the words and to allow memory and imagination to wander. These approaches undeniably can be valuable for some. But if, like me, you want reasonable answers, then you must be more patient. You must endure the distinctions and definitions. You must resist the temptation to accept the answers that make it seem easy. You must engage in painstaking philosophical reflection. Anything less will surely be fruitless.

I cannot hope that all readers will agree with all my answers. But I do hope that at least some will find something useful in these reflections on the most baffling questions about the nature and value of death.

Notes

Introduction

1. Paul Edwards, "Existentialism and Death: A Survey of Some Confusions and Absurdities."
2. Epicurus, "Letter to Menoeceus."
3. Op. cit., 30–31.

Chapter 1

1. James van Evra, "On Death as a Limit," 25.

Chapter 2

1. "Lives" are discussed again later, in Chapter 7.
2. Ernst Mayr, *The Growth of Biological Thought,* 53.
3. Op. cit., 74–5.
4. Aristotle, *De Anima,* 416a18.
5. Op. cit., 424a17.
6. Op. cit., 434b14.
7. Op. cit., 434b25.
8. Op. cit., 413b26.
9. Op. cit., 434a23.
10. Op. cit., 414a28.
11. This chart is derived from one presented by Thomas S. Hall in his *Ideas of Life and Matter,* Volume 1, 109.
12. Aristotle, *De Anima,* 415a27.
13. Op. cit., 413b1.
14. Op. cit., 415a23–25.
15. Op. cit., 415a28.
16. C. Brooke Worth and Robert K. Enders, *The Nature of Living Things,* 91–92.

17. James Christian, *Philosophy: an introduction to the art of wondering*, 415.
18. Richard Goldsby et al., *Biology*, 2.
19. James Christian, op. cit., 415.
20. Gary Matthews, "*De Anima* B2–4 and the Meaning of *Life.*"
21. Op. cit., mss14.
22. Op. cit., mss14.
23. William T. Keeton and James L. Gould, *Biological Science* 4th ed., 602.

Chapter 3

1. Aristotle, *De Anima*, 413a21; (Book II, Chapter 2; page 557 in the Jowett edition).
2. For a good general introduction to vitalism, see Morton Beckner's article "Vitalism" in the *Encyclopedia of Philosophy*, Volume 8, 253–6. The books by Driesch are cited in the Bibliography, below.
3. Hans Driesch, *History and Theory of Vitalism*, 209.
4. Ernst Mayr, *The Growth of Biological Thought*, 53.
5. Ibid.
6. Mayr, op. cit., 55–56.
7. *The Oxford Paperback Dictionary*, 1983, 22.
8. Francis Crick, *Life Itself*, 61–62.
9. Crick, op. cit., 62.

Chapter 4

1. Quite a few commentators seem to identify death with the permanent cessation of consciousness. Thus, for example, James van Evra apparently finds it reasonable to say that ' . . . dying is simply a matter of ceasing to think and experience.' "On Death as a Limit," 25.
2. Roy Perrett, *Death and Immortality*, 14.
3. Ibid.
4. Ibid.
5. Ibid.
6. Perrett, op. cit., 17.
7. Perrett, op. cit., 18.
8. Jay Rosenberg, *Thinking Clearly about Death*, 23.
9. Rosenberg, op. cit., 21.
10. Rosenberg, op. cit., 106. (Emphasis added.)
11. The relevance of suspended animation to standard analyses of death is discussed by Michael Wreen in "The Definition of Death."

12. In light of the fact that no analysis of the concept of life seems fully adequate, it is difficult to *prove* that the frozen blastula is not alive. However, many commentators share this intuition. In "A Piece of Yourself in the World," James Lieber says that such a frozen fetus is "not fully alive." In this context, he remarks that "nothing can live in liquid nitrogen." (page 77).

13. For details concerning the laboratory techniques of cryopreservation, see *Low Temperature Preservation in Medicine and Biology,* ed. by M. J. Ashwood-Smith and J. Farrant. A very interesting discussion of the technical, legal, and moral problems that arise in connection with cryopreservation of human fetuses can be found in James Lieber, "A Piece of Yourself In the World."

14. Rosenberg, op. cit., 23.

15. A number of others share my intuition about suspended animation. Michael Wreen seems to be one. In "The Definition of Death," he says, "Suspended animation is a state not readily assimilated to either life or death. . . . ' (89). Lieber makes the same point.

16. Rosenberg, op. cit., 106.

17. Op. cit., 21–22.

18. Op. cit., 21.

19. Op. cit., 22.

20. Op. cit., 33, 104. For a slightly different account of the same phenomenon, compare Roy Perrett's discussion of metamorphosis (and other changes) in *Death and Immortality,* 16.

21. Aristotle is generally credited with being the first to distinguish substantial change from mere alteration. See, for example, *Generation and Corruption,* Bk. I, Ch. 4. Once again, it may be interesting to compare the interpretation of substantial change proposed here with the one given by Perrett in *Death and Immortality,* Chapter 1.

22. D6 is consistent with my view about the caterpillar example, too. I agree with Rosenberg that the caterpillar does not die when it undergoes metamorphosis. Perhaps Rosenberg would describe the case by saying that the caterpillar turns into another living thing and so does not die because it does not satisfy the *third* conjunct of D6. As I see it, the caterpillar does not undergo substantial change, but continues to exist through the amazing alterations in shape, etc., and it continues to live. Thus, it does not satisfy the *first* conjunct of D6. That, according to me, is approximately why it doesn't die.

23. Keeton and Gould, *Biological Science,* 1064. I thank Dick Goldsby and Barbara Osborne for telling me about chlamydomonas.

24. There are other actual reproductive practices that refute D6 (and variants). One of these (described in Keeton and Gould, 1055) concerns certain cellular slime molds. These creatures are single-celled, amoeba-

like individuals. Under certain conditions, large numbers of these individuals "aggregate," forming one large living cell. Each former individual is thoroughly assimilated into the new individual. Each thus seems to go out of existence, but I for one would be uneasy about saying that any of them dies in this process.

25. Gary Matthews has presented a possible difficulty for this argument. I have presupposed that the various transplantable organs of the victim's body are genuinely "living"—that when we say that the skin cells or kidneys (for example) are still alive, we use 'alive' in the same sense as when we say that the organism as a whole is alive. If this presupposition is false, then the example fails to refute D7. I think that the presupposition is true, but I see no way to prove it.

Chapter 5

1. Gilbert Ryle, *The Concept of Mind,* 149.
2. Roy Perrett, in *Death and Immortality,* 17, says that "Dying, then, is a process that if uninterrupted by external forces will normally end in death; but dying does not necessarily eventuate in death." Perrett's view seems to be quite like the one expressed by D3, except for the absence of mention of "short times."
3. These considerations also serve to refute D1, D2, and D3.
4. Ninian Smart, "Philosophical Concepts of Death," 27.
5. Op. cit., 28.
6. Ibid.
7. Ibid.
8. Op. cit., 27.
9. Ibid.
10. Op. cit., 27.
11. Ibid.
12. Ibid.
13. Op. cit., 29.
14. Ibid.
15. In *"De Anima* B2–4 and the Meaning of *Life,"* Gary Matthews presents an account of "psychic powers" based on remarks Aristotle makes in various places. According to Matthews, a property, F, is a psychic power if and only if there is some species, S, such that in order for S to be preserved, individual organisms that belong to S must have F. It should be clear that Matthews's psychic powers are not quite the same as my vital capacities. For one thing, every vital capacity must be a *biological* capacity, but Matthews places no such restriction on psychic powers. Furthermore, though the loss of vital capacities might make it impossible for

individuals to live in the manner appropriate to their kind, it might still be possible for them to live. This is not so for psychic powers. Thus, the disease-fighting capacity is not a psychic power (because we *could* live without it). But it is a vital capacity, because we can't live in the manner appropriate to our kind without it.

16. Aristotle presents his list of vital properties in Bk. II, Ch. 3 of *De Anima,* and he discusses those properties in detail in the chapters that follow. Although he gives different lists in different places, he seems to count nutrition, appetition, reproduction, sensation, growth, locomotion, and thought as vital properties. I discussed Aristotle's views in Chapter 2.

17. A point of clarification concerning causal processes: it is not necessary that the causal chain contain defeasible links. If there is a sequence of events in which each event "leads to" its successor, whether defeasibly or strictly (i.e., they *causally necessitate* their successors) then the sequence as a whole is still a concrete causal sequence.

18. Perhaps I should also mention that the analysis makes use of the somewhat obscure notion of "kinds" of organism. I said that certain properties are vital for organisms of certain "kinds," yet I did not say precisely what I mean by this term. I fear that I would not be able to do so. I should point out, however, that by 'kind' I do not mean 'species'.

19. Smart agrees that one can die even though one was never formerly dying2. He cites the case of a person who dies instantaneously as the result of a burst blood vessel in the brain. See "Philosophical Concepts of Death," 29. Perrett, in *Death and Immortality,* 17, also agrees, but cites no example.

Chapter 6

1. For a rough characterization of the biological concept of death, see the beginning of Chapter 4.

2. For a thorough and insightful discussion of this issue, see Peter van Inwagen's *Material Beings.*

3. Epicurus, op. cit., p. 30.

4. Epicurus, op. cit., p. 31.

5. Lucretius, op. cit., p. 131.

6. Peter Dalton, "Death and Evil."

7. In "A Matter of Life and Death," L. W. Sumner says, "The death of a person is the end of that person; before death he *is* and after death he *is not.* To die is therefore to cease to exist" (153). In "The Evil of Death," Harry Silverstein says, " . . . when one is dead one does not exist . . . " (402).

8. Roy Perrett, *Death and Immortality,* 15.

9. Jay Rosenberg, *Thinking Clearly about Death,* 33.

10. Rosenberg, op. cit., 96.

11. Rosenberg, op. cit., 27.

12. I have to admit that there is a problem concerning this story. While I do indeed have the cited recollection, it also seems to me that there never was any occasion on which I visited the Chesapeake Bay. The problem is this: why would a seafood restaurant adjacent to some other bay, such as Naragansett Bay (which I have visited often), put the quoted motto on its napkins?

13. Dictionaries say the same thing. For example, the *Oxford Paperback Dictionary,* New Edition, 1983, gives, as the first sense of the word "dead," "no longer alive" (160).

14. Perrett, op. cit., 14.

15. Ibid.

16. Ibid.

17. Perrett, op. cit., 18.

18. Perrett, op. cit., 15.

19. There is one minor difficulty. It seems to me that we sometimes say that something has been "destroyed" even though it has not gone out of existence. Thus, if an automobile has been utterly wrecked beyond any hope of repair, we say that it has been destroyed. It still exists. Thus, line (2) is open to some further quibbles.

20. Lucretius presupposes this view throughout Book III. A particularly clear expression can be found in the passage in which he speaks of the moment when the soul " . . . passes away into the air and leaves the cold limbs in the chill of death" (122–3).

21. Lucretius, op. cit., 119.

22. Lucretius, op. cit., 131.

23. Ibid.

24. The argument can be found on p. 131.

25. Rosenberg, for example, vigorously rejects dualism but accepts the termination thesis.

26. Rosenberg, op. cit., 27.

27. There are of course other versions of the argument that make use of one concept of personality in one line and another concept of personality in other lines. Since such versions are not formally valid, I shall not discuss them here.

Chapter 7

1. For further discussion of the idea that the time of death is like a limit toward which moments within life may approach, see James van Evra's "Death as a Limit."

2. Rosenberg, *Thinking Clearly about Death,* 96ff.

3. I have suggested that psychological personality is a matter of degree, so that it makes sense to say that something gradually becomes more and more a person. This sort of view is suggested also by W. R. Carter in "Once and Future Persons." Carter associates his view with the notion that there are degrees of truth to such statements that Adam is a person. I see no clear connection between the two doctrines, and I do not mean to commit myself to the second of them.

In "Abortion: Identity and Loss," Warren Quinn discusses an ontological scheme according to which existence itself is a matter of degree. In this view, we could say that a just-conceived zygote exists only very slightly; the week-old fetus is more real; the fetus gradually becomes more real as it develops. Quinn tries to show that such a view is, despite appearances, coherent. I, for one, find myself unable to understand what might be meant by saying that there are two objects, but one of them "exists more" than the other. This sort of gradualist view is discussed also by Lawrence Becker in "Human Being: The Boundaries of the Concept," and it is criticized by Roderick Chisholm in "Coming into Being and Passing Away: Can the Metaphysician Help?"

Chapter 8

1. Epicurus, "Letter to Menoeceus," 31.

2. Op. cit., 35.

3. Lucretius, *On the Nature of Things,* 131.

4. For an interesting comparison, see Stephen Rosenbaum, "How to Be Dead and Not Care: A Defense of Epicurus." Several other relevant articles are listed in the Bibliography.

5. In the "Letter to Menoeceus," (32), Epicurus says "When, therefore, we maintain that pleasure is the end, we do not mean the pleasures of profligates and those that consist in sensuality. . . . For it is not continuous drinkings and revellings, nor the satisfaction of lusts, nor the enjoyment of fish and other luxuries of the wealthy table, which produce a pleasant life. . . ."

6. It might be interesting to consider the relevance of the intrinsic/extrinsic distinction to premise (A) in Rosenbaum's reconstruction of the Epicurean argument in "How to Be Dead and Not Care: A Defense of Epicurus" (218). See also the "first conclusion" discussed by Peter Dalton in "Death and Evil" (196).

7. Notice that this version of the argument is no longer about the state of being dead. It is, rather, about the event of death—the event that necessarily takes place precisely when a person dies.

8. For references to several philosophers who have defended the deprivation approach, see Note 2, Chapter 9.

Chapter 9

1. Epicurus, "Letter to Menoeceus," 30–31.

2. I am by no means the first to defend this sort of answer. Similar views are defended (or at least discussed with some enthusiasm) by a number of philosophers. See, for example, Jeff McMahan, "The Evil of Death"; Thomas Nagel, "Death"; Roy Perrett, *Death and Immortality;* L. S. Sumner, "A Matter of Life and Death"; Douglas Walton, *On Defining Death;* and Bernard Williams, "The Makropulos Case: Reflections on the Tedium of Immortality."

3. For the most vigorous presentation of the claim that the standard view involves an illegitimate comparison, see Harry Silverstein, "The Evil of Death," Part I.

4. Epicurus, "Letter to Menoeceus," 31.

5. Lucretius, *On the Nature of Things,* 134.

6. I assume that for each axiology, there are "basic intrinsic value states." These are states of affairs that contain neither more nor less information than is needed (according to the axiology) to determine how much value has been enjoyed (or suffered). On the simple hedonism under discussion, *Dolores suffering pain of intensity 10 from t1 to t3* would be basic; but *Dolores suffering pain of intensity 10 from t1 to t3 while observing a bad performance of her favorite opera* would not. The latter contains excess information. On the other hand, a state of affairs such as *Dolores suffering pain* is not basic because it contains too little information—it doesn't tell us the precise amount of pain she suffered, or the time at which she suffered it. For more discussion, see *Doing the Best We Can* in Chapter 2.

7. I am suppressing consideration of certain complexities. One that should be addressed concerns cases in which there is no particular possible life in which a certain state of affairs occurs that is precisely the one that would exist if that state of affairs took place—several possible lives are tied for this distinction. What shall we say then?

Suppose that in her actual life Dolores does not move to Bolivia. Then her actual life is the life she would lead if she were not to move to Bolivia. Suppose that among possible lives in which she does move to Bolivia, there are two that are equally similar and most similar to her actual life. Then I want to say this: if each of these lives is worse for Dolores than her actual life, then moving to Bolivia would be bad for her; if each is better for her than her actual life, then moving to Bolivia would be good for her; if one is better and the other is worse, then it's not the case that moving to if one is better and the other is worse, then it's not the case that moving to Bolivia would be good for her, and it's not the case that moving to Bolivia would be bad for her; moving to Bolivia might be good for her and might be bad for her.

In what follows, I shall write as if there is always a unique possible life that is the one she would lead if she were to move to Bolivia. My main points are not affected by this simplifying assumption. For further discussion, see my "Some Puzzles about the Evil of Death."

8. A number of philosophers have explicitly discussed the principle that evils can befall a person only at times when he or she exists. McMahan, for example, calls it "the existence requirement". See Jeff McMahan, "Death and the Value of Life" (33).

9. By Harry Silverstein in "The Evil of Death," 414.

10. For other views on the Lucretius Problem, see Anthony Breuckner and John Martin Fischer, "Why is Death Bad?" and F. M. Kamm, "Why Is Death Bad and Worse Than Pre-natal Non-existence?" For a criticism of Kamm's view, see my "F. M. Kamm and the Mirror of Time."

Chapter 10

1. W. D. Ross, *The Right and the Good,* 19ff.

2. Ross, op. cit., 28–29.

3. Ross, op. cit., 41.

4. Ross, op. cit., 41.

5. For an extended discussion of Ross's theory, see my *Introductory Ethics,* Chapter 10.

6. For an extended discussion of the formulation and evaluation of hedonistic act utilitarianism, see Chapters 2, 3, and 4 of my *Introductory Ethics.*

7. A vigorous attempt to show that utilitarianism cannot account for the wrongness of killing can be found in Richard Henson's "Utilitarianism and the Wrongness of Killing."

8. R. E. Ewin, "What is Wrong with Killing People?," 126.

9. Don Marquis, "Why Abortion is Immoral," 189. It is interesting to note that Marquis begins his paper by saying that he will present an argument for the conclusion that abortion is "seriously immoral" (183). In the passage quoted, he suggests that he is going to tell us "why killing is wrong" (189). These passages suggest that Marquis is engaged in a discussion of the *all-in* normative status of abortion. But later, when it comes time to give the answer, Marquis says that his argument "shows only that abortion is *prima facie* wrong, not that it is wrong in any and all circum-

stances" (194; emphasis added). This leads me to think that Marquis has argued for a vastly weaker and much less controversial conclusion than the one he hints at in his title.

Chapter 12

1. The relevant distinctions were drawn above in Chapter 7.

2. In Section II of "Why Abortion Is Immoral," Don Marquis discusses the idea that a theory about the morality of abortion ought to be in this way based on a more abstract theory about the morality of killing in general.

3. In Section V of "Why Abortion Is Immoral," Marquis insists that his own view does not yield the result that nonconception is just as bad as abortion. I find it difficult to follow the details of his reasoning.

Chapter 13

1. St. Thomas Aquinas, *Summa Theologiae* Question 64; Article 5; "Is it legitimate for somebody to kill himself?" Volume XXXVIII, 31–37.

2. For a very useful discussion of the literature on this topic, see the article "Suicide" by Glanville Williams in *The Encyclopedia of Philosophy,* Volume 8, 43–46.

3. Aquinas, op. cit., 33.

4. David Hume, "Of Suicide."

5. Hume, op. cit., 411–412.

6. John Donnelly, "Suicide and Rationality," 96.

7. Ibid.

8. Donnelly, op. cit., 100. " . . . the suicidist would have no way adequately to determine that his plan would be successful."

9. Philip Devine, *The Ethics of Homicide,* 24.

10. Ibid.

11. Devine, op. cit., 27.

12. Devine, op. cit., 26.

13. Ibid.

14. This example was suggested to me by Julie Petty.

15. Devine, op. cit., 25.

Bibliography

Aquinas, St. Thomas. *Summa Theologiae,* Latin text, English translation, Introduction, Notes, Appendices, and Glossary by Marcus Lefebure (London and New York: Blackfriars and McGraw-Hill, 1975).

Aristotle. *The Basic Works of Aristotle,* edited by Richard McKeon (New York: Random House, 1941).

Ashwood-Smith, M. J., and J. Farrant, eds. *Low Temperature Preservation in Medicine and Biology* (Tunbridge Wells: Pitman Medical Ltd., 1980).

Becker, Lawrence. "Human Being: the Boundaries of the Concept," *Philosophy and Public Affairs,* 4 (1975): 334–359.

Beckner, Morton. "Vitalism," in *The Encyclopedia of Philosophy,* ed. Paul Edwards (New York: Macmillan and the Free Press, 1967), Volume 8, 253–256.

Brueckner, Anthony L., and John Martin Fischer. "Why is Death Bad?" *Philosophical Studies,* 50 (1986): 213–221.

Carter, W. R. "Once and Future Persons," *American Philosophical Quarterly,* 17, 1 (January, 1980): 61–66.

Chisholm, Roderick. "Coming into Being and Passing Away: Can the Metaphysician Help?" in John Donnelly, *Language, Metaphysics, and Death,* 13–24; originally published in *Philosophy and Medicine,* Volume III, eds. H. Tristram Englehardt, Jr., and Stuart Spicker (Dordrecht: Reidel, 1977).

Crick, Francis. *Life Itself: Its Origin and Nature* (New York: Simon and Schuster, 1981).

Dalton, Peter C. "Death and Evil," *The Philosophical Forum,* XI, 2 (Winter, 1979–80): 193–211.

Devine, Philip E. *The Ethics of Homicide* (Ithaca and London: Cornell University Press, 1978).

Donnelly, John, ed. *Language, Metaphysics, and Death* (New York: Fordham University Press, 1978).

Driesch, Hans. *The Science and Philosophy of the Organism,* The Gifford Lectures delivered before the University of Aberdeen in the year 1907 (London: Adam and Charles Black, 1908).

Driesch, Hans. *The History and Theory of Vitalism,* trans. C. K. Ogden (London: MacMillan and Co., Ltd., 1914).

Edwards, Paul. "Existentialism and Death: A Survey of Some Confusions and Absurdities," originally published in *Philosophy, Science, and Method,* eds. S. Morgenbesser, P. Suppes, and M. White (New York: St. Martin's Press, 1969); reprinted in John Donnelly, *Language, Metaphysics, and Death,* 32–61.

Epicurus. "Letter to Menoeceus," trans. C. Bailey, in *The Stoic and Epicurean Philosophers,* edited and with an introduction by Whitney J. Oates (New York: The Modern Library, 1940), 30–34.

Ewin, R. E. "What is Wrong with Killing People?" *Philosophical Quarterly,* 22 (1972): 126–139.

Feldman, Fred. *Introductory Ethics* (Englewood Cliffs: Prentice-Hall, 1978).

Feldman, Fred. *Doing the Best We Can: An Essay in Informal Deontic Logic* (Dordrecht: Reidel, 1986).

Feldman, Fred. "On Dying as a Process," *Philosophy and Phenomenological Research,* L, 2 (December, 1989): 375–390.

Feldman, Fred. "F. M. Kamm and the Mirror of Time," *Pacific Philosophical Quarterly,* 71, 1 (March, 1990): 23–27.

Feldman, Fred. "Some Puzzles about the Evil of Death," *The Philosophical Review,* C, 2 (April, 1991): 205–227.

Feldman, Fred. "The Enigma of Death," *Philosophia* (forthcoming).

Fischer, John Martin. *Essays on Death* (Stanford: Stanford University Press, forthcoming).

Goldsby, Richard A., et al. *Biology* (New York: Harper & Row, 1976).

Hall, Thomas S. *Ideas of Life and Matter* (Chicago: University of Chicago Press, 1969).

Hare, R. M. "Abortion and the Golden Rule," *Philosophy and Public Affairs,* 4 (1975): 201–222.

Henson, Richard G. "Utilitarianism and the Wrongness of Killing," *The Philosophical Review,* LXXX (1971): 320–337.

Hume, David. "Of Suicide," in *Essays: Moral, Political, and Literary by David Hume,* eds. T. H. Green and T. H. Grose (London: Longmans, Green, and Co., 1898).

Kamm, F. M. "Why is Death Bad and Worse and than Pre-natal Nonexistence?" *Pacific Philosophical Quarterly,* 69 (1988): 161–164.

Keeton, William T., and James L. Gould. *Biological Science,* 4th ed. (New York: W. W. Norton & Co., 1986).

Ladd, John. *Ethical Issues Relating to Life & Death* (New York and Oxford: Oxford University Press, 1979).

Lieber, James. "A Piece of Yourself in the World," *The Atlantic Monthly,* (June, 1989): 76–80.

Lovelock, J. E. *Gaia: A New Look at Life on Earth* (Oxford and New York: Oxford University Press, 1979).

Lucretius. *On the Nature of Things,* trans. H. A. J. Munro, in *The Stoic and Epicurean Philosophers,* ed. and with an introduction by Whitney J. Oates (New York: The Modern Library, 1940), 69–219.

Marquis, Don. "Harming the Dead," *Ethics,* (1985): 159–161.

McMahan, Jeff. "The Evil of Death," *Ethics,* 99, 1 (October, 1988): 32–61.

Marquis, Don. "Why Abortion is Immoral," *The Journal of Philosophy,* LXXXVI, 4 (April, 1989): 183–202.

Matthews, Gareth. *"De Anima* B2–4 and the Meaning of *Life,"* in *Essays on Aristotle's De Anima,* eds. M. Nussbaum and A. Rorty (Oxford: Oxford University Press, forthcoming).

Mayr, Ernst. *The Growth of Biological Thought* (Cambridge: The Belknap Press of Harvard University Press, 1982).

Moore, G. E. *Principia Ethica* (Cambridge: Cambridge University Press, 1962).

Nagel, Tom. "Death," *Nous* IV, 1 (February, 1970), 73–80; revised version in *Moral Problems,* ed. James Rachels (New York: Harper & Row, 1971); also reprinted in John Donnelly, *Language, Metaphysics, and Death,* 62–68.

Parfit, Derek. *Reasons and Persons* (Oxford: Oxford University Press, 1984).

Perrett, Roy W. *Death and Immortality* (Dordrecht: Martinus Nijhoff Publishers, 1987).

Pitcher, George. "The Misfortunes of the Dead," *The American Philosophical Quarterly,* 21, 2 (April, 1984): 183–188.

Puccetti, Roland. "The Conquest of Death," originally published in *The Monist,* 59 (1976), 249–263; reprinted in John Donnelly, *Language, Metaphysics and Death,* 163–175.

Quinn, Warren. "Abortion: Identity and Loss," *Philosophy and Public Affairs,* 13, 1 (Winter, 1984): 24–54.

Rosenbaum, Stephen. "How to Be Dead and Not Care: A Defense of Epicurus," *American Philosophical Quarterly,* 23, 2 (April, 1986): 217–225.

Rosenbaum, Stephen. "The Symmetry Argument: Lucretius Against the Fear of Death," *Philosophy and Phenomenological Research,* L, 2 (December, 1989): 353–373.

Rosenberg, Jay. *Thinking Clearly about Death* (Englewood Cliffs: Prentice-Hall, Inc., 1983).

Ross, Sir William David. *The Right and the Good* (Oxford: The Clarendon Press, 1930).

Ryle, Gilbert. *The Concept of Mind* (New York: Barnes and Noble, 1949).

Schrodinger, Erwin. *What is Life? & Mind and Matter* (London and New York: Cambridge University Press, 1967).

Silverstein, Harry. "The Evil of Death," *The Journal of Philosophy,* LXXVII, 7 (July, 1980), 401–424.

Smart, Ninian. "Philosophical Concepts of Death," in Arnold Toynbee, *Man's Concern with Death,* 25–35.

Sumner, L. W. "A Matter of Life and Death," *Noûs,* 10 (1976): 145–171.

Sumner, L. W. *Abortion and Moral Theory* (Princeton: Princeton University Press, 1981).

Toynbee, Arnold, et al., eds. *Man's Concern with Death* (London: Hodder and Stoughton, 1968).

van Evra, James. "On Death as a Limit," *Analysis,* 31 (1971): 170–176; reprinted in John Donnelly, *Language, Metaphysics and Death,* 25–31.

van Inwagen, Peter. *Material Beings* (Ithaca: Cornell University Press, 1990).

Walton, Douglas N. *On Defining Death* (Montreal: McGill-Queen's University Press, 1979).

Wild, John. *The Challenge of Existentialism* (Bloomington: Indiana University Press, 1955).

Williams, Bernard. "The Makropoulos Case: Reflections on the Tedium of Immortality," in B. Williams, *Problems of the Self* (New York: Cambridge University Press, 1973).

Williams, Glanville. "Suicide," in *The Encyclopedia of Philosophy,* ed. Paul Edwards (New York: Macmillan and The Free Press, 1967), Volume 8, 43–46.

Wreen, Michael J. "The Definition of Death," *Public Affairs Quarterly,* 1, 4 (October, 1987): 87–99.

Wreen, Michael J. "The Definition of Euthanasia," *Philosophy and Phenomenological Research,* XLVCIII, 4 (June, 1988): 637–653.

Wreen, Michael J. "The Definition of Suicide," *Social Theory and Practice,* 14, 1 (Spring, 1988): 1–23.

Wreen, Michael J. "The Logical Opaqueness of Death," *Bioethics,* 1, 3 (1987): 366–371.

Yourgrau, Palle. "The Dead," *The Journal of Philosophy,* LXXXIV, 2 (February, 1987): 84–101.

Index